THE EDUCATING ICON

THE EDUCATING ICON

Teaching Wisdom and Holiness in the Orthodox Way

Anton C. Vrame

HOLY CROSS ORTHODOX PRESS
Brookline, Massachusetts

© Copyright 1999 Holy Cross Orthodox Press
Published by Holy Cross Orthodox Press
50 Goddard Avenue
Brookline, MA 02445

On the cover: Christ the Teacher by Athanasios Clark

LIBRARY OF CONGRESS CATALOGING-IN-PUBLICATION DATA

Vrame, Anton C.
The educating icon: teaching wisdom and holiness in the
Orthodox way / Anton C. Vrame.
        p.   cm.
Includes bibliographical references.
ISBN 1-885652-28-3
1. Icons—Cult. 2. Catechetics—Orthodox Eastern Church.
3. Orthodox Eastern Church—Doctrines. I. Title.
BX378.5.V73   1999   99-29557
268'.819—dc21   CIP

To my parents
George and Maria Vrame

TABLE OF CONTENTS

Preface

This book, a modified version of my doctoral dissertation in religion and education, began as an exploration of two issues. The first issue was answering basic questions about religious education that continually confronted me, such as, What are your educational aims and, How do those aims guide your educational practice? While my fellow students had elaborate explanations to offer, I realized that the Orthodox Church did not possess an overall educational theory or theology that informed aims, curriculum, learning outcomes, and teaching approaches. Upon reviewing the past and discovering that even though there have been many initial offerings, most of which have influenced my thinking and have been incorporated into this work, we still seemed to lack a distinctively Orthodox approach that answered these simple yet profoundly significant questions.

The second impetus for this work came in a discussion about popular culture and media and their influence on persons. A colleague of mine stated, "We live in a visual world. We should live in a visual Church." I realized at that moment that as an Orthodox Christian I did live in a visual Church. Issues about the role of the media in our lives today, how it affects us, how we encountered it, and others, were issues that the iconoclastic controversy and the theology of the icon struggled with. For example, both the encounter with television or film and the encounter with the icon are "live" encounters, placing the viewer within the frame of the depiction. This realization led me to begin to explore the icon, its art and theology.

This exploration led me to the realization that icons, their art form, their use in the life of the Church, and the theology that has developed about them, offered a number of ideas central to Orthodox thinking that could serve as a way to reflect upon educational concerns. Over time, an educational theory or educational theology began to emerge. The same investigations also have led me into a study of the power of the visual culture upon our lives as well.

This book is a product of these investigations. They were initially expressed in my doctoral dissertation. That work is the basis for this book, although now in edited form. In places the changes are minor; in others it is a new work completely, reflecting more thought on the issue and the input of others. While the work is complete and I stand by it, I must concede that it is still a "work in progress" and "a first statement" about Orthodox catechesis, with every hesitation and qualification that both statements include. Even as I read it today, I am struck by how much more could be said, how many more scholars' works could be engaged, and ultimately, how much work needs to be done in all areas of Orthodox education. Thus, my hope is that this work will spark a conversation among Orthodox about education in the life of the Church.

Acknowledgements

While this work was written in the privacy of my home, I realize that many persons were "present" as I prepared this text. Their input, whether through conversation, written remarks, or simply encouragement to "get it done" has been invaluable.

When this was prepared as a dissertation, it could not have been accomplished without the guidance and support of Professors Thomas Groome and Michael Schiro of Boston College, and Rev. Stanley Harakas of Holy Cross Greek Orthodox School of Theology. They challenged me to think and think some more about what I was proposing, nudging me to explore areas that I had not considered initially. Their encouragement to publish this as a book was also significant. As I reflect upon my work in religious education I am struck by how their collective wisdom has been deeply informative, formative, and transformative of my journey as a religious educator.

The hospitality of the Institute of Religious Education and Pastoral Ministry at Boston College was significant as it provided most fertile ground to pursue studies in theology and education. The encounters with so many gifted persons, especially through the doctoral seminar, were nurturing, inspiring, and challenging. It was there that the ideas in this work were first articulated, probably badly, and I thank them for their collegial patience as well as their input.

As this project moved to development into a book I am extremely grateful for the comments and input of Professors John Boojamra of St. Vladimir's Orthodox Theological Seminary and John Elias of Fordham University. Presenting pieces of this work at academic conferences and in the classes I have taught have been helpful to clarifying my ideas and developing them further. Conversations with colleagues at Holy Cross Greek Orthodox School of Theology were also supportive. My conversations with iconographers, especially Athanasios Clark, whose works form the majority of the examples, helped me understand the mind of the iconographer better. These examples are located in St. Basil Greek Orthodox Church in Chicago, and I am very thankful for the opportunity to examine them closely and photograph them for this work. The superb editorial work of George Sioras and Presvytera Kerry Pappas cannot be underestimated.

Finally, I must confess to the most surprising outcome of this endeavor. I set off to explore the icons so that others might learn from them and gain some guidance about the practice of education in the Church. While I hope that others may benefit from this effort, now that I have finished, I realize that it is I who have been taught by the icons.

Chapter One

Introduction: Preparing the Surface

Icons, the sacred art of the Eastern Orthodox Christian Church, are one of its most distinguishing characteristics. They are a significant aspect of the Orthodox Tradition and, since the conclusion of the iconoclastic controversy in the mid-ninth century, they have had the status of doctrine. In that conflict, icons were defended, in part, for their educational impact on the believer. One of the primary apologists for icons, John of Damascus, writing about A.D. 730, called them, "the books of the illiterate, the never silent heralds of the honor due the saints, teaching without use of words those who gaze upon them."[1] According to the Fathers of the Seventh Ecumenical Council in 787, icons depict the life of Christ, events of Scripture, the lives of the saints, and events in the history of the Church, "so that our mind may remember them, and so that we may be lifted up to the level of their conduct."[2] Since that time, Orthodox Christians have been socialized with icons in their churches and homes. However, their educational potential has not been sufficiently explored or developed by contemporary Orthodox Christian educators.

The purpose of this study is to address this deficiency, to turn our attention to the icons of the Orthodox Church and, in conversation with theology, educational theory, and the social sciences, to consider and enhance their potential for education in Christian faith. I believe through such dialogue we can begin to recover principles for understanding the vision of – and renewing – "iconic catechesis" in the Orthodox Church.

Our focus here is neither on iconic catechesis as a methodology of instruction nor on a better way to use art within the Sunday school classroom. Our purpose is, rather, to develop a series of principles that form the basis of catechetical endeavors in the Orthodox Church. These principles are suggested by the artistic style of icons, the use of icons in the life of the Church, the theology of icons, and the place of icons in the lives of the people who interact through them for spiritual nourishment. The reasons for developing these principles are discussed below, along with some basic assumptions that will assist the reader. However, like the prayerful painter of icons, our first step is to "prepare the surface."

The Need for an Orthodox Approach

Principles of Orthodox catechesis derived from iconography will provide Orthodox Christian educators with coherent and compelling guidance that has been sorely absent in the educational praxis of Orthodoxy. The situation in Orthodox catechesis is that Orthodox religious educators have been too occupied with their praxis – developing programs, writing textbooks, conducting seminars, etc. – to devote sustained attention to the foundational issues of Christian education and their development, in part due to a serious deficiency of resources. Of the three major Orthodox jurisdictions in the United States (Greek Archdiocese, Antiochian Archdiocese, and Orthodox Church in America), the Greek Orthodox Archdiocese has a small department with a staff, and the Orthodox Church in America has a small department as part of its Unit in Education and Community Life. The Antiochian Archdiocese has just recently elevated its "department" of one person to a full-time position. Despite their small size, all three are very active, with numerous projects in development. At the two major Orthodox theological schools in the United States (Holy Cross Greek Orthodox School of Theology, Brookline, MA and St. Vladimir's Orthodox Theological Seminary, Crestwood, NY), there are no full-time professors of religious education. St. Vladimir's Seminary offers a Master of Arts in religious education. However, recruitment is difficult because of the "general lack of interest in education among Orthodox and the lack of salaried positions,"[3] although in the 1997-98 academic year, there was an increase in students. The overall situation is that Orthodox Christian education is a seriously underdeveloped field of study and practice. At the parish level, it remains largely a "lay" activity, inadequately supported, and generally unaware of the rich heritage on which improvements in *praxis* need to be rooted.

In one respect this situation may appear surprising. Education was a very early concern of the first Orthodox to arrive in North America. The missionaries who began coming to Russian Alaska in the 1790s saw education as vital to spreading the Gospel and teaching native Americans who were converting. The missionaries were quick to establish schools.[4] But this situation was exceptional. For the most part, Orthodox Christianity came to America in waves of immigration during the early twentieth century. In this new land, handing on the Orthodox faith to children of immigrant families was a central concern, and although church leaders urged parishes to begin catechetical instruction, few programs were implemented. Equally important, few resources were developed and made available for use in the parishes. Some of those resources came from other Christian traditions. For example, in 1927, George Alexander, the first Director of Religious Education for a Greek Orthodox Diocese in the United States, recommended to the Archdiocese that the Episcopalian curriculum program, "with appropriate changes," could be adopted by Greek Orthodox Sunday schools.[5] In those early days no systematic attempts were made toward understanding and articulating a distinctive Orthodox approach to Christian education.

The development of an Orthodox approach can be traced back to 1956, when religious educators from the various ethnic jurisdictions formed the Orthodox Christian Education Commission (OCEC). The OCEC was organized to pool resources and combine efforts to address the educational concerns of the churches. By this time, there was a growing realization that the "Protestant model," the Sunday school, was inadequate and inconsistent with Orthodox concepts of religious education. The primary aims of the OCEC were to "find an Orthodox approach" to Christian education, to relate Orthodox life and teaching to the American environment, and to create an inter-Orthodox forum for the exchange of ideas.[6] Despite these lofty aims, the challenges of educating individuals in Orthodox faith and identity continued to be the overwhelming activity of the OCEC, and no foundational Orthodox approach was articulated. In 1975, Sophie Koulomzin, a guiding force of the OCEC from its inception, wrote that: "The Orthodox Church today faces a challenge. It needs to discover an approach to religious education that is rooted in the total church tradition."[7]

Various attempts have been made in the last twenty years to respond to this need for an Orthodox approach to religious education. While an exhaustive presentation of these efforts is beyond the aim of this chapter, in order to situate the present discussion on Orthodox Christian education, major contributions to this conversation are reviewed, including the work of Alexander Schmemann, Constance Tarasar, George Nicozisin, Kyriaki FitzGerald, and John Boojamra.

Alexander Schmemann sought to provide a foundation for religious education by locating it within the liturgical life of the Orthodox Church. In his book, *Liturgy and Life: Christian Development through Liturgical Experience*, he identified examples of how aspects of the liturgical cycle of the Church are catechetical in nature, noting that "liturgical catechesis" is the traditional method of education in the Church.[8] For Schmemann, the aim of catechesis is "to bring the individual into the life of the Church."[9] This means that catechesis is more than imparting religious knowledge and moral training; it also involves "edifying," literally "building up," a member of the Body of Christ, the chosen race, and the holy nation. "Religious education is nothing else but the disclosing of that which happened to man when he was born again through water and Spirit, and was made a member of the Church."[10] Schmemann also identifies the process by which Orthodox should educate: "O taste and see that the Lord is good!" (Ps. 34.8). Experience before understanding, participation before explanation, is advocated as the way of catechesis in the Church.[11]

While Schmemann, correctly I believe, identifies liturgy as central to Orthodoxy's approach to religious education, the remainder of his presentation is an explanation of the liturgical life of the Orthodox. Schmemann's influence is great and can be seen in the liturgical emphasis of the textbooks published by the OCEC, as well as in the effect it has had on others who have connected religious education with the liturgical life of the Orthodox Church, including Constance Tarasar, George Nicozisin, and Kyriaki FitzGerald.

Constance Tarasar is probably the most widely published and best known of all Orthodox religious educators, having been active in the field since the 1960s. She has written on a wide range of topics, presenting and expanding the liturgical perspective inherited from Schmemann. For example, in one essay she applies the "taste and see" principle to children's experience of worship: "The child learns to worship through experience from the very first moments in the Church. The child's first 'understandings' come through the senses."[12] Elsewhere, she uses this principle to reestablish the connection between doctrine and liturgical experience, thus reintegrating catechesis into the life of the Church in the fullest meaning of that phrase.[13] In her doctoral dissertation, she proposes a curricular plan based on the liturgy of initiation according to educational goals and developmental levels.[14] Most recently, she has made a cogent articulation of the theology of Orthodox religious education, focusing on three foundational premises:

(1) theology and religious education are fundamentally of
the church, (2) theology and religious education are grounded
in an understanding of God in Trinity, and our relationship
to God and to each other as persons, and (3) theology and
religious education must be communicated in their fulness.[15]

In a book that deals largely with the historical development
of religious education in the Greek Orthodox Archdiocese of
North and South America, George Nicozisin articulates an understanding of religious education that is rooted in the distinctive
nature of Orthodox Christianity. As he points out, the Orthodox in America, with their immigrant roots, came to see
themselves as different from other Christians. For Nicozisin,
this difference is rooted in the *phronema* (φρόνημα) of the Orthodox Tradition. *Phronema*, according to him,

> is an attitude, a position and/or posture which reflects a par-
> ticular spirit, a theological sentiment or frame of mind. An
> Orthodox Christian *phronema*, in Christian education then,
> is a program which postulates a scriptural, traditional, doc-
> trinal spirit, a sentiment and frame of mind which is reflected
> and existentialized in the liturgical life of the individual both
> within and without the church.[16]

Nicozisin identifies the *phronema* of the Orthodox as a living
tradition of liturgical practices and customs, which has been
passed down from one generation to the next by example and
personal instruction, over and above what is found in manuals
of theology. *Phronema* is not merely the external "forms" of
Orthodoxy – vestments, icons, candles, incense, etc. – but its
inner spirit, its way of thinking, its way of living. Instead of
paradosis (παράδοσις), or tradition, he uses the term
parakatatheke (παρακαταθήκη, literally deposit, or heritage).
The term *parakatatheke* is rooted in the sacrament of ordination. When the bishop places the consecrated eucharistic bread
in the hands of the newly ordained presbyter he says, "Receive
this deposit (*parakatatheke*), preserve it until the parousia of our

Lord Jesus Christ ... "[17] Viewed in this way, our Orthodox heritage can be seen to be pulsating with a dynamism far greater than might be implied by the term tradition. Sacramentally, the eucharistic bread is the living body of Christ. Tradition could be merely a collection of practices and intellectual study. *Parakatatheke* and *phronema* are that, but they are more – much more. Nicozisin wants this living *phronema* to permeate all educational efforts. He wants a pedagogy fully integrated with the sacramental life of the church – not merely an intellectual exercise – and a church life that interconnects with and permeates all aspects of life. The Orthodox *phronema* must be lived to "give life, vitality, and meaning" to each Orthodox Christian.[18]

In her efforts toward an Orthodox theory of religious education, Kyriaki FitzGerald examines the liturgical context of *phronema* and the interactions of liturgical life with, as she calls it, "religious formation".[19] Influenced by the work of faith development theorist James Fowler and religious educator John Westerhoff, FitzGerald seeks to better understand the process of religious formation by which this distinctively Orthodox *phronema* is born and matures in the person of the believer by working from the liturgical life itself and citing its texts and practices. The process is seen as one of socialization or enculturation resulting from personal participation in the liturgical life of the Church, both in the assemblies of the eucharistic community and in the family life of the Orthodox home.

In the home, "the liturgical life is the medium of family formation."[20] The religious practices, disciplines, and rituals that are part of family life help each family member become aware that all of life is to be guided by this particularly Orthodox framework (*phronema*). The liturgical calendar of the eucharistic community, with its seasons of feasting and fasting, is the calendar of the home. Family life, as a primary expression of the Orthodox "context and structure to life," involves all aspects of the believer's life within its "sacred rhythm" and orients the person towards *theosis*.[21] FitzGerald, with Schmemann, Tarasar, and

Nicozisin, sees the liturgical life of the Orthodox Tradition as central to the development of approaches to religious formation.

John Boojamra takes a modified approach to religious education or, as he refers to it in the title of his book, *Orthodox Christian Education*.[22] Boojamra sees socialization as the preferable model for the Orthodox. He does not deny the significance of liturgy. However, he feels that the "liturgical captivity" of education materials has "distorted both the nature of the Church and Christian education" because Orthodoxy is "more than liturgy."[23] The socialization model is preferable because "both children and adults become Christians not by learning *about* Christianity but by being integrated *into* an existing Church through experiencing the rites, symbols, and stories of the community."[24] He feels that socialization is congenial to Orthodoxy because Orthodoxy has always favored a formational approach over an informational approach to learning. Boojamra also sees the family as educator, considering the family as an extended system of relationships. However, in this larger system of relationships, he does not see children as the central focus. He does not consider children to be the sole desirable outcome of marriage, but only one of its benefits.[25] This is, perhaps, the reason for his belief that the primacy of children in religious education is one of its dysfunctions. For Boojamra, Christian education has been reduced to memorization of names, dates, and places, intended to be digestible in forty-five-minute sessions that we "do" to the young. However, he believes that "Christianity is an adult's religion" and that "its concepts and stories are not suited to the child's mental structure."[26]

In his writing, Boojamra has identified the *person* as the focus of the educational process and, with this orientation, he advocates that *theosis* "be the primary goal of any educational process and material that we devise."[27] He has even suggested that pedagogy be renamed "hypostagogy," in keeping with the notion that education for the entire person (that is, a *hypostasis*) is the central concern. Boojamra's brief comment on icons as a major insight into the Orthodox understanding of personhood was an important stimulus for the work reported here.[28]

Perhaps the most significant recent development in Orthodox religious education has been the publication of the *Living Our Orthodox Faith* textbook series by the Greek Orthodox Archdiocese of America's Department of Religious Education. Begun in 1985 under the leadership of Ernest Villas, with materials being produced each year from 1989 to 1994, this effort marks a shift in Orthodox thinking about religious education, which is expressed in its colorful pages.[29]

Before publication of textbooks and supplementary materials began, the Department of Religious Education, with extensive involvement of theologians, professional educators, and curriculum developers, articulated a philosophy of Orthodox Christian education in a document titled *Orthodox Catechesis*. This statement provided the guidance for the development of the series. It begins with:

> The purpose of Orthodox Christian Education (*catechesis*) is to help build up the Church, the Body of Christ, by nurturing every person in the life of personal communion with the Holy Trinity (*theosis*), and thus, through this ministry, to bear joyful witness to God's loving and redeeming work in the world. Being only one part of the total life of the Church, Christian education is effective in the context of living faith in the home and the local parish. Living faith is concretely expressed through all believers – bishops, priests, parents, teachers, parish leaders, youth leaders, and all Orthodox Christians seeking to know and to live the new life in Christ by the power of the Holy Spirit.[30]

Orthodox Christian education is recognized as having a dual nature: 1)*orthodoxia* – the objective content of Scripture, Tradition, doctrine, ethics, spiritual wisdom, and liturgics; 2)*orthopraxia* – the formation of Christian character in the "living and application of Christian truth."[31] The goals of Christian education are inherent in the organizing structures of the life in Christ (*orthopraxia*) and include worship (*latreia*), community (*koinonia*), discipleship (*matheteia*), service (*diakonia*), and witness (*martyria*). Under each of these, the statement articulates certain goals of catechesis. For example, under "service" the following are listed:

1) To be able to serve God and humanity in the light of the example and teachings of Christ, the Apostles, and Saints. 2) To be motivated and serve God and humanity in the spirit of sacrificial love (*agape*), self-giving or self-emptying (*kenosis*), and faithful fulfillment of the specific needs of others in local and global settings. 3) To be able to identify and serve through the variety of ministries in the life of the Church under the guidance and power of the Holy Spirit. 4) To be able to recognize and to fulfill God's call (*klesis*) through various vocations, professions, and responsibilities in the Church, family, and society. 5) To know the meaning of and to live as God's stewards returning to Him in gratitude His gifts of time, talent, and treasure.[32]

The next step in the development of the series was the articulation of various learning objectives. Using a taxonomy of "What one needs to know," "What one needs to believe," and "What one needs to do," the group of theologians, educators, and curriculum developers, who were continuously involved, began listing specific items.[33] These individual items were then sorted under fifteen topics ranging from "God the Father," "the Saints," to "Other Religions" and graded from pre-school to the twelfth grade. This became the "Scope and Sequence" or the blueprint out of which each grade level of materials began to be developed.

Though this may seem an uneventful moment, it marked a radical departure from past efforts in Orthodox textbook development. In this endeavor, questions pertaining to religious education were systematically asked, and the answers generated were used to develop materials. In earlier efforts, materials had been developed first, and then a scope and sequence that fit the existing tools was put together.

While the framers of *Orthodox Catechesis* have not offered any further explanations of this guiding document, one attempt has been made to reflect on the shift in thinking that took place with the introduction of this curriculum series; it is summarized here. Religious education, as an effort of the entire community, strives to nurture all of its members in all stages of life toward whole personhood through the ministries and curricula of the Church. In the *Living Our Orthodox Faith* series, these components of religious education were expressed in "living examples" via high quality art, integration of content both with the life experiences of the learners and from grade to grade, reliance upon narrative, and an experience-based, active approach to education and Christian living. The series is seen as nurturing the Orthodox identity of the learner while, over time, challenging the community in areas of diversity, marginalized voices – especially those of women and the non-ordained, on social issues, and on the idealized Church versus the real church.[34]

With the gains of the last two decades, an emerging consensus on the aims of Orthodox religious education can be seen. Three elements are now consistently present in Orthodox thinking and writing on the subject. First, *theosis* is seen as the aim of Orthodox education – although careful reading indicates there is difference of opinion regarding whether *theosis* is to be considered "process" (*Orthodox Catechesis*, Tarasar) or "end-product" (Boojamra, FitzGerald, Nicozisin). As Orthodox theology favors the generally "both/and" over the "either/or" approach to questions, the difference here is resolved by emphasizing that *theosis* is both. Apparent differences are probably just in emphasis. Second, religious education is seen as a deeply social process, involving the entire life of the community and all of its members as lifelong students and teachers. Third, religious education is seen holistically, that is involving: a) the whole person – mind, body, spirit; b) the whole community – all believers and their collective wisdom, knowledge, and experience of past and present; and c) the whole Tradition – *orthodoxia* and *orthopraxia*.

There are, I believe, several reasons that Orthodox religious education has not developed further. First, as was pointed out above, the few Orthodox religious educators have been too busy "doing" religious education to pause and reflect upon their ministries.

Second, the paths that the pioneers have followed have tended to be too broad to yield a clear and compelling foundation for what follows. The liturgical life seems an obvious starting point for understanding Orthodox catechesis, but FitzGerald notes that the "infinite number of ways the liturgical life may be expressed" presented major difficulties in her work.[35] Paradoxically, it may simultaneously be too narrow an approach. Unless liturgical formation makes connections to other dimensions of life, it can reduce to the academic study of liturgy – and as Boojamra reminds us, the Church is more than liturgy. On the other hand, socialization comes across as an approach that is truly massive – extremely challenging to organize, analyze, and implement. Also, in taking either approach, there are difficulties in identifying specifics that are readily manageable. How does one "lift up" an aspect of liturgy? How do we focus on the extensive vistas inherent in socialization? I believe that concentration on icons – a central aspect of the Tradition with clear, objective content (*orthodoxia*), an established role in people's lives (*orthopraxia*), and characteristics that are theoretical yet specific enough to "pin down" will contribute significantly to an enhanced vision of the future of Orthodox catechesis.

A third reason is that Orthodox writings on religious education are oftentimes not widely accessible to Orthodox catechists. Boojamra's published book is the most widely available. Much of Tarasar's work is published in collections of essays – she provides the Orthodox perspective – which are not readily available to many Orthodox readers. (Part of the problem here may be economic; these collections also reflect on the status of non-

Orthodox thought in the matters addressed, and there may be reluctance to purchase large books for single essays.) FitzGerald's work is a dissertation, and Nicozisin's work is long out of print. Compounding this inaccessibility to available literature is the lack of positions in Orthodox organizations that could nurture additional thought and discourse on these topics. Nevertheless, in spite of the difficulties, the work of Schmemann, Tarasar, Nicozisin, FitzGerald, and Boojamra constitute a significant baseline to which I hope to make a small contribution through the exploration of the educational potential of the iconic aspect of our Tradition with respect to both its theory and its ability to direct our paths as educators.

The Orthodox Tradition has many sources that contribute to a discussion of catechetical foundations: Scripture, liturgy and sacrament, councils, the Fathers, etc. Hopefully, one day all of them will be fully explored from a catechetical perspective. The prominent role that the educational function of icons played in their traditional justification convinces me, as a religious educator, to begin my study of Orthodox catechesis with the icons. Furthermore, in the visual culture of the present day, the icons seem particularly appropriate, not only to the Orthodox, but to all religious educators concerned with the impact of the visual arts – and by extension, the symbolic "materials" of all traditions – on religious education. To this wider audience, the present study has the potential to be a source of insight and renewal.

Basic Assumptions

Even though this work contains an explanation and elaboration of a number of Orthodox principles, many of them are already operative. Therefore, permit me to identify and briefly touch on a few of them.

An **icon** is a sacred image depicting Jesus Christ, the Virgin Mary (the "Theotokos" of Orthodox Tradition), one or more saints, prophets of the Old Testament, events in their lives, milestones in the history of the Church, etc. As Philip Sherrard points out, any work of art could be considered "religious" because of its source or subject matter, such as the painting of a scene from Scripture by Giotto, Rembrandt, or Chagall, but "it cannot be called an icon unless its form derives from spiritual vision, spiritual understanding, and is fused (although not confused) with this spiritual content."[36] Icons are a central, highly visual feature of Orthodox churches and chapels – an integral part of liturgical worship. Icons are also central to the personal prayer and devotional life of Orthodox Christians. They are found in homes, places of business, automobiles, classrooms, etc., where they serve as expressions of the personal faith and piety of the individual Orthodox Christian.

Icons are traditionally painted according to a style established during the Byzantine era; yet this style has evolved into various schools that reflect, for example, a Russian or a Cretan iconographic tradition. In addition to paintings, icons are executed as frescoes, mosaics, embroidery, relief carvings, etc. Frequently icons are photographed, printed, and mounted for use; these too are icons. While icons can be executed in non-Byzantine styles (e.g., Ethiopian), the illustrations used in this book are from the more traditional styles, although from various periods and schools.

During the iconoclastic controversy, icons were referred to as "books" that teach illiterate believers the content of their Christian faith. In modified form, this viewpoint has become remarkably contemporary. In recent decades, theologians, philosophers, cultural anthropologists, and art historians have extended the understanding of "texts" to include the visual as well as the literary arts. Films, television programs, and print advertising, as well as works of art have come to be of particular interest and are included among the "texts" that are analyzed, for example, to understand a particular culture. In a similar vein, Orthodox theologians have often spoken of "reading icons" – a process of viewing icons and reflecting on their content, constituent parts, artistic style, etc. in order to apprehend their

.dational notion of this study, derived from both
w that icons are indeed "texts" that can be "read"
.ks of art that elicit responses from beholders. This
.ing is deeply embedded within the Tradition, hav-
eloquently expressed in defense of the icons. Today,
hear an iconographer talking about "writing" an icon,
than "painting" one, and it is not uncommon to see a
cional icon that has been signed, "Written by the hand of
The insights of Orthodox writers who have "read the icons"
a., well as those of contemporary students of the visual texts of a
culture have made invaluable contributions to the work that is
unfolding in this study.

Theosis is the term used in Orthodox theology to express the
ultimate destiny of human existence. It means participation in
or union with God according to the model set forth in the person of Jesus Christ, the God–man. In fact, through union with
God, humanity's characteristics are made "even more real and
authentic by contact with the divine model, according to which
they were created."[37] *Theosis* is the vision of the deification or
divinization of the human person – becoming like God.

While clearly a theological or spiritual vision of humanity,
theosis is a holistic vision involving the whole person, body, mind,
and spirit.[38] It is to live *in* Christ and not just externally imitate
him. It is the ultimate destiny of humanity achieved in Christ
through the unilateral action of the Father's love and an open
invitation for human response and effort.[39] *Theosis* is both the
way of life of the Christian and the goal of Christian life, the
process and end-point. *Theosis* is living, acting, knowing – the
totality of one's being – as God lives, acts, and knows. Because
this manner of being is depicted in the icons, in this work, *theosis*
is called "iconic living and knowing."

Synergy involves the cooperation of the human and the divine wills. As Stanley Harakas points out, the concept of *synergy*
is the "patristic affirmation that while human beings can do
nothing without God, God does nothing regarding goodness,

righteousness, and holiness, without human cooperation."[40] As in *theosis*, God invites us to union with him yet does not impose himself on us, honoring and even authenticating the essential freedom of the person. *Synergy* does not imply that the human and divine wills are equal partners. The human will is a fallen, created will. The divine will is holy and uncreated and thus the greater partner. Yet, the concept of *synergy* rejects any notion of predestination or its opposite, Pelagianism. The person is free to follow and to conform to the divine will while never losing his or her freedom.[41]

Catechesis. Orthodox educators have not generally been caught up in the debates of educators from other faith traditions about what to call education in faith. As a result, they have not had to locate themselves on the map of the discipline of religious education.[42] One can find a whole range of terms in Orthodox writings on the subject: "religious education," "Christian education," "Christian religious education," "catechesis" and occasionally others, often prefixed by "Orthodox."

"Catechesis" would appear to be the preferable term to be used by Orthodox educators, given its roots in the patristic tradition – some of the great discourses of the Fathers were catechetical orations – as well as its association with liturgical life. However, in the literature, all of the terms mentioned above can be found. But, despite the term or terms used, the explanations provided by the various authors reflect a vision similar to that of Kieran Scott's relative to catechesis: "Catechesis is unabashedly confessional. Its constitutive interest is to awaken, nourish, and develop one's personal belief, to hand on the tradition, solidify one's religious identity and build up the ecclesial body. It is 'enculturation in a transforming community.'"[43]

In this work, "catechesis" is the preferred term used to refer to "Orthodox religious education." It is viewed as a complex of processes that encompass, among others, the socialization of Orthodox family and community life, classroom education, liturgical and sacramental cultivation, ethical and moral development, and one's personal devotional life.

As indicated earlier, the focus of *iconic catechesis* is neither a better means of using art in the Sunday school classroom nor a methodology for religious instruction. Rather, the emphasis is on a series of principles, emerging from the theology of icons and their use in the Orthodox Tradition, which motivate and guide the processes involved in faith education. A first principle to be addressed in the chapters that follow is the goal of iconic catechesis. From the icons we can discern that this goal is iconic living and knowing – becoming an icon in the process of attaining communion with God – *theosis*. Another is that a sacred curriculum, comprised of visible and invisible elements, emerges from our encounters with the icons: sacred place, sacred time, sacred presence, and personal communion. The visible sacred curriculum is the visual content of the icon, depicting the story of the community and its members who have lived iconically. The invisible sacred curriculum relates to the place, time, presence, and communion with which the icon mystically engages us. A third principle is that the icon has the potential to inform, form, and transform the believer into the likeness of God – and the community and cosmos into a manifestation of the kingdom of God. A fourth is, as "iconic catechesis" becomes praxis, the act of education can become sacramental, with "rubrics" for the teaching and learning encounter.

The Chapters

Before beginning our exploration of the principles of iconic catechesis and the educational commitments that emerge in subsequent chapters, Chapter Two will situate the icon historically and theologically through a review of the iconoclastic controversy. Readers already familiar with this history and the debate regarding icons and the imagery that it spawned, may want to skip this chapter and proceed directly to the educational issues that follow.

In Chapter Three, "iconic living" and "knowing" will be the focus as we seek the aim of iconic catechesis. The connection between the icon and the Orthodox concept of *theosis* will be explained, along with the holistic epistemology – body, mind, heart, and soul – that is engaged through the icons.

Chapter Four will present the visible and the invisible curricula – of sacred place, time, presence, and communion – that are derived from the icons and will begin to outline their implications for "iconic catechesis."

Chapter Five will continue with the final set of principles of "iconic catechesis." Drawing upon educational thought, the work of cultural anthropologists, and building on the material of the earlier chapters, the potential of the icon to inform, form, and transform the believer will be presented.

In Chapter Six the presentation becomes fully pastoral, applying the principles from the earlier chapters to the "sacrament of education" – the praxis of the education of Orthodox Tradition in liturgical assemblies and in other meetings of the members of the community of faith, in their homes and in their personal lives.

Throughout this work, examples of icons will be presented and analyzed to illuminate the issues discussed.

NOTES

[1] John of Damascus, *On the Divine Images*, First Apology, Ancient Documentation; p. 39. Translated by David Anderson (Crestwood, NY: SVS Press, 1980). This text contains the three apologies of John in edited form, omitting repetitions from one apology to the next. I shall refer to St John's writings as "First, Second, or Third Apology" cite the chapter, and provide the page references from Anderson.

[2] Sixth Session, of the Seventh Ecumenical Council, Vol. 4 (Mansi, Vol 13, 277b). As found in Daniel Sahas, *Icon and Logos: Sources in Eighth Century Iconoclasm*, (Toronto: University of Toronto Press, 1986), p. 104. Sahas' work has become a standard translation of the Sixth Session which read the Definition of the Iconoclastic Council of 754 at Hieria and refuted it paragraph by paragraph, as well as the Definition of Nicea II and is an excellent introduction to iconoclasm.

[3] John L. Boojamra, "Report of the Department of Christian Education," *The Word* (November, 1995), p. 16.

[4] See Constance Tarasar, ed. *Orthodox America 1794-1976: Development of the Orthodox Church in America* (Syosset, NY: Orthodox Church

in America Department of History and Archives, 1975), p. 17.

[5] George Nicozisin, *The Road to Orthodox Phronema: Christian Education in the Greek Orthodox Archdiocese of North and South America* (Brookline, MA: Greek Orthodox Archdiocese of North and South America Department of Religious Education, n.d.), pp. 34-35.

[6] Tarasar, *Orthodox America*, p. 234.

[7] Sophie Koulomzin, *Our Church and Our Children* (Crestwood, NY: SVS Press, 1975), p. 14.

[8] Alexander Schmemann, *Liturgy and Life: Christian Development through Liturgical Experience* (Syosset, NY: Orthodox Church in America Department of Religious Education, 1983), p. 11.

[9] Ibid.

[10] Ibid.

[11] Ibid., p. 13.

[12] Constance J. Tarasar, "Taste and See: Orthodox Children at Worship" in *The Sacred Play of Children*, ed., Diane Apostolos-Cappadona (New York: Seabury Press, 1983), pp. 51-52.

[13] Constance J. Tarasar, "The Orthodox Experience" in *A Faithful Church: Issues in the History of Catechesis*, ed. O. C. Edwards and John Westerhoff (Wilton, CT: Morehouse-Barlow, 1981), pp. 255-256.

[14] Constance J. Tarasar, *A Process Model for the Design of Curriculum for Orthodox Christian Religious Education* (Ed.D. Dissertation, SUNY-Albany, 1989).

[15] Constance J. Tarasar, "Orthodox Theology and Religious Education," in *Theologies of Religious Education*, ed., Randolph C. Miller (Birmingham, AL: Religious Education Press, 1995), p. 84.

[16] G. Nicozisin, *Road to Orthodox Phronema*, pp. xii-xiii.

[17] *Euchologion to Mega* (Athens: Astir, 1980, in Greek), p. 165. Translation by the author.

[18] G. Nicozisin, *Road to Orthodox Phronema*, p. xiv.

[19] Kyriaki FitzGerald, *Religious Formation and Liturgical Life* (Ph.D. Dissertation, Boston University, 1985).

[20] Ibid., p. 94.

[21] Ibid., pp. 106-107.

[22] John Boojamra, *Foundations for Orthodox Christian Education.* (Crestwood, NY: SVS Press, 1989), p. 29. FitzGerald relied heavily on the work of Boojamra. The *Foundations* text is a collection of material that was published between 1981 and 1984.

[23] Ibid., p. 30.

[24] Ibid., p. 31.

[25] Ibid., see ch. 3, "The Family as Educator."

[26] Ibid., p. 81.

[27] Ibid., p. 31. See also "The Liberation of Christian Education," *Phronema* 6, 1991: 39-49.

[28] John Boojamra, "The Liberation of Christian Education," *Phronema* 6, 1991: 40.

[29] The titles in the series (pre-school to grade 5) are: *God Loves Us*, *Happy with God*, *Me and My World*, *Loving God*, *Sharing God's World*, *Growing with God*, and *God Calls Us*. Materials for grades six and up continue to be produced along topical themes, rather than by grade level exclusively. Titles so far produced are: *Facing Up to Peer Pressure*, *Stewardship*, and *Knowing Christ*.

[30] *Orthodox Catechesis* Greek Orthodox Archdiocese of America Department of Religious Education, Brookline, MA. (mimeographed, n.d.), p. 1.

[31] Ibid.

[32] Ibid., p. 4.

[33] To my knowledge, this process has never been documented before. I am aware of it from my personal conversations with the men and women who were involved with the process. I became involved informally in 1986 and formally in 1989 when textbook development dominated the focus.

[34] Anton C. Vrame, "Forming Orthodox Identity in the Curriculum of the Greek Orthodox Church" in *Personhood*, ed., John T. Chirban (Westport, CT: Bergin and Garvey, 1996), 173-184.

[35] K. FitzGerald, *Religious Formation*, p. 135.

[36] Philip Sherrard, *The Sacred in Life and Art* (Ipswich, U.K.: Golgonooza Press, 1990), p. 73.

[37] John Meyendorff, *Byzantine Theology: Historical Trends and Doctrinal Themes* (New York: Fordham University Press, 1987), p. 164.

[38] Stanley S. Harakas, *Toward Transfigured Life* (Minneapolis: Light and Life, 1983), p. 28

[39] Meyendorff, *Byzantine Theology*, p. 164.

[40] S. Harakas, *Transfigured Life*, p. 232.

[41] Ibid.

[42] The map image belongs to Mary Boys, *Educating in Faith: Maps and Visions* (San Francisco: Harper and Row, 1989). As she stated in her 1994 Presidential Address to the Association of Professionals and Researchers in Religious Education (APRRE) the discipline of religious education has generally left out the Orthodox Christian perspective.

[43] Kieran Scott, "Three Traditions of Religious Education," *Religious Education* 79 (1984), p. 325.

Chapter Two

✳

The Theological Rationale of the Icons

While present in the Christian Church from its beginnings,[1] the place of art and icons in the Church was fiercely challenged in the eighth and ninth centuries by the iconoclastic controversy – a theological convulsion that shook the Eastern Roman Empire. Ultimately, the iconophiles prevailed and, since that time, icons have been an even more significant aspect of the Orthodox Tradition. Indeed, the Seventh Ecumenical Council, held at Nicea in 787, incorporated icons into dogmatic Orthodoxy. To deny the icons is to deny Orthodox Christianity.

The purpose of this chapter is not to reopen the iconoclastic debate, to secure the triumph of Orthodoxy once again, or to discover anything "new" in the debate about the historic period from about 726 to 843. The bibliography on the history, the theological debate, the socio-political climate, and other aspects of the iconoclastic period is extensive, and to cover it thoroughly would be a major undertaking. The scope of this chapter is much more modest: to present the historical background and the theological justification of the icons in order to help the reader become familiar with the Orthodox position. Then, because our concern is with the implications of the icons on catechesis, some initial educational observations based on this ancient debate will be presented. Accordingly, this chapter consists of three sections: The Historical Conflict; The Theological Rationale; and Educational Implications.

THE HISTORICAL CONFLICT

To refer to the one-hundred-seventeen-year period under question (ca. 726–843) as the iconoclastic "controversy" gives the impression of a long series of meetings, treatises, and debates about the place of icons in the religious life of the Byzantine Empire. In reality, the time was filled with political intrigue and skullduggery, excommunication and anathematization, depositions and exiles, torture and martyrdom – on both sides of the conflict. In this period we can see the shrinking fortunes of the Byzantine Empire: the Eastern frontiers were gradually lost to Arab and Turkish invaders while Italy and Western Europe severed their ties with Constantinople. We can also see acceleration in the estrangement of Eastern and Western Christianity, which led to formal schism in later centuries.

The iconoclastic controversy occurred in two distinct phases. The first phase began in 726 during the reign of Emperor Leo III and ended with the decrees of the Seventh Ecumenical Council, held in Nicea in 787 under the reign of Empress Irene. The second phase began in 813 with Leo V "the Armenian" and ran until the "Triumph of Orthodoxy" under Empress Theodora in 843. It is notable that orthodoxy was defended and restored to the Byzantine Church during the rule of two women, both of whom served as emperors in their own right.

The first phase[2] of the conflict began when, in 726, Emperor Leo III (717 - 741) publicly spoke out against icons and characterized those who venerated them as idolaters. His aim was religious reform: to purify the Church and Empire by eliminating idols. Shortly thereafter, he sent a representative to remove the icon of Christ from the *Chalke* (Bronze) Gate of the imperial palace in Constantinople and replace it with a Cross. In Leo's mind, Constantine the Great had triumphed under the Sign of the Cross – *en touto nika* – and this action would mark the beginning of the empire's return to its past glory.[3] An angry mob of iconophiles ("friends of icons," also identified in the literature as "iconodules"), mostly women, stormed the gate, killing the agent. Leo retaliated against the mob, by severely punishing the iconophiles. More significantly, however, the news of these events reached Hellas, a separate imperial district or "theme" of Byzantium. The rulers of the Hellas district proclaimed their own iconophile emperor and planned an attack upon Constantinople, which Leo had no difficulty suppressing.

Responding to letters from Leo on these matters, Pope Gregory II rejected Leo's theological arguments for iconoclasm, which were based upon the Decalogue prohibition of idol-worship,[4] but Gregory did not break his ties with him. In fact, Pope Gregory tried to boost Leo's popularity in Italy because the support of Byzantine armies against the approaching Lombards was needed. It is around this time that John of Damascus (ca. 675 - ca. 750) wrote his three apologies, *Against Those Who Attack the Divine Images*,[5] from the St. Sabbas monastery in Moslem-controlled Jerusalem. Also, from the beginning of the eighth century, there is more frequent use of the term "orthodox," meaning upright or truthful, to describe the Church.[6]

In 730 Leo issued an edict ordering the destruction of icons and called an assembly of secular and religious leaders to support him. The iconophile Patriarch of Constantinople at the time, Germanus, refused to attend and was deposed. An iconoclast loyal to the emperor, Anastasius, replaced him as patriarch. Anastasius signed the edict, giving it ecclesial sanction. Pope Gregory III (who succeeded Gregory II in 731) officially condemned iconoclasm, and Leo responded by imprisoning the papal envoys. A rift between Rome and Constantinople opened. Byzantine influence in Italy steadily declined from this point, with middle Italy completely detaching itself from the Byzantines and allying with the papacy and western Europe.

With Leo's son, Emperor Constantine V (741 - 775), the iconoclastic policies of the empire intensified. In 742 Constantine lost his throne to his brother-in-law Artabasdus, an iconophile, who seized the throne in battle and restored the icons to the empire. However, Constantine successfully reclaimed his throne in 743, capturing Artabasdus and his sons and parading them seated backwards on donkeys after blinding them. Victorious, Constantine took the offensive, recovering territory lost to Arabs. However, Italy was lost permanently in 751 as the Lombards took control of Ravenna. In 754 the Papacy formally allied itself with the Frankish King Pepin, establishing the foundation for a separate Western Empire.

Convinced that the victory over his iconophile rival was a sign that iconoclasm was the correct policy, Constantine began an all-out persecution of iconophiles. An articulate theologian, he wrote a number of treatises supporting his iconoclast views. However, only fragments of two have survived. In them Constantine argued for the consubstantiality (ὁμοούσιος or *homoousios*) of the image with its prototype. He rejected any images of Christ on the grounds that they could not depict his divine nature – a monophysite leaning. Also, in keeping with the Decalogue, images and the devotion paid to icons were idolatrous. The only acceptable image of Christ was the bread and wine of the Eucharist. To support his claim, Constantine called a council.

Three hundred thirty-eight carefully selected iconoclast bishops, with no representatives from Rome or the other patriarchates (Alexandria, Antioch, or Jerusalem), were called to meet in Hieria (February 10 to August 8, 754), although the final session was held in Constantinople. The council followed Constantine's theological arguments but avoided his monophysite leanings and anything that might conflict with previous ecumenical councils. The council's argument was that the iconophile position separated the dual nature of the person of Christ. If only the human nature of Christ was being depicted, then one fell into the Nestorian heresy. On the other hand, depicting his divine nature was impossible because the divinity of God could not be represented. However, if the iconophiles believed that the divinity had been subsumed in the human nature, they were monophysites. "The only admissible figure of the humanity of Christ ... is bread and wine in the holy Supper. This and no other form, this and no other type has he chosen to represent his Incarnation."[7]

As Milton Anastos points out, the council preferred an "ethical" concept of images, that is, one that saw the biographies of the saints and their virtues as living images to be imitated by the average Christian. Anastos indicates that for this reason the fathers of the council cited a patristic line of reasoning, emphasizing that Christians ought to remember God in their hearts and not rely upon icons for their spiritual edification.[8] One of the Church fathers cited by the Council was Theodotus of Ancyra (a fifth century contemporary of Cyril of Alexandria), who said:

> we have been taught not to fashion images of the saints by means of material colors, but rather to imitate their virtues, which are really living images, with the aid of what has been recorded about them in books, so that we may be stimulated in this way to a zeal like theirs.[9]

The council prohibited both the production and veneration of icons on August 29, 754. John of Damascus was excommunicated. The total destruction of icons was ordered. Although the council called itself "ecumenical," it would not be recognized as such by local councils in Jerusalem (760), at the Lateran in Rome (769), and in Antioch (781).[10]

Constantine followed the mandate of his handpicked council and pursued his iconoclastic policies vigorously. Icons were destroyed and replaced by various forms of secular art. Constantine paid particular attention to the monasteries, strongholds of iconophile theology. Monasteries were forcibly closed, and the monks imprisoned, tortured, exiled, or killed. Constantine then attempted to extend his iconoclastic policies to include rejection of the veneration of the Theotokos, saints, and relics, but he died before these additional proscriptions could take hold. Constantine's son Leo IV (775-780), was a moderate

on iconoclastic issues and abandoned the anti-monastic persecutions. His wife Irene probably exerted her influence; she was
an iconophile from Athens.

Leo IV died prematurely in 780, and Irene was proclaimed
"coemperor" with and regent for their ten-year-old son
Constantine VI (who had been named Emperor and thus sole
heir in 776). Resolute, Irene faced down an initial challenge to
her regime. Then, as head of the empire for her minor son,
Empress Irene proceeded with her iconophile policies, working
to restore icons to the Church. The patriarch selected during
her husband's life was forced to resign, and she persuaded Church
leaders to select her secretary, Tarasius, to become patriarch in
784.

Irene and Patriarch Tarasius proceeded deliberately to con-
vene a new council. There was still substantial support for
iconoclasm, which had been in place nearly fifty years, and they
had to work slowly. On July 31, 786, a first attempt at a council
in Constantinople was broken up by soldiers who had supported
Constantine V and favored iconoclasm. Irene ordered the regi-
ments involved to Asia Minor on the pretense of Arab attack.

In May 787, invitations to a new council were issued. This
council of 350 bishops convened in Nicea, away from
Constantinople, and deliberated in seven sessions from September 24 to October 13. It read the decree of the 754 council at
Hieria and condemned both the council and iconoclasm as he-
retical. The destruction of iconoclast writings was ordered.[11] John
of Damascus was restored along with the icons, which were to
be properly venerated in accordance with his theological rationale. This theological rationale is the subject matter of the next
section.

There is a postscript to the first phase of this conflict. Irene
overthrew her son and became the sole ruler of Byzantium in
797 with the title *Basileus* – Emperor (not the feminine *Basilissa*
– Empress).[12] In 802 the Holy Roman Emperor (of Western
Europe), Charles the Great (Charlemagne), offered to marry

Irene. His objective was the reunification of the Eastern and Western Roman Empires. In his mind the throne in Constantinople was vacant because a woman claimed to be emperor. However, shortly after the proposal, Irene was deposed and exiled to a monastery where she died.

The second phase of iconoclasm began with the ascendancy of Leo V, "the Armenian," to the throne in 813 (d. 820). Leo was from Asia Minor, where iconoclasm still flourished, and restoration of iconoclasm to the empire was one of his goals. As he noticed, iconoclast rulers had prospered and lived long lives, while iconophile emperors were deposed and killed in battle. Before attending to ecclesial matters, he planned to restore the military fortunes of the empire against the advancing Bulgars. Once peace at the borders was secured, Leo began to implement his iconoclast policies.

Leo V retained John Grammaticus, now the theological voice of iconoclasm, to accumulate theological arguments for a new iconoclast council. Two ecclesiastical rivals, Patriarch Nicephorus of Constantinople and Theodore of the Studios Monastery, united to oppose the emperor. Initially Leo prevailed; Theodore was exiled, and Nicephorus was deposed and replaced by an iconoclast relative of Constantine V, who was loyal to Leo.

In the spring of 815, a council met in the Great Church of St Sophia (Hagia Sophia) under the leadership of the new patriarch. It summarized and condemned the 787 council and summarized and restored the 754 council.

A debate exists about the theological rationale offered at the Council of St Sophia. Anastos asserts that the 815 Council did not advance anything greater than the 754 Council had already articulated, while Paul Alexander argues that the Definition (*Horos,* the definition is the decree explaining the theological position of the council) of 815 represents the climax of the iconoclast controversy in that it focused on the "nature of the true religious image."[13] While never calling them idols – apparently as a compromise – the council rejected the production of icons and any acts of devotion involving them. It also blamed the "feminine simplicity" of Empress Irene for the restoration of icons in 787. However, it said little in its own theological voice except: "Embracing the straight doctrine we banish from the Catholic church the invalid production, presumptuously proclaimed (by the Seventh Ecumenical Council of 787), of the spurious images." The council called the icons "soulless" and pointed to the saints as "sharers in the form of Christ."[14] According to Alexander, the council moved beyond the Christological arguments of the earlier phase of the conflict and moved the argument to the nature of the images themselves because calling the icons spurious is a significant innovation. As he points out, for the Council of St Sophia "the true representation of Christ and of the saints was the virtuous man."[15] Yet even Alexander acknowledges Patriarch Nicephorus' contention that the St Sophia Council, while rejecting the 787 definition, offered no definition of its own, thus making its definition (*horos*) ill-defined (*aoristos*).[16]

For these reasons it seems reasonable to conclude that iconoclasm, as an ideology, had become exhausted and weak. Furthermore, in the second phase the resistance was greater and better organized. Theodore the Studite was particularly influential, among the people, writing and speaking openly against iconoclasm, despite the severe persecution of iconophiles by Emperor Leo.

If support for iconoclasm was weak, it was even weaker for Leo who began to fear for his throne, becoming quite paranoid. His fears were not unfounded. On Christmas Day 820, he was murdered in church by followers of Michael "the Amorian."

Michael II "the Amorian" (820-829) was also an iconoclast but did not continue the persecution of iconophiles. He recalled Theodore and Patriarch Nicephorus from exile, although Nicephorus did not return to his see. Patriarch Methodius openly challenged Michael's iconoclast policies, calling for the restoration of icon veneration. Michael responded by having Methodius scourged and imprisoned, although supposedly for the political reason of being an iconophile allied to Rome. Michael did not recognize any of the councils – 754, 787, or 815 – and actually forbade all discussions about icons.

His successor, Theophilus (829-842), was a harsh iconoclast and openly resumed persecutions. Fueled by his tutor John Grammaticus, whom Theophilus convinced the Church to elect as patriarch in 837, the monasteries were particularly targeted. Throughout both phases of the conflict, the monks had been iconophiles, with many icon painters and defenders of "orthodoxy" among them.[17] However, the iconoclast sphere of influence was confined to Constantinople; in the rest of the empire, icon veneration flourished. Upon Theophilus' death on January 20, 842, his wife Theodora became regent for their minor son Michael III (842-867).

Despite being from an iconoclast region of Armenia, Theodora saw the restoration of the icons as her most urgent task. In one year, she had the iconoclast patriarch, John Grammaticus, deposed and Methodius reinstated. She had a council convened in 843, which decreed the restoration of icons in accordance with the 787 Council of Nicea and was recognized as "ecumenical."[18] On the first Sunday of Lent, March 11, 843, the decree was solemnized in St Sophia as the "Triumph of Orthodoxy." With this decree the conflict finally ended. Ever since, the Orthodox Church has celebrated the restoration of icons on the first Sunday of Lent, the "Sunday of Orthodoxy."

THE THEOLOGICAL RATIONALE

The Seventh Ecumenical Council refuted the Council at Hieria, relying on the patristic witness from antiquity and the more contemporary writings of John of Damascus. John's voice was particularly powerful in the debate, as he was alternately anathematized and restored by the various councils on images.

Yet, by the time of the triumph of Orthodoxy in 843, the body of writings in defense of icons had expanded to include, among others, those of the influential Theodore the Studite and Patriarch Nicephorus. The theology of images presented by these three fathers of the Church is our concern in this section. This theology can be seen in four areas: 1) the argument about the Mosaic prohibition of idols (Ex. 20.4-5); 2) the argument about the nature of the image itself; 3) the Christological argument; and 4) the issue of worship (λατρεία, *latreia*) versus veneration (προσκύνησις, *proskynesis*).

A comment must be made on the methodology of the iconophiles and the iconoclasts. To this day, any debate within Orthodoxy will look to the "Tradition," both written (primarily Scripture, patristic writings, and other authorities) and unwritten (liturgical practices, the oral tradition, the argument of silence), for its support. This is very apparent in the iconoclast controversy. Both sides saw their position supported in the Tradition. There was merit on both sides, for the Tradition included support for both arguments.

The iconoclasts cited passages claiming that icons and their veneration were not in the Tradition handed down from Christ or the Apostles and that the ancient authorities steadfastly supported this position. Thedotus of Ancyra has already been identified. The iconoclasts also found supportive statements made by Asterius of Amasea, Origen, Epiphanius, Eusebius, and many others.[19]

The iconophiles also cited the fathers, for many authorities favored the images. However, their argument also included an argument from silence. The iconophiles noted that the Church had always used images and found no problem with them. Thus, history itself was evidence of their position; had there been an issue with the icons, the Church had had many opportunities to speak on the matter. Yet, in the six Ecumenical Councils only one mention of images had been made. Canon 82 of the Quinisext (the Council "in Trullo" of 691) prohibited the image of the Lamb, insisting on the image of the human Christ in artistic depiction. Thus, history itself was evidence for the authenticity of icon veneration. As Jaroslav Pelikan wryly asks: "were the iconoclasts willing, despite the promise of Christ that the gates of hell would not prevail against the church, to claim that the church had been in error for seven hundred years until they came along?"[20]

The Mosaic Prohibition

> You shall not make for yourself a graven image, or any likeness of anything that is in heaven above, or that is in the earth beneath, or that is in the water under the earth; you shall not bow down to them or serve them; for I the Lord your God am a jealous God (Exodus 20.4-5a).

This text is repeated verbatim in Deuteronomy 5.8-10, and the meaning appears clear: there were to be no images in Israel. The word used by the Septuagint is *eidolon* (εἴδωλον), meaning picture or copy, from which the word idol is derived. The text itself does not specifically state that God could not be depicted but that images of any kind are prohibited.[21] The word *eidolon* is clear; it refers to images of the gods or any of the pagan deities, and thus the Mosaic injunction can be seen as a command against paganism. In Jewish thought, idols and pagan gods were identical, for there is no reality to either. "The idol is not merely an alternative god; it is an unreal god, and therefore false as distinct from true and real."[22] Pictorial representation of God was prohibited to preserve God's spiritual nature in the minds of the Israelites. The meaning of the Hebrew Scriptures appears clear: the pagan worship of idols was prohibited because the idols were meaningless representations, but imagery used in the aid of worship was an acceptable practice.

We can assume that this understanding was clear to the Israelites because even the Hebrew Scriptures have references to pictorial depiction, especially in connection with the worship

of God. The Tabernacle and the Ark of the Covenant were signs
of God's presence (Ex. 40.34-38), and both were decorated with
cherubim (Ex. 36.8; 37.7-9) as was the Temple of Solomon (1
Kg. 6.23; 31; 35). Nowhere, however, were there depictions of
God. Elsewhere in the Scriptures, the prohibition of God's depiction was reinforced by contrast with the pagan use of empty,
lifeless, idols.

> Why should the nations say,
> "Where is their God?"
> Our God is in the heavens;
> he does whatever he pleases.
> Their idols are silver and gold,
> the work of men's hands.
> They have mouths, but do not speak;
> eyes, but do not see.
> They have ears, but do not hear;
> noses but do not smell.
> They have hands, but do not feel;
> feet, but do not walk;
> and they do not make a sound in their throat.
> Those who make them are like them;
> so are all who trust in them (Psalm 115.2-8).

An additional argument against idols was that they were made
by human hands. The logic behind this was that God could
neither be controlled nor mastered by human efforts, especially
in a visible form. Furthermore, the materials used in the fabri-
cation of idols are profane and could be used in the production
of other objects. All things are the creation of God and subject
to him; thus they can not be used to depict him. It was "ridiculous to seek a likeness of Yahweh in the created order."[23]

The iconoclasts justified their position scripturally on the
Mosaic prohibition. Exodus 20.4-5 was sufficient biblical proof
for the prohibition of icons and their veneration, showing clearly
that the iconophiles were idolaters. The Decalogue command

had special authority for the iconoclasts, having been handed down from Moses "the lawgiver" himself, and it was used by some of the fathers to show the differences between pagan and Christian worship. "This seemed to prove that the reverence appropriately paid to God could not be transferred to images, even if this were done on the pretext of Christian devotion to so-called images of Christ and the saints."[24] This argument was sufficiently persuasive to stimulate the major apologists of icons to refute the iconoclast interpretation of the passage.

The iconophile apologists began by pointing out that the Hebrew Scriptures had more to say about images than only prohibiting them. They urged their readers to look at the entire text, to look beyond the letter of the law, at its spirit.[25] The iconophile argument was straightforward. God was clearly to be first in a Christian's life, and worship is due God alone. Placing an object, even one depicting God, as an object of worship is idolatrous. However, an artistic object placed in the service of the worship of God is acceptable and a practice to be encouraged. The apologists pointed out the inconsistency of the prohibition with the reality recorded in the Scriptures. They wondered, rhetorically, why God commanded Moses to decorate the tabernacle with images if their use was prohibited. An example is the following passage, cited by John of Damascus, from Leontius of Neapolis, a seventh century bishop in Cyprus (d. ca. 650):

> Truly this command is awesome: God, who commands Israel to make no image, or carving, or likeness of anything in heaven or on earth, Himself commands Moses to make graven images of cherubim which are living creatures. He shows a vision of the temple to Ezekiel, and it is full of the images and carved likenesses of lions, men and palm trees. Solomon knew the law, and yet he made images, filling the temple with metal figures of oxen, and palm trees, and men, but God did not reproach him on this. Now, if you wish to condemn me on this subject, you are condemning God, who

ordered these things to be made, that they might be remind-
ers for us of Himself.[26]

The apologists pointed out that the reason for the Mosaic
injunction was to lead Israel to greater worship of God and to
avoid the pagan episodes that marked the history of Israel. John
of Damascus wrote, "You see that the one thing aimed for is
that no created thing can be adored in place of the Creator, nor
can adoration be given to any save Him alone. ... For again He
says, 'You shall have no other gods before Me.'"[27] Theodore the
Studite made the connection to the spiritual nature of worship
even closer: "Is not the very pattern of the whole tabernacle a
distinct prefiguration of worship in the Spirit, roughly sketched
in a symbolic vision for the great Moses by the God of all?"[28]

That God used images to reveal himself was certainly a powerful argument for the iconophiles. However, they also asserted,
arguing from Scripture, that God made images of himself. First
and foremost, the Son is an image of the Father. As St Paul
taught: "Christ, ... is the likeness of God" (2 Cor. 4.4) and "He
is the image of the invisible God" (Col. 1.15). The English translation (RSV) here is misleading. In the original, both texts use
the same word – image, in Greek εἰκών – icon. As John of
Damascus explained: "The Son is the natural image of the Father, precisely similar to the Father in every way, except that He
is begotten by the Father, who is not begotten."[29] Of one essence with the Father, according to the Nicene-Constantinopolitan
Creed, Jesus is an image of God.

By mentioning Christ in conjunction with the Mosaic prohibition, John of Damascus pointed out the general Christian
understanding, especially of his day, of the differences between
the revelation of the Old Testament and that of the New. The
Incarnation of Jesus as the Second Person of the Trinity did not
contradict the Mosaic injunction but, rather, transformed it.
God the Father still could not be depicted, but his image – the
Son – could.

Yet, there was still more to the argument. "God Himself first made an image, and presented images to our sight, for 'God created (the first) man in His own image' (Gen. 1.27)."[30] Humanity itself was "made in the image and likeness of God," and thus God had made an image of himself. John asked and wondered how the image of God is present in humanity, an issue we shall take up in more detail in the next chapter. In his *Third Apology* he systematically listed the images made by God. About humanity he wrote:

> The third kind of image is made by God as an imitation of Himself: namely, man. How can what is created share the nature of Him who is uncreated, except by imitation? Just as the Father, and the Son who is the Word, and the Holy Spirit, are one God, so also mind and spirit constitute one man, according to God's dominion and authority. For God says, "Let us make man according to our own image and likeness," and immediately He adds, "and let him have dominion over the fish of the sea, and over the birds of the air, and over all the earth."[31]

From these passages we can see that the iconophiles considered the icons as means to greater worship of God, that the Hebrew Scriptures argued against paganism yet advocated imagery in worship, that the Incarnation of Jesus had surpassed the revelation of the Old Testament, and that images of God existed – namely Jesus and humanity. These final points will be important in the Christological argument over images. At a more fundamental level, however, the argument rested with the nature of the image itself.

The Nature of the Image

For the iconoclasts, a true image must have the same essence (*homoousios*) as the original person (prototype) being depicted. The icons were not *homoousios* with their prototypes. "This definition of the relation between the image and the thing or person imaged ... meant that an image of Christ being used in worship was in fact 'the falsely so-called image of Christ,' since it obviously could not be 'identical in essence' with the person of Jesus Christ himself."[32] Therefore, to venerate an icon is to worship "as God a thing which is not God, that is, of idolatry,"[33] Also, if the images were *homoousios*, then with each new image produced, say of Christ, many Christs were being depicted and many forms of worship were being created before them, thus leading to polytheism.

However, the iconophiles neither believed nor argued that the images were *homoousios* with the prototype.

> An image is a likeness, or a model, or a figure of something, showing in itself what it depicts. An image is not always like its prototype in every way. For the image is one thing, and the thing depicted is another; one can always notice differences between them, since one is not the other, and vice versa. I offer the following example: An image of a man, even if it is a likeness of his bodily form, cannot contain his mental powers. It has no life; it cannot think, or speak, or hear, or move. A son is the natural image of his father, yet is different from him, for he is a son, and not a father.[34]

The argument of the iconophiles was that the image was "similar to" yet different from the original. At the Seventh Council, the fathers argued,

> The icon resembles the prototype, not with regard to the essence, but only with regard to the name and to the position of the members which can be characterized. ... No one of sound mind who sees an icon of a man thinks that ... man is separated from his soul. An icon lacks not only a soul but also the very substance of the body ... If these were seen in the icon, we would call this a "man" and not an "icon of a man."[35]

The iconophiles relied upon an Aristotelian logic of similarity, that is, "to what" (πρός τι) is the image related. This meant that there was a close relationship between the prototype and the image, like father to son, but that there were clear differences as well.[36] To the question that naturally arises from this line of reasoning, "What then is being depicted, either Christ or Christ himself (in essence)?" Theodore the Studite answered: "We say that Christ is one thing and His image is another thing by nature, although they have an identity in the use of the same name."[37]

As for the issue about many images creating many Christs, the iconophiles saw this as a ridiculous outcome of the iconoclast position. To refute the argument, the iconophiles, relying upon the writings of St Basil the Great (d. 379), turned to the respect that the people paid to the image of the emperor. People paid homage to the image, but it was understood that the homage was to the emperor, not the image. At the enthronement of a new emperor, his bust would be carried into all the major cities, and people would come out to see the image. There was also a legal precedent for seeking asylum at the statue of the emperor, which was established by Emperor Theodosius; if someone took refuge there, one was safe from removal for ten days.

Based on these practices, St Basil had written "that the image of the emperor is also called 'emperor' and yet there are not two emperors."[38] In a statement that would become central to the iconophile refutation of iconoclasm, Basil had also written: "The honor given the image passes to the prototype. The image of the emperor is an image by imitation … in works of art the likeness is dependent on its original form."[39]

Using the Aristotelian principle of similarity, the iconophiles were able to develop it to refute both the idea that many images lead to polytheism, as well as the idea that the image creates multiple deities. Theodore wrote that:

> We call the image of Christ "Christ" because it is also Christ, yet there are not two Christs. It is not possible to distinguish one from the other by the name, which they have in com-

mon, but by their natures. (He next repeats the above statement of Basil the Great).

"It happens," the heretics say, "that as many are called Lords
and Christ as there are different icons, and from this comes
polytheism"...

So what? Is not the Father Lord? Is not the Son Lord? Is not
the Spirit Lord? As each of them is also God? Of course. So
then are there three Gods and Lords? What impiety! There is
one God and Lord. And, sir, you must understand the same
in the case of icons. Even if there are many representations,
still there is only one Christ and not many; just as the same
one is Lord, and not different individuals.[40]

The Christological Argument

As Sahas points out, the end of the iconoclast controversy
was the culmination of the Christological doctrines articulated
by the Church over the centuries.[41] Both parties to the debate
knew the Tradition, and both claimed to be in harmony with it,
particularly the doctrine of the Fourth Ecumenical Council of
Chalcedon (451), which defined the position of the Church
regarding the two natures of Christ. Jesus Christ – the God-
man – was both God and human, two natures in one person
(*prosopon*) and *hypostasis* "without confusion, without change,
without division, without separation."[42] For the iconoclasts, the
icons were a clear departure from this doctrine. As has been
pointed out, there were three possibilities. First, the icons depicted the humanity of Christ, which had subsumed or
overwhelmed his divinity. If this was the case then the iconophiles
were monophysites. Second, if the icons depicted only the humanity of Christ, then they fell into Nestorianism. Third, if the
icons somehow depicted the divinity of Christ, then Christ was
not divine. It was impossible to depict the divinity of Christ
because divinity cannot be circumscribed or contained in any
fashion.

The iconophiles completely agreed with the last option. God could not be depicted, for he was "utterly uncircumscribable" and "no thought can comprehend, no sound can designate" him.[43] As John of Damascus wrote: "If anyone should dare to make an image of the immaterial, bodiless, invisible, formless, colorless Godhead, we reject it as a falsehood."[44]

Yet the iconophiles also saw a new reality being expressed in the new covenant established by Christ. "In former times God, who is without form or body, could never be depicted."[45] Here John of Damascus refers to the period of the Old Testament and, continuing in the same, often cited statement, points out the crucial difference:

> But now when God is seen in the flesh conversing with men, I make an image of the God whom I see. I do not worship matter; I worship the Creator of matter who became matter for my sake, who willed to take His abode in matter, who worked out my salvation through matter. Never will I cease honoring the matter which wrought my salvation! I honor it, but not as God.[46]

For the iconophiles, the Incarnation of divinity in the person of Jesus not only made the icons possible; it made them a requirement of true Christian faith.

Reflecting on the Incarnation, we can see within this argument two Christological issues being raised by the iconophiles: the historicity and the humanity of Christ. In the following statement of John of Damascus these are evident in his thinking:

> The flesh assumed by Him is made divine and endures after its assumption. Fleshly nature was not lost when it became part of the Godhead, but just as the Word made flesh remained the Word, so also flesh became the Word, yet remained flesh, being united to the person of the Word. Therefore I boldly draw an image of the invisible God, not as invisible, but as having become visible for our sakes by partaking of flesh and blood.[47]

The iconophile position emphasized the historicity of Christ, made possible by the Incarnation and clearly manifested by the icons. Theodore the Studite quotes the First Epistle of John, "That which ... we have seen with our eyes, which we have looked upon and touched with our hands..." (1 Jn 1.1) and then lists events of Christ's life. "As the Gospel writers had been able to 'write of Christ in words (λογογραφεῖν),' so it was also possible to 'write in gold (χρυσογραφεῖν)' by depicting these scenes in icons."[48] For the iconophiles, the content of icons and of the Gospels were the same. At the Seventh Council, the fathers stated that, "The representation of scenes in colors follows the narrative of the gospel; and the narrative of the gospel follows the narrative of the paintings. Both are good and honourable."[49]

John's statement also dealt with the issue of the humanity of Christ, for He was the Word made flesh, and this flesh had not been lost in the Ascension nor had divinity somehow been lessened by dwelling in the flesh. The iconophile argument was that flesh had been sanctified through the union with divinity in Christ. The Seventh Council declared: "Even though the catholic Church depicts Christ in human form, she does not separate this from the divinity united with it. ... We confess the Lord's flesh to be deified."[50] An implication of this view, evident throughout the thinking of the iconophiles, was that matter is good. The implications of this will be addressed in the discussions on veneration, the body, and the environment. However, the view of the humanity of Christ as refined by Theodore the Studite deserves attention.

Theodore systematically refuted the iconoclast argument that Christ is uncircumscribable by discussing the humanity of the Christ revealed in Scripture. He asked, how, if Christ does not have a human nature, can the Scriptures describe him as suffering blows (Is. 53.3), being spat upon (Is. 50.6), having his hands and feet pierced (Ps. 21.16-17), dwelling in Nazareth (Mt. 2.23), or having someone say of him, "See the Lamb of God..." (Jn. 1.14)?[51] He concluded:

If Christ is not circumscribable, He is not of two natures, divinity and humanity, since He does not have the property of each. For circumscribability is characteristic of humanity. But if He is of two natures, how can He avoid having the properties of those whose natures He has?[52]

Theodore also raised the issue of Jesus' birth as evidence of his humanity. If Christ could not be circumscribed, then he could not have been conceived in Mary's womb. "But if He was not only conceived … but even born as an infant, then He is circumscribed without shame."[53] Although his divinity, coming from the uncircumscribable Father, could not be circumscribed, his humanity, which comes from a circumscribable mother, could be circumscribed. Jesus was *homoousios* with his Father and *homoousios* with his mother. Thus Jesus, from two origins, possessed the properties of each and is uncircumscribable and circumscribed in his person.[54]

As a final point in this argument, Theodore very briefly reflected on the maleness of Christ. Theodore argued that maleness and femaleness can only exist within bodies. If Christ did not have a body, he reasoned, then he could not be circumscribed. However, he continued, we know that Jesus was born as a male, for so the Scriptures testified. Therefore, Jesus had a body. Adding weight to his argument, Theodore noted, was that Jesus was circumcised on the eighth day (Lk. 2.21). Theodore could conclude decisively that Jesus had a human body – that of a male – and was circumscribed.[55] Hence, Jesus could be depicted in images.

The entire Christological argument about the Incarnation, the historicity, and humanity of Christ centered on the understanding of the *hypostasis,* or person of Christ. As the definition of the Council of Chalcedon declared, Jesus was one *hypostasis* (person) in two natures. The iconophiles understood that the *hypostasis* of Christ, preserving what was distinct to the two natures, could be depicted. John of Damascus wrote, "God's body is God because it is joined to His person by a union which shall never pass away."[56] Theodore refined this view by arguing that only a *hypostasis* could be depicted, not nature in general. Humanity is the species, but each individual differs in his or her *hypostasis* and therefore is called Paul, George, or Katherine. Jesus had not assumed humanity in general, but a specific *hypostasis* that differentiated him from others. Theodore wrote:

> If Christ does not represent an individual, as you (the iconoclasts) say, but man in general, how can He say to His disciples, "Who do men say that I, the son of man, am?" (Mt. 16.13) Therefore He is one like us, although He is God and one of the Trinity. Just as He is distinguished from the Father and the Spirit by the property of sonship, so He is differentiated from all other men by His hypostatic properties.[57]

Thus, the only option was to depict the divine and human natures together, in the *hypostasis* of Jesus, the mystery in whom the invisible God took on visible flesh.[58]

Veneration (proskynesis) versus Worship (latreia)

The distinction between veneration and worship may seem obscure or a "hairsplitting" matter of semantics. To an observer, the practices of Orthodox toward icons – bowing, kneeling, making prostrations, kissing, lighting candles before them, offering incense before them, decorating them, and carrying them in processions – may seem idolatrous because the outward act is directed at the icon. Yet, each of these acts is an act of veneration, of honoring the person or persons depicted through the image. The person being honored is represented by the image. The honor being paid does not stop at the icon but passes through to the original person. The iconoclasts and iconophiles argued over this point.

The iconoclasts believed that the acts of honor associated with images were idolatry because the images were the object of worship. Rather than worshipping God, the people were worshipping lifeless, soulless objects. The iconoclasts preferred to worship God through mental contemplation, in spirit and truth (Jn. 4.23). They believed true spiritual worship was being perverted by the use of images and the adoration of material objects, leading the Church into idolatry.

There was one major exception to the iconoclasts' position: the cross. Iconoclasts paid a special respect to the image of the cross. Recall that Leo III, the first iconoclast emperor, had the image of Christ at the *Chalke* Gate replaced with the image of the cross. The iconoclast devotion to the cross was sincere, but when challenged with the apparent inconsistency by iconophiles, the iconoclasts argued "we worship the symbol (*typos*) of the cross on account of him who was fastened to it."[59]

The iconophiles responded to the accusations of the iconoclasts on many fronts. They challenged the singular devotion paid to the cross as well as the idea that worship in spirit could not be aided by material objects. Most significantly, they challenged the iconoclast understanding of worship, making careful distinction between worship, due only to God, and the veneration offered to images.

On the matter of the cross, John of Damascus located a passage from Leontius of Neapolis:

As long as wood is fastened together in the form of a cross, I venerate it because it is a likeness of the wood on which Christ was crucified. If it should fall to pieces, I throw the pieces into the fire. When a man receives a sealed order from the emperor, he kisses the seal. He does not honor clay, paper, or wax for their own sake, but he gives honor and veneration to the emperor. Likewise, when Christian people venerate the form of the cross, they are not worshipping the nature of wood, but they see that it is marked with the imprint of the hands of Him who was nailed upon it, and so they embrace and honor it.[60]

This argument by Leontius was consistent with the position

of the iconoclasts: because of the crucifixion of Jesus, Christians honor the cross. To refute the charge of idolatry, Leontius noted the relative nature of the image (the cross) being honored. The wood that constitutes the image is not the focus of reverence. The materials can be discarded when they wear out. However, John of Damascus was more incisive regarding the inconsistency of the iconoclasts: "If we bow down before the cross, no matter what substance it is made from, shall we not bow down before the image of Him who was crucified upon it?"[61]

The iconophiles argued that icons and material objects were aids to worship, leading the believer to the prototype of what was depicted. Their argument was based on the statement of Basil the Great about honoring the image of the emperor in his absence, "The honor given the image passes to the prototype."[62] For the iconophiles, devotion to the icon, although directed to the image, does not remain with the image but passes through to the original – to the prototype being depicted. This was very evident to the iconophiles, and they argued along a fairly simple line. John of Damascus noted, "I have often seen lovers gazing at the garments of their beloved, embracing the garments with their eyes and their lips as if the garment were the beloved one."[63] For the twentieth century reader, the modern example is the individual who kisses the photograph of a loved one. Is the object of affection the paper of the photograph, or is the affection really being directed toward the person being depicted? As Theodore the Studite summarized it, "The mind does not remain with the materials, because it does not trust in them. Through the materials … the mind ascends toward the prototype: this is the faith of the orthodox."[64]

This point is not to be taken lightly. It is an essential concept in the veneration of images as well as in the use of material objects in worship and devotional life. The appropriate encounter with the icon, despite its powerful presence as a visual image, is an encounter that goes beyond the icon itself to the greater transcendent reality of God. Going back to the Mosaic injunction against idolatry, graven images of deities were prohibited because they depicted something beyond which there was no reality, making them false gods. When Christians venerate icons, their thoughts and prayers are properly directed to that which is depicted, not the depiction itself, even though the act of veneration is directed toward the object. To the uninitiated observer, this veneration may appear to be an idolatrous act. For the Orthodox Christian, the distinction is understood, even though, paradoxically, the icon itself is considered a holy object. An interesting question that this issue raises is how Orthodox Christians personally perceive this subtlety and how the perception might vary from childhood to adulthood.

In advocating the correctness of using material objects in the worship of God, the iconophiles offered three arguments. The first was that matter was essentially good because it was a creation of God. John of Damascus wrote, "Do not despise matter, for it is not despicable. God has made nothing despicable."[65] A second argument was that through the Incarnation of Christ, matter had become an instrument of salvation. In one now famous passage John writes: "I do not worship matter, I worship the Creator of matter who became matter for me ... I worship that through which my salvation has come, I honor it, not as God, but because it is full of divine grace and strength."[66] The third was directed toward the inconsistency of the iconoclasts who, the iconophiles noted, neither accepted all material objects of religious devotion nor rejected them completely. If incorporeal worship was the only acceptable form of worship, then all forms of material objects should be eliminated from worship. But, because as human beings we have bodies and senses, our bodies and senses must be engaged in the worship of God – it is an unavoidable concomitant of being human. In the lengthy but significant passage that follows, John postulated the conditions necessary for exclusively spiritual worship, noted shortcomings of this viewpoint, and ironically challenged the position taken by iconoclasts:

If you say that only intellectual worship is worthy of God, then take away all corporeal things: lights, the fragrance of incense, prayer made with the voice. Do away with the divine mysteries which are fulfilled through matter: bread, wine, the oil of chrism, the sign of the cross. All these things are matter! Take away the cross and the sponge of the crucifixion, and the spear which pierced His lifegiving side. Either give up honoring all these things, or do not refuse to honor images. Matter is filled with divine grace through prayer addressed to those portrayed in images. Purple cloth by itself is a simple thing, and so is silk, and a cloak is woven from both. But if the king should put it on, the cloak receives honor from the honor given to him who wears it. It is the same with matter. By itself it deserves no worship, but if someone portrayed in an image is full of grace, we become partakers of the grace according to the measure of our faith. The apostles saw the Lord with bodily eyes; others saw the apostles, and others the martyrs. I too desire to see them both spiritually and physically and receive the remedy by which the ills of both soul and body (for I am composed of both) may be healed. What I see with my eyes I venerate, but not as God; I revere that which portrays what I honor. You, perhaps, are superior to me, and have risen so far above bodily things that you have become virtually immaterial and feel free to make light of all visible things, but since I am human and clothed with a body, I desire to see and be present with the saints physically. Condescend from your heights to my lowly state of mind, for by doing so you will make your lofty position safe. God accepts my longing for Him and for His saints.[67]

Theodore the Studite put the argument in fewer words when he stated that if only mental worship was sufficient, then God did not need to become human and endure the cross; He could have communicated with humanity mentally.[68]

On the issue of whether an icon was being worshipped, John of Damascus defined the terms the Orthodox would use to discuss the question. The key terms are *latreia* (adoration or absolute worship) and *proskynesis* (veneration or relative worship). He described five forms of *latreia*: The first type of absolute worship is adoration for God alone, "for only He by nature deserves to be worshipped." The second worship of God is the "awe and yearning we have of Him" because of His glory. Third is thanksgiving for all that God has given us. Fourth is the worship that is "inspired by our needs and hopes for His blessing." Fifth is the worship that is "repentance and confession."[69] His point was simple: absolute worship – *latreia* – is due God and God only, involving no material objects. "Worship" directed toward anyone or anything else must be of a relative nature.

John used the term *proskynesis* – veneration – to discuss relative worship. He defined seven forms of veneration, giving the first type – that due the saints and the icons – the fullest explanation.

What are the different ways we offer this relative worship to created things? First of all, those places where God, who alone is holy, has rested. He rests in holy places: that is the Theotokos, and all the saints. These are they who have become likenesses of God as far as is possible, since they have chosen to cooperate with divine election. Therefore God dwells in them. They are truly called gods, not by nature, but by adoption, just as red-hot iron is called fiery, not by nature, but because it participates in the action of the fire ... Therefore ... they are to be venerated, not because they deserve it on their own account, but because they bear in themselves Him who is by nature worshipful. We do not back away and refuse to touch red hot iron because of the nature of the iron, but because it has partaken of what is hot by nature. The saints are to be venerated because God has glorified them, and through Him they have become fearful to the enemy, and are benefactors for the faithful. ... Therefore we venerate them, because the king is given honor through the worship given to his beloved servants. They are obedient servants and favored friends, but they are not the King Himself. When someone prays with faith, offering his petition in the name of such a favored friend, the King receives it, through the intercession of the faithful servant, because He accepts the honor and faith which the petitioner has shown to His servant.[70]

The second type of veneration is given to places and the things "by which God has accomplished our salvation." The third kind is due to "objects dedicated to God, such as the holy Gospel and other books ... patens, chalices, censers, altars should all receive respect." The fourth kind is due to "images which were seen by the prophets (for they saw God in the images of their visions). These images were of future things, such as Aaron's rod, which prefigured the mystery of the Virgin ..." The fifth kind of relative worship is "our veneration of each other, since we are God's inheritance, and were made according to His image, and so we are subject to each other, thus fulfilling the law of love." The sixth kind of veneration "is given to those who have been given authority to rule over us," and the seventh is "given to benefactors who grant the requests of their petitioners.."[71]

In all the forms of veneration, the relativity of worship should be clear. As John stated near the conclusion of his treatise: "We venerate images; it is not veneration offered to matter, but to those who are portrayed through matter in the images. Any honor given to an image is transferred to its prototype."[72] By honoring an image, it is God who is honored, even as the material image is the vehicle of grace and blessings. But, as stated above, the icons themselves are holy objects; they are not mere symbols.

EDUCATIONAL IMPLICATIONS

Three basic educational issues emerging from the historical debate on the icons are noted. They serve as a foundation for

the principles of iconic catechesis and will be developed further
in light of later theological and educational reflection, but they
are introduced now in their historical context. The iconophiles
recognized the formative power of images in the life of believers, moving and challenging them to a new way of life. In this
passage, John of Damascus raised the key issues related to the
educational significance of icons:

> What more conspicuous proof do we need that images are
> the books of the illiterate, the never silent heralds of the honor
> due the saints, teaching without use of words those who gaze
> upon them, and sanctifying the sense of sight? Suppose I have
> few books, or little leisure for reading, but walk into the spiritual hospital – that is to say, a church – with my soul choking
> from the prickles of thorny thoughts, and thus afflicted I see
> before me the brilliance of the icon. I am refreshed as if in a
> verdant meadow, and thus my soul is led to glorify God. I
> marvel at the martyr's endurance, at the crown he won, and
> inflamed with burning zeal I fall down to worship God
> through His martyr, and so receive salvation.[73]

This statement expresses the three basic educational themes
of icons. One, images are books, proclaiming the Gospel equally
with the written word and perhaps more formatively. Two, there
is a psychological dimension to the icons in that they sanctify
vision, and through it, all bodily senses, pointing to a holisitic
approach to knowledge and Christian living. Three, to encounter the icons is to be taught by them through personal
engagement. The content of the icons' teaching is a healing,
salvific message that invites a response.

Books Equal to Scripture

Even prior to the iconoclast conflict, images were defended
for their educational utility. The earliest defense of icons was
that they were books for the illiterate; many patristic writers
describe them thus. In keeping with his remarks above, John of
Damascus expressed this view: "What the book is to the liter-

ate, the image is to the illiterate. Just as words speak to the ear, so the image speaks to the sight; it brings us understanding."[74]

That this perspective has the potential to be both minimalist and elitist cannot be overlooked. To suggest that icons are only books minimizes their potential. As we have already noted and shall continue to emphasize, the icons offer a great deal more for catechesis. At a basic level, visual information presented by icons can be perceived and understood without a great deal of sophistication. A preliterate child with minimal guidance can learn to recognize persons and events depicted in icons. However, with the help of a catechist, the ability to discern and appreciate the subtleties and nuances of icons in depth can develop.

Furthermore, the notion that icons are only books can be an elitist position. If, in the Byzantine Empire, the practice of religious education was to direct some to icons while reserving the study of sacred texts and writings – requiring literacy and more advanced knowledge – then for others, the position on icons as books would be a highly elitist, discreditable perspective. However, at its best, Byzantine education flourished within that society, being encouraged for all boys and men, and also being accessible to some women.[75] While the same standards for equal access to education that exist today did not apply, the Byzantines fared considerably better in this respect than was normative for that time period.

Even when icons are referred to as "books," the significance of integrating visual and verbal messages, so that jointly they will yield greater knowledge, was understood. At the Seventh Ecumenical Council, the assembled fathers pointed out the interrelationship of the visual and the verbal, and the synergistic benefits that result.

> The representation of scenes in colors follows the narrative of the gospel; and the narrative of the gospel follows the narrative of the paintings. Both are good and honorable. Things

which are indicative of each other undoubtedly speak for each other ... When we see on an icon the angel bringing the good news to the Virgin, we must certainly bring to mind that 'the angel Gabriel was sent from God to the virgin. And he came to her and said: "Hail, O favoured one, the Lord is with you. Blessed are you among women" (Cf. Lk. 1.26-28).' Thus from the gospel we have heard of the mystery communicated to the Virgin through the angel, and this way we are reminded of it. Now when we see the same thing on an icon we perceive the event with greater emphasis.[76]

Notice that the icons achieve their goal more powerfully – "with greater emphasis" – than the verbal message because of the dynamism of an artistic presentation. By examining the icon of the Annunciation we can see what the Council meant. The moment of the encounter is presented vividly (see Figure 1). The angel is moving toward Mary. The wings are extended, and the garments have a great deal of motion in them. Mary appears startled by the angel's appearance. Her spinning has fallen; her hand is raised in surprise. The art focuses on the most important point of the story – the moment of the encounter between the angel and Mary – presenting it dramatically, colorfully, and clearly.

The iconophiles also made a claim that modern readers may find shocking: the content of the image is equal to the content of the word. This claim is consistent with Eastern Christian views on the relationship of revelation to Scripture. Scripture is not the equivalent of revelation. Rather, it is the verbal record of how God chose to reveal himself to us so that, by faith, it becomes a medium of God's revelation. However, God has chosen to reveal himself in many ways, through actions and images as well as words.[77] At the Seventh Ecumenical Council this idea was used to articulate the purpose of icons. The high value of both the visual and the verbal allowed the Fathers to use a very natural line of reasoning. Whether the believer hears the Gospel or sees the icon, the reaction is the same; both lead to doxology of God.

For, when they hear the gospel with the ears, they exclaim "glory to Thee, O Lord"; and when they see it with the eyes, they send forth exactly the same doxology, for we are reminded of his life among men. That which the narrative declares in writing is the same as that which the icon does [in colors].[78]

In the definition of the Seventh Council, the equality of visual and verbal was made dogmatic. The Council definition describes the icons as being "of equal benefit to us as the Gospel narrative. For those which point mutually to each other undoubtedly mutually signify each other."[79] The benefit is that both icon and word, but especially the icon, help us know that the Incarnation of God the Logos "was real" and "not imaginary."

Theodore the Studite was earlier cited as saying that the Gospels write the message of Christ in words while the icons write in gold. Based on the decision of the Council, Patriarch Nicephorus of Constantinople wrote, "If the one is worthy of honor, the other is worthy of honor also." If the icons could not be venerated, then neither could the Gospels. As he argued, "Either accept these [icons], or get rid of those [Gospels]."[80]

A Psychology of Icons

For the early Church, as for all people of the time whose view of humanity was Hellenistic, vision was the primary sense. John of Damascus and Theodore the Studite both recognized vision as the "noblest of the senses."[81] The Church also had the words of Jesus to support the primacy of sight: "Blessed are your eyes, for they see, and your ears, for they hear. Truly, I say to you, many prophets and kings longed to see what you see, and did not see it, and to hear what you hear, and did not hear it" (Mt. 13.16-17). John of Damascus reflected on these words and expressed the desire to see Christ face to face, which was only made possible by the icons.

We too desire to see, and to hear, and so be filled with gladness. They saw Him face to face, since He was physically present, we hear His words read from books and by hearing our souls are sanctified and filled with blessing, and so we worship, honoring the books from which we hear His words. So also, through the painting of images, we are able to contemplate the likeness of His bodily form, His miracles, and His Passion, and thus are sanctified, blessed, and filled with joy. Reverently we honor and worship His bodily form, and by contemplating His bodily form, we form a notion, as far as is possible for us, of the glory of His divinity.[82]

In the time of Christ, when people heard and saw Jesus, the verbal and visual messages were coordinated. The Apostles described what they saw and heard, and their descriptions are recorded in Scripture. While the verbal message could be maintained through reading and hearing the proclamation of the Gospel, without images the visual message would be diminshed. Icons provide the means by which the believer maintains visual contact with the embodied, incarnate, historical Jesus. They remind us that He is always in our midst and help us grasp opportunities for fellowship with Him. Matter has been sanctified by the Incarnation and, therefore, is an appropriate channel for contemplation, veneration, and worship.

The iconophiles recognized that to come to the knowledge of Christ all the senses had to be engaged. This is consistent with the view of the totality of the humanity of Christ. Since Christ's humanity included all the senses of the embodied state, all the senses and the body were sanctified through union with the divine in the person of Christ. John of Damascus wrote, as quoted above, that only through the bodily senses can a person contemplate the bodily form of Christ and form an idea of his divinity. Thus, for the believer, the way to Christ is through the bodily senses.

John emphasized that the body and the senses must be engaged in worship in order to come to knowledge of Christ. He rejected the over-rationalistic approach favored by iconoclasts who worshipped only in "spirit and truth." Recall that in a statement cited earlier, he challenged the iconoclasts to eliminate all vestiges of the material world in their worship – lights, incense, oral prayer, bread, oil, etc. – to be consistent with their line of reasoning and to limit themselves to exclusively intellectual worship, with no images at all.

A second psychological aspect of icons is the emotional response they generate in the viewing believers. The art of the icon intends to evoke an emotional response from the viewer. The iconophiles felt that the emotions evoked by material objects were natural and perfectly appropriate in the case of images. At the Seventh Council, the deliberations included a reference to a sermon by St. Gregory of Nyssa, in which he said, "I saw an icon of the Passion and I was not able to pass by the sight without tears, because the art was conveying the story vividly."[83]

Imitation of Depicted Virtue

The emotional response stimulated by the icon is not purposeless – just "feeling" something for the sake of the feeling. It is intended that the emotion will lead the person to action, to imitate the virtues depicted by the icons. The Church recognized the power of art to form one's behavior. The Seventh Council also stated this clearly:

> These holy men of all times who pleased God, whose biographies have remained in writing for our benefit and for the purpose of our salvation, have also left to the catholic Church their deeds explained in paintings, so that our mind may remember them, and so that we may be lifted up to the level of their conduct.[84]

The Council noted that the story of the bravery of the forty martyrs of Sebaste, who froze to death on an Armenian lake during the reign of Emperor Licinius (320) for their unwillingness to renounce Christianity,[85] would be retold by the image and would inspire others to imitate their courage. The Seventh Ecumenical Council recognized that the whole purpose of retelling or re-presenting the stories of the saints and Christ was to lead believers to imitate them. Retelling the stories of the saints, remembering their deeds, and painting their icons were instructive, not because people needed to recall their physical characteristics, but because Christians should attempt to imitate their virtue. There is a singularity of purpose in art, story, and praise. They exist to lead people to salvation.[86]

Salvation comes not abstractly, but person by person, and the Council recognized this. Virtue was understood to be personal, bound up in the identity and agency of a believer, and not a concept simply agreed to cognitively. John of Damascus expressed this view by uniting human salvation with the Incarnation of Christ. Through this event, humanity received the opportunity for divinization or to become "partakers of divine nature" by union with God through the life of the Church. In a few lines he explained Orthodox anthropology:

> The person of the Son of God did not assume angelic nature, but human nature. Angels do not share in this; they do not become partakers of the divine nature. But by the operation of grace, men do share in and become partakers of the divine nature ... We do not become the same person as He is, for we also first exist as individual persons.[87]

This concreteness of the transformed human person is graphically displayed in the icons. In the icon of the Transfiguration of Christ (Figure 7), the human person of Christ radiates the uncreated light of His divinity without destroying or damaging, but showing the perfection of, humanity. The saints are concrete and of this world; yet they possess the qualities of the transfigured world brought about by Christ. In the icons of saints, we see the concreteness of their human person depicted in its transformed manner, achieved stylistically in the art of the icon. The image of the human person transformed by grace is venerated.

The saints, as vessels of divine grace, show the potential of human life for union with God. However, like the iron in the fire, the saints do not lose their personal identity in the union.

They are transfigured and filled with the divine fire, the divine light, which is the energy of God. The saints are the particular, concrete examples of the life in Christ for believers to learn from, imitate, and ultimately to be transfigured themselves. The goal is not to *know about* the saints but to *become* saints. The icon graphically displays the possibility for all human beings to be united with God, achieving *theosis*, in and through the community. The icon, then, depicts the goal of life and education in the Church. Its meaning shall be the subject of the next chapter.

To attain the personal goal of *theosis*, the ancient Church recognized that each person begins in a different place, dependent upon the person's life situation, and that the icons constitute resources that can be applied to unique situations. Each person could be personally engaged by an icon. For the non-believer, the icons were a first step to learning the message of the Gospel.

> If, for example, a pagan were to say to a Christian, "Show me your faith, so that I too may believe," the Christian would begin at the point where his hearer stood, leading him from the data of sense experience to things invisible. Specifically, he would take his friend to church and show him the icons there, so that the pagan would ask about these figures and in this way open himself to the Christian message.[88]

The picture creates an open space for the learner to enter and begin the process of discovery without forcing any one particular point. In the internal, personal dialogue that can ensue, either through the verbal commentary offered in liturgical services or through the instruction of a teacher, the learner can bring his or her assumptions and questions to the icon, see and hear the message of the community, and arrive at a point for response, decision, and action.

Through the use of all means possible, the Church worked to actively engage the person and bring about the continual conversion of Christian life with the hope that the believer would not return to its old ways. At the Seventh Council, the fathers noted:

Thus, the holy catholic Church of God, using many different means, attracts those who are born within her to
repentance and to the knowledge of how to keep the commandments of God. She hastens to guide all our senses to
the glory of the God of all, as she works out a rectification
through both hearing and sight, by displaying to the gaze of
those who come forward what has taken place. Thus, when
she takes someone away from greediness and avarice, she presents him with an icon of Matthew, who from a tax collector
became an Apostle, abandoning the madness of avarice and
following Christ; or of Zacchaeus climbing a sycamore because he wanted to see Christ, and making a commitment to
Him to give half of his goods to the poor and, if he had
defrauded anyone of anything, to return four times as much.
In this way, the continuous looking at pictorial drawings serves
to preserve one's conversion and keeps one constantly mind-
ful of it, so that one may not return to one's own vomit.[89]

By engaging with the image of a saint, the believer saw that it
was possible to repent and begin living a faithful Christian life.
The community facilitated the conversion by presenting the icon
to the believer. Conversion or *metanoia* was nurtured by the
continual presence of the image, with or without the living presence of other members of the community.

NOTES

[1] Frescoes in catacombs date from around the end of the first century A.D. By the fourth century, images or icons depicting individuals
were the preferred form of personal piety. Examples of icons pre-
dating the iconoclastic controversy are few, given the ferocity of the
conflict. Nevertheless, the sixth-century Monastery of St. Catherine
in the Sinai houses many of them. In Ravenna, by the fifth and sixth
centuries, artistic decoration of churches had reached full bloom. See
Charles Murray, "Art and the Early Church," *Journal of Theological
Studies* 28 (1977), pp. 303-345; Norman H. Baynes, "The Icons Before Iconoclasm," *Harvard Theological Review* 44 (1951), pp. 93-106;

Robert Milburn, *Early Christian Art and Architecture* (Berkeley: University of California Press, 1988).

[2] I am following the sequence of events found in George Ostrogorsky, *History of the Byzantine State*, trans. Joan Hussey (New York: Rutgers University Press, 1969), pp. 147-221 and A. A. Vasiliev, *History of the Byzantine Empire,* vol. 1 (Madison: University of Wisconsin Press, 1973), pp. 234-299.

[3] Christoph Schönborn, "Theological Presuppositions of the Image Controversy," in *Icons Windows on Eternity: Theology and Spirituality in Color*, ed. Gennadios Limouris (Geneva: WCC Publications, Faith and Order Paper No. 147, 1990), p. 88.

[4] Daniel Sahas, *Icon and Logos: Sources in Eighth Century Iconoclasm* (Toronto: University of Toronto Press, 1986), pp. 26-28.

[5] Georges Florovsky dates their authorship between 726 and 730. However, we cannot be certain of the dates. Also, only the barest of facts are known about the life of this very important defender of Orthodoxy. He is chiefly remembered for his defense of the icons, his treatise "The Font of Knowledge," the first attempt at a systematic theology, and the numerous hymns he wrote for the liturgical life of the Orthodox Church – hymns that are still in use today. *The Byzantine Fathers of the Sixth to Eighth Century*, vol. IX of the Collected Works (Vaduz: Buchervertriebsanstalt, 1987), pp. 245-257.

[6] D. Sahas, *Icon and Logos*, p. 30.

[7] *Epitome of the Definition of the Iconoclastic Conciliabulum, held in Constantinople, A.D. 754. Nicene and Post-Nicene fathers* vol. XIV (Grand Rapids: Eerdman's, 1956), p. 544.

[8] Milton Anastos, "The Ethical Theory of Images Formulated by the Iconoclasts in 754 and 815," *Dumbarton Oaks Papers* No. 8 (1954), p. 153. See paragraph 16 of *Epitome*.

[9] J. D. Mansi, *Sacrorum conciliorum nova et amplissima collectio*, 13, 309 E-312 as cited in M. Anastos, "Ethical Theory of Images," p. 155.

[10] D. Sahas, *Icon and Logos*, p. 34.

[11] The iconophiles were quite successful in eliminating iconoclast writings, as virtually none survive. If the decision of the 754 Council had not been read and recorded in the meetings of the 787 Council, we would have no record of it.

[12] The significance of her title was that as a woman, her right to

rule and lead the military would be questionable in the eighth century. By taking the masculine title, Irene hoped to dissuade challengers to her authority. See G. Ostrogorsky, *History of the Byzantine State*, p. 181.

[13] M. Anastos, "Ethical Theory of Images," p. 159; Paul Alexander, "The Iconoclastic Council of St. Sophia (815) and its Definition (*Horos*)," *Dumbarton Oaks Papers* No. 7 (1953), p. 37. My purpose is not to enter their debate but to present the story as it appears to have happened and leave the textual analyses and arguments to the historians.

[14] P. Alexander, "Iconoclastic Council of St. Sophia," p. 41.

[15] Ibid., p. 44. This is the point of contention between Anastos and Alexander. Anastos feels that this is still the "ethical" theory of the 754 Council while Alexander disagrees.

[16] Ibid., p. 46.

[17] Of the monks' place in the overall conflict, Meyendorff writes, "Whatever role was played in the Orthodox victory over the iconoclasts by high ecclesiastical dignitaries ..., the real credit belonged to the Byzantine monks who resisted the emperors in overwhelming numbers." John Meyendorff, *Byzantine Theology* (New York: Fordham University Press, 1983), p. 51.

[18] The status of Nicea II appears to vary over time in the Western Church. In the eighth century, the Council of Frankfurt of 794 saw images only as didactic tools, while the *Libri Carolini* refuted the theological points of the council. In more recent times, Leo Davis discusses the council in his treatment of the theology of the Seven Ecumenical Councils [Leo Donald Davis, S.J., *The First Seven Ecumenical Councils (325-787): Their History and Theology* (Wilmington, DE: Michael Glazier, 1987)]. On the other hand, the 1981 edition of Richard McBrien's *Catholicism*, (San Fransciso: Harper Collins, 1981, revised 1994) does not even mention the council, while the 1994 edition does at least include references to it. Perhaps the change of perspective came about as a result of the 1987 Apostolic Letter of Pope John Paul II on the council, *On the Twelfth Centenerary of the Second Council of Nicaea, Duodecimum Saeculum*, where the Pope calls Nicea II "the last council fully recognized by both the Catholic Church and the Orthodox Church," Preface, 1.

[19] For a compendium of patristic writings both for and against icono-

clasm, see Cyril Mango, *The Art of the Byzantine Empire 312-1453* (Medieval Academy of America, Toronto: University of Toronto Press, 1986).

[20] Jaroslav Pelikan, *The Christian Tradition, vol. 2, The Spirit of Eastern Christendom (600-1700).* (Chicago: University of Chicago Press, 1974), p. 98..

[21] Mosche Barasch, *Icon: Studies in the History of an Idea* (New York: New York University Press, 1992), p. 15.

[22] G. Kittel, "Εἴδολον," *Theological Dictionary of the New Testament* Vol. 2, ed. by. G. Kittel, trans. by G. W. Bromiley (Grand Rapids: Eerdman's, 1964), p. 377.

[23] G. von Rad, "Εἰκών," *Theological Dictionary of the New Testament,* vol. 2, ed. G. Kittel, trans, G. W. Bromiley (Grand Rapids: Eerdman's, 1964), p. 382.

[24] J. Pelikan, *Spirit of Eastern Christendom,* p. 107.

[25] John of Damascus, *On the Divine Images, First Apology,* 5, trans. David Anderson (Crestwood, NY: 1980), p. 16.

[26] John of Damascus, *Third Apology, Ancient Documentation,* p. 97.

[27] John of Damascus, *First Apology,* 6, p. 17.

[28] Theodore the Studite, *First Refutation of the Iconoclasts,* 6. In *On the Holy Icons,* trans. Catharine Roth (Crestwood, NY: SVS Press, 1981), p. 25. This text contains the three refutations by Theodore. In this dissertation I shall refer to these as "First, Second, or Third Refutation," citing the appropriate chapter and the page reference from Roth.

[29] John of Damascus, *Third Apoloy,* 18, p. 75.

[30] John of Damascus, *Second Apology,* 20, p. 65.

[31] John of Damascus, *Third Apology,* 20, p. 76.

[32] J. Pelikan, *Spirit of Eastern Christendom,* p. 109.

[33] C. Roth, "Introduction" in Theodore the Studite, *On the Holy Icons,* p. 10.

[34] John of Damascus, *Third Apology,* 16, pp. 73-74. See also where John writes, "An image is of like character with its prototype, but with a certain difference." *First Apology,* 9, p. 19.

[35] D. Sahas, *Icon and Logos,* p. 77.

[36] Paul J. Alexander, *The Patriarch Nicephorus of Constantinople* (Oxford: Clarendon Press, 1958), pp. 200-201. See also Pelikan, p. 119.

[37] Theodore the Studite, *First Refutation,* 11, p. 31.

[38] Basil of Caesarea (the Great), *Hom.* 24.4 (PG 21:608) in Pelikan, *Spirit of Eastern Christendom,* p. 103.

[39] Basil the Great, *On the Holy Spirit*, 18.45, trans. David Anderson (Crestwood, NY: SVS Press, 1980), p. 72.

[40] Theodore the Studite, *First Refutation*, 8-9, pp. 28-29.

[41] D. Sahas, *Icon and Logos*, p. 7.

[42] Henry Bettenson, ed., *Documents of the Christian Church Second Edition* (London: Oxford University Press, 1967), p. 51.

[43] Theodore the Studite, *First Refutation*, 10, p. 31.

[44] John of Damascus, *Second Apology*, 11, p. 58.

[45] John of Damascus, *First Apology*, 16, p. 23.

[46] Ibid.

[47] Ibid., 4, pp. 15-16.

[48] J. Pelikan, *Spirit of Eastern Christendom*, p. 131.

[49] D. Sahas, *Icon and Logos*, p. 98.

[50] Ibid., p. 159.

[51] Theodore the Studite, *Third Refutation*, 27-31, pp. 88-89.

[52] Ibid., 32, p. 89.

[53] Ibid., 35, p. 91.

[54] Ibid., 39, p. 92.

[55] Ibid. 45-46, p. 94.

[56] John of Damscus, *First Apology*, 16, p. 23.

[57] Theodore the Studite, *Third Refutation*, 19, pp. 84-85.

[58] John of Damascus, *First Apology*, 8, p. 18. For an excellent treatment of this issue, see John Meyendorff, *Christ in Eastern Christian Thought* (Crestwood, NY: SVS Press, 1975), p. 173ff.

[59] J. Pelikan, *Spirit of Eastern Christendom*, p. 110,

[60] John of Damascus, *Third Apology, Ancient Documentation*, p. 98.

[61] John of Damascus, *First Apology, Ancient Documentation*, p. 41.

[62] See note 39.

[63] John of Damascus, *Third Apology*, 10, p. 71.

[64] Theodore the Studite, *First Refutation*, 13, p. 34.

[65] John of Damascus, *First Apology*, 16, p. 24.

[66] John of Damascus, *Second Apology*, 14, pp. 61-62.

[67] John of Damascus, *First Apology, Ancient Documentation*, pp. 36-37.

[68] Theodore the Studite, *First Refutation*, 7, p. 27.

[69] John of Damascus, *Third Apology*, 28-32, pp. 82-84.

[70] Ibid., 33, pp. 84-85.

[71] Ibid., 34-39, pp. 85-88.

[72] Ibid., 41, p. 89.

[73] John of Damascus, *First Apology, Commentary*, pp. 38-39.

[74] Ibid., 17, p. 25.

[75] Tamara Talbot Rice, *Everyday Life in Byzantium* (New York: Barnes and Noble Books, 1994), p. 192.

[76] D. Sahas, *Icon and Logos*, p. 98.

[77] The Orthodox theologian, Dumitru Staniloae, writes, "The essential unchanging core of Christian revelation is identified with the series of acts through which the revelation was effected. These acts moreover were expressed without alteration by a number of particualr words and images. Even were we to use other words and images they would have to express the same essential core of acts which the original words and images set forth..." Dumitru Staniloae, "Revelation Through Acts, Words and Images" in *Theology and the Church* (Crestwood: SVS Press, 1980), p. 112.

[78] D. Sahas, *Icon and Logos*, p. 69.

[79] Ibid., p. 178.

[80] J. Pelikan, *Spirit of Eastern Christendom*, p. 131.

[81] John of Damascus, *First Apology*, 17, p. 25. See also Theodore the Studite, who in the first (ch. 17; p. 37) and third refutations (ch. 2, p. 78) points out that sight precedes hearing but both are necessary in the correct appropriation of the content of the images. In a recent essay, Mary Charles Murray has discussed the understanding of the Early Church (100-600). See Mary Charles Murray, "The Image, the Ear, and the Eye in Early Christianity," *Arts* 9:1 (1997), pp. 17-24.

[82] John of Damascus, *Third Apology*, 12, p. 72

[83] PG 44 1292-1301 in D. Sahas, *Icon and Logos*, p. 143. This would seem to show that images assist not only the unlettered. St Gregory of Nyssa was a sophisticated viewer of images as well as a brilliant theologian.

[84] D. Sahas, *Icon and Logos*, p. 104.

[85] George Poulos, *Orthodox Saints* Vol. 1, (Brookline, MA: Holy Cross Orthodox Press, 1990), pp. 217-218.

[86] D. Sahas, *Icon and Logos*, pp. 125-126

[87] John of Damascus, *Third Apology*, 6, p. 81.

[88] John V of Jersualem, *Against Constantinus Cabalinus on the Images*, 10 (PG 96: 325) as cited in J. Pelikan, *Spirit of Eastern Christendom*, p. 121.

[89] D. Sahas, *Icon and Logos*, pp. 171-172.

Chapter Three

The Aim of Iconic Catechesis:
Iconic Knowing and Iconic Living

In the previous chapter we reviewed the iconoclastic controversy during which icons were defended – in part for their educational potential – and we examined the implications of the eighth century understandings that were involved in that historical context. For today's reader, two additional questions arise as we seek to recognize the potential of icons in the context of contemporary educational methodology. 1) What are the icons educating for? 2) How might the icons be educating? Our focus in this chapter will be on the first – the question that asks "what for?"

The aim of iconic catechesis is to nurture, instruct, and direct each member of the community of faith – the Church – in Christian living, or as Orthodox writers typically call it, the life in Christ, so that each person grows "in the grace and knowledge of our Lord and Savior Jesus Christ" (2 Pet. 3.18) and becomes "a partaker of the divine nature" (2 Pet. 1.4). Alternatively stated, the goal of iconic catechesis is for each person to become an icon, a living image of God, a person who lives in continual fellowship – communion – with God, reflecting a particular way – the Christ-like way – of knowing and living in the world, hence "iconic knowing and living."

In the theological language of Orthodox Tradition, this is

theosis – divinization or deification – achieving union or fellowship with God – restoring divine likeness to the fallen person.

Paul Evdokimov enriches our understanding by pointing out, with such arresting simplicity, that "The doctrine of *theosis* as set forth by the eastern fathers is not a logical doctrine, not a concept but rather a *vision* of life and grace."[1] The icon is the artistic expression of this vision, literally held up for all to see, to engage, and to offer a response.

The aim of catechesis in the Orthodox Tradition is integral to and expressed by the icon. This vision of the icon is a vision of the human person transfigured by the Holy Spirit, so that:

> Christ may dwell in your hearts through faith; that you, being rooted and grounded in love, may have power to comprehend with all the saints what is the breadth and length and height and depth, and to know the love of Christ which surpasses knowledge, that you may be filled with all the fulness of God (Eph 3.17-19).

In an interplay of reciprocity, this vision of the person, articulated systematically in the language of theological anthropology, is alternatively expressed by the artistic depictions of the icons themselves. Theological anthropology holds a key to understanding iconic catechesis because it is persons who are being engaged in catechesis, and the icons depict a vision of personal existence.

The remainder of this chapter will first endeavor to articulate "the Orthodox doctrine of the person." Then, by exploring the icon as an art form and considering artistic modes of knowing, the meaning of "iconic knowing" in the perspective of Orthodox Christian faith will be explored. Finally, these two areas will be brought together to help clarify the combined term "iconic living and knowing."

THE ORTHODOX DOCTRINE OF THE PERSON

As we begin this discussion, it is important to note that Orthodox Christianity has no creedal, dogmatic statements on the nature of the human person, as it possesses for the person of Jesus Christ or the Trinity. However, patristic writings of the centuries, intended primarily to deal with other topics, provide a rich source of material out of which our understanding of the human person is developed. Drawing from various treatises and other writings in Trinitarian theology, Christology, soteriology, and pneumatology, theologians have synthesized and articulated the Orthodox Christian view of the human person.

While many statements relate to the Orthodox understanding of the person, two are dominant within the Tradition:

"Then God said, 'Let us make man in our image, after our likeness'" (Gen. 1.26).

"God became human so that humans could become god." (St Athanasios).[2]

These two statements summarize everything that Orthodoxy teaches about human nature and existence. Once we understand and accept the content and implications of these two statements, everything else follows logically.

Both statements begin with God. To understand the nature of the human person, we must first reflect on the nature of God. In the statement of Genesis, "Let us," the fathers saw a direct revelation of God as Trinity. What may seem an unrelated and abstract issue is fundamental to the Orthodox understanding of person. God exists as three identifiable unique persons.

According to John Zizioulas, the fathers realized that "divinity" could not exist outside a person. That is, the person is the way of being, the *hypostasis* of divinity. As they continued to reflect on the Trinity, they realized that the Trinity – the one God – is a communion of persons. God is a social being, three persons relating freely to one another in love, totally open and receptive to one another, yet never losing their distinctiveness and concreteness.[3]

From this affirmation, the Orthodox understanding of the

human person flows. It is the first glimpse of "image and like-ness." Humanity, as such, is only an abstraction – a concept. For humanity to exist, it must have a mode of existence – a *hypostasis* – that applies to specific, identifiable persons. Thus, humanity exists only in persons. As children become images of their parents from the genetic material given them, so human persons embody the image of God, with which He endowed them. Specifically, humanity is the image of Christ, who is the image of the Father (Col. 1.15). As the person of Jesus Christ was both divine and human, the fathers saw communion with divinity as intrinsic to human nature.

The fathers often attempted to describe the characteristics of the divine image of God within each person. First, since hu-manity was originally created in the image and likeness of God, humanity has always retained its essential connection with God and is inherently good. As Gregory of Nyssa writes, "If ... man came into being ... to participate in the divine goodness, he had to be fashioned in such a way as to fit him to share in this goodness."[4] The fall of humanity – in the sin of Adam and Eve – broke the relationship, and the likeness was lost. That is, the fullness of the relationship that results in God-like living had been broken. However, the eastern fathers insist that the image of God within humanity was not lost in the Fall, only the like-ness. The connection with the divine having been broken, the likeness of God within humanity was marred, defaced, and tar-nished. However, humanity retains the capacity for holiness, even while living in a sinful, fallen world – marked chiefly by death (Rom 5.12) – in which it strives to restore itself to its original luster. The Orthodox Tradition sees the dynamic of human existence as moving from God-image to God-likeness, restoring the likeness of God within each person.

This perspective is notable for its extremely optimistic vision of humanity, especially in light of others that consider human nature as "totally depraved" or "a mass of sin." Simultaneously, however, Orthodoxy is very realistic about human frailty. The

Tradition recognizes that human weakness accompanies the capacity for holiness and that human striving by itself is insufficient, as reflected in the following hymn from Great Lent: "The multitude of my transgressions is like the deep waters of the sea, and I drown in my iniquities. Give me Thy hand, O God my Savior: save me as Thou hast saved Peter, and have mercy on me."[5] The human vocation is seen as striving to ascend to the higher, more God-like dimensions of human life but, as noted by the hymn, it cannot be done alone. The intervention and assistance of God is needed to lift the human person from the fallen state.

What is the image of God in humanity? The fathers were never as definitive as we would like; they do not offer a descriptive list that provides the answer. On the one hand, a list would not be convincing; inevitably it would be challenged as too limited. On the other, since God is ultimately beyond knowing, we can only speculate about humanity's true connection with the image of God. Nevertheless, from the God revealed in Scripture and from their own reflections, the fathers offer many impressions of "the image of God" in humanity and the nature of the person. Based on patristic writings, modern theologians have explored these even further, making connections with other areas of study. Six major characteristics that have emerged are discussed below: uniqueness, freedom, growth, ecclesial relationship, creativity, and love. A seventh characteristic, the heart, will serve to introduce the second section – on epistemology – of this chapter.

A Person, Therefore Unique

As each person in the Trinity is unique, with distinct qualities and characteristics, so each human person is unique and unrepeatable. Recalling a child who commented that he was an endangered species because, as the child noted "There is only one of me," Kallistos Ware writes on the uniqueness of each person:

We are not interchangeable tokens or programs on a computer, but within each of us there is a priceless treasure not to be found in anyone else. From before our birth – indeed, from all eternity – God the Creator foreknows each one of us in our particularity, and for each one He has a special love and a different plan. In each of us He discerns possibilities not to be realized by any other person in the universe. Each has the vocation of creating something beautiful in his or her own unrepeatable way.[6]

This simple fact is underscored by the icon, which is a witness to a unique person or group of persons who lived a particular life in a particular place and time or who jointly participated in a particular event. There has been only one St Katherine the Great Martyr (3rd c.), St Basil the Great (4th c.), St Gregory Palamas (14th c.), or St Nektarios of Aegina (20th c.). Their lives have been imitated by others but never repeated. To step into a church is to enter an environment overflowing with images of men and women from all times and places, who responded to God's call to fulfill their unique vocations in the world. They include apostles, teachers, martyrs, hierarchs, monastics, ascetics, theologians, wonder workers, etc.

The uniqueness of each saint is depicted artistically. The written name of the saint near his or her figure on the icon crystallizes his or her unique identity. Yet, each person is also recognizable through his or her appearance. As you and I recognize one another through our unique physical characteristics, the saints are recognized by the particularities of their iconic depictions. The icons do not attempt photographic reproduction; yet certain physical characteristics associated with each saint have been retained and have remained remarkably stable over time. This is amplified by Leonid Ouspensky:

The iconography of saints is distinguished by extraordinary stability. This is due not only to the desire to preserve the image sanctified by Tradition, but also to the need to preserve a living and direct connection with the person in the icon. Therefore, the icon perforce shows the nature of the service of a saint, whether he be an Apostle, a bishop, a martyr ... and reproduces with particular care his characteristic, distinctive traits. This iconographic realism lies at the basis of the icon and is thus one of its most important elements.[7]

The depiction of St Basil the Great (see Figure 2) in various icons has remained relatively stable – balding with a tuft of hair on his forehead and a long black beard. Maintaining the connection to the actual person's features is very evident in the icon of St Gregory Palamas, Archbishop of Thessalonike in the fourteenth century. The icon (see Figure 3) was produced not too long after his death in 1359 and canonization in 1368. The icon's provenance is Thessalonike, Gregory's home, and it depicts features of the saint, most likely from the memory of the iconographer. An interesting comparison is the photo of St. Nektarios (d. 1922) and his icon (See Figure 4). Nektarios was declared a saint in 1967. The icon picks up characteristics of Nektarios. In some ways then, it could be argued that it is a portrait of the saint and has probably determined how the saint has been depicted ever since.[8]

In God's Image, Therefore Free

Freedom is a significant aspect of being created in the image and likeness of God, interconnected with our uniqueness as persons. Ware notes that:

> As God is free, so likewise man is free. And being free, each human being realizes the divine image within himself in his own distinctive fashion ... Each, being free, is unrepeatable; and each being unrepeatable is infinitely precious.[9]

In his freedom, God acts in a unique manner, according to his person. Human persons are likewise free to uniquely exercise their freedom, according to the sum of their personal characteristics.

Yet, God's freedom, as it is connected to his existence as Trinity, raises an apparent contradiction, especially for modern thought. God is three free persons existing as an interdependent communion. The contradiction stems from the fact that, in modern Western thought, the notion of freedom has focused on individual independence to the point where dependence and interdependence are virtually excluded. According to much that is found in modern thinking, freedom is *from* others; it is a freedom of separation. Critics have pointed out that in the situation where we presently find ourselves, this "individualized freedom," taken to its logical outcome, ultimately becomes a freedom of alienation "of person from society, of people from each other, of humanity from the natural world, of the personal ego from the higher Self or spiritual essence."[10]

Many today are searching for a way of understanding freedom in a way that reconnects people with themselves, with one another, with the world, and with God. They seem to find their answer in a conceptual framework that considers freedom as a freedom *for* relationship, freedom *for* a communion of persons.

Human freedom is not an abstraction but a complex of personal actions, usually directed toward and typically involving other persons. Directing one's life to a future project – a goal of some type – is achieved within a world of other people. In order to become ourselves, others must be involved; without commitment to the freedom of others, our personal freedom is an illusion. We cannot become ourselves by ourselves, despite the perceptions created by self-centered individuality or individualism. The philosopher, John Macmurray, addresses this concern:

> We need one another to be ourselves. This complete and unlimited dependence of each of us upon the others is the central and crucial fact of personal existence. Individual independence is an illusion; and the independent individual, the isolated self, is a nonentity ... It is only in relation to others that we exist as persons.[11]

True personal freedom is a freedom that chooses communion and fellowship with others, enabling and empowering persons to connect and unite with one another in order to transform themselves, one another, and the world.

Fallen, Yet Meant to Grow toward God-likeness

From the patristic exegesis of "image and likeness," the Orthodox Tradition sees human persons as dynamic, growing beings. From their creation, human persons are meant to grow toward God-likeness, toward restoration of their fellowship with God. As far back as the time of Irenaeus, the Orthodox have made a distinction between image and likeness, which is beyond the Hebrew parallelism of Genesis. In this understanding, as Ware writes,

> the image ... indicates our essential humanity, the endowment conferred on every one of us simply by virtue of the fact that we are human beings; and even though it is obscured by sin it is never entirely lost. The likeness ... is attained only by the saints who have reached the fullness of *theosis* (deification). Image is to likeness as starting point is to end point, or as potentiality is to realization.[12]

The human vocation, in this view, is to grow from God's image towards God-likeness. Growth and progress are not only possible but essential to human existence. Each person is on a journey: "to be human is to be a traveler, always on the move. Personhood implies constant discovery, ever new beginnings, increasing self-transcendence."[13]

Within the Orthodox Tradition, there is an understanding that the goal of education is to form "a whole person" and that achieving this goal involves a dynamic and endless process of growth. Growth and development are seen positively; in terms of personhood, they are endless. Growth in personhood has as its aim growth towards God-likeness, which is ultimately endless because God is a mystery: "ineffable, beyond comprehension, invisible, existing forever and always the same."[14] Growth in personhood is growth and development of one's humanity and is consistent with growth toward God-likeness. "How could you be God when you have not yet become human?" St Irenaeus asks.[15] To grow in humanity is to grow toward God-likeness, and to become more like God is to grow in one's humanity.

The journey toward God-likeness has no limits for the person; it extends into eternity. According to St Paul, humanity's manifestation of God-likeness is to grow "from glory to glory" (2 Cor. 3.18). Growth is endless; each personal discovery leads to another, learning never ceases, relationships continue to develop. Our present personal existence ultimately becomes mystery, like God, since each person is "an indissoluble psychosomatic unity with unfathomable psychic depths."[16] In the kingdom of God, the mystery continues, for eternity is "but an ascending spiral, and to this ascending spiral there is no final limit. God is inexhaustible, and so the potentialities of our human personhood according to the divine image are likewise inexhaustible."[17]

Relational, Therefore Ecclesial

Running through the characteristics discussed so far has been the thread that to be a person is to be in relation. In the Orthodox Tradition this signifies more than the simple wisdom that human beings are social creatures. A conscious emphasis has been made here to use the term "person" and to avoid "individual," even though some readers may see them as synonymous. There is a distinction pointing to the relational character of humanity that Ware identifies as follows:

A "person" is not at all the same as an "individual." Isolated, self-dependent, none of us is an authentic person but merely an individual, a bare unit as recorded in the census. Egocentricity is the death of true personhood. Each becomes a real person only through entering into relation with other persons, through living for them and in them. There can be no man, so it has been rightly said, until there are at least two men in communication.[18]

An individual is solitary, someone not in relationship with others. To be a person one must be in relationship.

Recalling earlier statements, divinity does not exist in abstraction but in the personal existence of the members of the Trinity dwelling freely in communion with one another. In our earthly existence, the Orthodox Tradition identifies the locus of communion as the Church, where an ecclesial mode of being – the foretaste of God's way of living – is meant to be lived and experienced. The fathers remind us that the sacramental way of living – the life in Christ – involves our being in communion with God, self, one another, and the world. Through the sacraments, especially the Eucharist, we are offered the opportunity to participate in that divine mode of existence.

The sacramental or ecclesial way of life begins with the initiatory sacraments of Baptism, Chrismation (Confirmation), and Eucharist. "As many as have been baptized into Christ have put on Christ" (Gal. 3.27) is sung at Orthodox baptisms. Baptism initiates the Christian into the "new network of relationships which transcends every exclusiveness."[19] We are joined to the Church and begin a new way of being. We move from being an isolated individual to being a person who is a member of the body, part of the community of Christ.

In Chrismation, which completes the baptismal rite, our bodies are sealed with the gift of the Holy Spirit, giving life to all our actions and indicating that the path to sanctification involves our whole selves: body, mind, and spirit. We become "christs" – "anointed ones" – and the priestly, prophetic, and royal ministry of Christ becomes our vocation to the world, exercised according to our unique talents and abilities. In the Eucharist, the third sacrament of initiation, which we repeat throughout life, we are nourished and enter into communion with the divine. As Panagiotis Nellas writes:

The Eucharist is the center of the spiritual life in Christ and its source. Here the union with Christ is complete and full. The whole person in all its dimensions, with all its psychosomatic senses and functions, is joined in a deep union with Christ, is transformed and christified.[20]

In the Eucharistic assembly – the Divine Liturgy – our relational way of being is manifested fully. All the members of the community take their respective places, according to the gifts and ministries each fulfills, and offer themselves to God on behalf of and for the life of the world. In return they receive life from the Father in the gift of the Holy Spirit and his Son.

The ways in which Christians are intended to express their fellowship and communion – with God, self, one another, and the world – include *askesis* (ascetic discipline), prayer, and ministry. *Askesis,* prayer, and ministry are not part of the image of God within the person *per se*, yet they show how the image becomes manifested in the life of Christians and leads them toward God-likeness. While each of these is a complete subject unto itself, a brief discussion of each is warranted.

Askesis. Given certain traditional descriptions of *askesis*, it can be seen as individual pursuit of spiritual discipline: fasting, work, chastity, following a rule of prayer, etc. Stanley Harakas introduces another dimension when he characterizes *askesis* as "struggle; it is the various methods used to fight the passions and evil habits, to overcome temptation. *Askesis* is exercise, practice and training."[21] Let us consider the practice of fasting as an example. An Orthodox Christian will follow the rule the Church prescribes for fasting: nothing from an animal (meat, dairy products, eggs, certain types of fish) nor oil on Wednesdays and Fridays, particular feast days, and during the fast seasons: Great Lent (40 days); Holy Week; the Nativity, also known as Advent (40 days); Dormition Fast (Aug. 1-15); Apostles Fast (the week after All Saints Sunday to June 29).[22] All of this appears to be individual effort for an individual good – to come closer to God.

However, *askesis* is not meant to be an individual effort but, rather, an ecclesial act. Ascetic practices are intended to reject the desire to remain independent in order to achieve self-salvation. Their purpose is to conform our will through the necessary self-discipline and relationship to others so that we will develop and grow ecclesially. In its various forms, *askesis* subordinates individual will to the will, life, and experience of the community. "Individual effort is transformed into a common effort; the struggle becomes an act of communion, taking its place in the life of the whole body of the Church."[23]

Prayer. The fourth century writer, Evagrius Ponticus, states, "Prayer is a continual intercourse of the spirit with God."[24] Another translation of this text substitutes "conversation" for "intercourse."[25] Whichever word one selects, the experience of prayer is personal, that is, relational. The Romanian theologian, Dumitru Staniloae, speaks about prayer as "being totally absorbed in the reality of God." He calls prayer an "encounter with the personal infinity of God who loves us."[26] Anthony Bloom writes:

> When a great joy has come upon us or a great pain or a great sorrow, we do not forget it in the course of the day. We listen to people, we do our work, we read, we do what we are supposed to do, and the pain of bereavement, the awareness of joy, of the exhilarating news is with us incessantly. This should also be the sense of the presence of God. And if the sense of the presence of God is as clear as that, then one prays while one does other things.[27]

As a personal event, the experience of prayer is characterized by the many facets of relationship: uniqueness, freedom, growth, etc. Each person's prayer experience is unique. For prayer to be authentic, the partners must be free and mutual. God freely chooses to join our prayer (or not) as we must freely choose to pray.[28] Over time, prayer grows in time, place, content, and quality.

In their ascetic life, monastics seek to follow St Paul's injunction to pray unceasingly (1 Thes. 5.17); they have set rules and specific times for corporate as well as private prayer. Through prayer, one seeks to see God in all created beings and things and to see the uncreated dimension of God's glory – the uncreated light that Christ revealed on Mount Tabor. When this level of prayer is experienced, the person becomes prayer and is continually in the presence of God. This achievement is not restricted to monastics. "The whole existence of a Christian can, even in its most everyday concerns become prayer, if hope and faith support it through all its vicissitudes, if in its entirety it is interpreted in the light of the cross and the Resurrection."[29]

Ministry. The example was set by Christ who washed the feet of his disciples and challenged them, "If I then, your Lord and Teacher, have washed your feet, you also ought to wash one another's feet" (Jn. 13.14). By this example all are called to minister to one another. Ministry in its various forms (the ministry of the *laos* or laity as well as the ministry of the clergy) is relational and ecclesial. As Zizioulas writes:

> The relational character of the ministry implies that the only acceptable method of mission for the Church is the *incarnational* one: the Church relates to the world through and in her ministry by being involved existentially in the world. The nature of mission is not to be found in the Church's *addressing* the world but in its being fully in *com-passion* (sic) with it.[30]

The variety of ministries in the Church reflects the variety of the networks of relationships in which the people of God, *laos* and clergy together, have gathered historically. Through the Eucharistic assembly these ministries are empowered, commissioned, and distributed, even as they are gathered, united, and offered to God, thus eliminating the possibility of separating the Church from the world. "The world is *assumed* by the community and referred back to the Creator."[31] This act, according to the Divine Liturgy of St Basil the Great is "for the life of the world,"[32] directing Christians to social and cosmic responsibilities.

Sharing in God's Creativity

The apparent need for humans to be creative and the capacity to create are aspects of the divine image within persons.[33] The Scriptures open with the acts of God, who created the cosmos – the world and its creatures – *ex nihilo* – out of nothing – with only a word: "And God said" (Gen. 1.3). St Paul writes that God has created in and through Christ "all things, in heaven and on earth visible and invisible" (Col. 1.16). The Psalmist glorifies God for his acts of creation, "You did set the earth on its foundations, so that it should never be shaken" (Ps. 104.5).

Being in God's image, humanity shares in his creativity. Human beings seek "to share in God's mastery over chaos and evil."[34] However, the ability of humans to create does not extend to creation *ex nihilo*. Human creativity is limited to extant materials, such as wood, and to certain abstractions, such as musical tones. This means that writing music or poetry, painting a portrait, building a table, making a tool, and many other abilities and capacities of self-expression, images of the divine ability of creation, are present within humanity. Human creativity resembles divine creativity in that a person can "realize the ideas that he conceives,"[35] whether they are simple tools, forms of artistic expression, or complex social organizations.

The arts, however, appear to hold a special place in the domain of human creativity. The poem, song, aria, or symphony, the painting, drawing, or sculpture have the appearance of coming from nothing. God's creative acts result in order and beauty emerging from a formless void. A person's artistic creation takes an idea and expresses it in a meaningful, orderly, beautiful manner. In the human dimension, artistic creations most closely reflect the divine ability to create *ex nihilo*.

Above All, Loving as God Loves

Of all the characteristics of the divine image within humanity, the capacity to love and be loved may be the supreme characteristic of the image of God. Love is what characterizes

God above all other attributes, "God is love, and he who abides in love abides in God, and God abides in him" (1 Jn. 4.16). Love is the greatest of the virtues mentioned by St Paul – "faith, hope, and love … and the greatest of these is love" (1 Cor. 13.13). In a homily I once heard, a preacher explained St Paul's comment as meaning that in the kingdom of God, faith and hope will be unnecessary; they will have achieved their fulfillment. Yet love will still be required and will grow.

Love raises individuals to the status of persons. In the Orthodox Tradition, the Trinity is the model of love, relationship, and ultimately, personhood. As Staniloae writes,

> We are aware that the most perfect and meaningful unity is unity in love, that is, unity between persons who retain their own individual identities. Any other unity is devoid of meaning and spiritual life. Hence the expressions 'one in being' and 'three in Persons' must not lead us to contemplate the divine being in itself as distinct from the Persons and from their mutual love, but rather as the love existing in persons and between persons.[36]

The three persons of the Trinity are united in a communion of love that affirms their personhood as it affirms the status of the others.

The love of the Trinity is the model for love among persons. Among human beings, love unites individual persons, bringing them into relationship and communion with one another. The chief human experiences of this model of love are the family and marriage. Marriage unites two persons "into a communion of love for their mutual companionship, support, enjoyment, and personal fulfillment and completion."[37] Through sexual intercourse – a gift of God – the partners are able to transcend themselves, "drawing husband and wife into a loving, caring and intimate communion of body and soul."[38] Through the sexual encounter, the partners may actualize their potential for becoming cocreators with God through child-bearing. The fruit of their love for one another extends to include yet another – a new person.

The more encompassing love that transcends familial bounds is the love born by entering into a relationship with God and the Church through baptism. Through baptism in water and Spirit – entry into the Church – a new mode of personal existence is generated. In the Church, "a kind of relationship with the world which is not determined by the laws of biology" is established.[39] In the Church, persons enter into a new network of relationships that transcend exclusiveness. Love is not limited to the natural limitations of bodily existence, but extends without exclusiveness, not because of any moral obligation, but out of the new mode of existence generated through the rebirth of water and Spirit.[40]

In "ecclesial existence," love is the ability to see and recognize another person as a person and neighbor, allowing each person to become the neighbor to all. In the parable of the Great Judgment (Mt. 25.31-46), Jesus makes the relationship to a neighbor a criterion of blessedness (v. 34). This concept is developed extensively in the writings of the desert fathers. "Abba Anthony said, 'Life and death depend on our neighbor. If we gain our brother we gain God. But if we scandalize our brother we are sinning against Christ.'"[41] In the ascetic tradition, the movement toward God is simultaneously a movement toward the other person. The sixth century desert father, Dorotheus of Gaza, offers what has become a classic analogy of this relationship:

> Imagine a circle with its center and radii or rays going out from this center. The further these radii are from the center the more widely are they dispersed and separated from one another; and conversely, the closer they come to the center, the closer they are to one another. Suppose now that this circle is the world, the very center of the circle, God, and the lines (radii) going from the center to the circumference or from the circumference to the center are the paths of men's lives. Then here we see the same. Insofar as the saints move

inward within the circle towards its center, wishing to come near to God, then, in the degree of their penetration, they come closer both to God and to one another; moreover, inasmuch as they come nearer to God, they come nearer to one another, and inasmuch as they come nearer to one another, they come nearer to God. It is the same with drawing away... Such is the property of love; inasmuch as we are outside and do not love God, so each is far from his neighbor. But if we love God, inasmuch as we come near to Him by love of Him; so we become united by love with our neighbors, and inasmuch as we are united with our neighbors, so we become united with God.[42]

The ability to love without exclusiveness empowers one to see self and others with new eyes, to see ourselves as we will be, or are intended to be. "The love which is *agape* discovers that each individual, and especially each one who is suffering, is a sacrament of Christ."[43] Of course, to live in this manner is a struggle, and the human vocation is to struggle with the many distractions, passions, and temptations that become obstacles along the journey. The Church recognizes those whom it believes have successfully achieved this love as saints. Clément describes sainthood in the following manner:

The sanctified person is someone no longer separated. And he is only sanctified to the extent that he understands in practice that he is no longer separated from anyone or anything. He bears humanity in himself, all human beings in their passion and their resurrection. He is identified, in Christ, with the "whole Adam." His own "self" no longer interests him. He includes in his prayer and in his love all humanity, without judging or condemning anyone, except himself, the last of all. He is infinitely vulnerable to the horror of the world, to the tragedies of history being constantly renewed. But he is crushed with Christ and rises again with him, with everyone. He knows that the Resurrection has the last word.[44]

ICONIC KNOWING – KNOWLEDGE OF "THE HEART"

The other major characteristic of humanity's divine image is traditionally referred to as the rational capability of the person. This has been understood in a relatively narrow sense, meaning intellectual and cognitive activities. Lately, however, the term "rational" has come to be seen as conceptually limiting. A term whose scope is more encompassing is needed – one that embraces the other aspects of a person's ability "to know." Orthodox thought has increasingly recognized that "the divine image embraces the total human being, body, soul and spirit together," not only the mind.[45] From the Tradition, "the heart" – a term with roots in the biblical, patristic, theological, and liturgical traditions of the Church – emerges as the expression that reflects this broader, more spiritual concept. The heart unites the rational and intellectual dimensions of the person with the physical, emotional, and spiritual. In the Orthodox Tradition, the heart is:

> not simply the physical organ but the spiritual center of man's being, man as made in the image of God, his deepest and truest self, or the inner shrine, to be entered only through sacrifice and death, in which the mystery of the union between the divine and the human is consummated. " 'I called with my whole heart,' says the psalmist – that is, with body, soul and spirit"… "Heart" has thus an all embracing significance: "prayer of the heart" means prayer not just of the emotions and affections, but of the whole person, including the body.[46]

Therefore, the human ability "to know in the heart" is a characteristic of the divine image of God. This ability encompasses: the mind and its ability to reason, imagine, and remember; the body, which is always involved in human activity; the emotions; and the soul of the person, that which is drawn to and relates to the transcendent God. Icons draw us into this manifestation of the heart as a way of knowing. They capture, portray, create, and express a realm of human experience that extends beyond the rational and speaks to all aspects of the person. Words and concepts cannot fully express, on their own, what can be expressed in and through the icon. What John Dewey points out about art in general is true for the icon:

> Because objects of art are expressive, they are a language. Rather, they are many languages. For each art has its own medium and that medium is especially fitted for one kind of communication. Each medium says something that cannot be uttered as well or as completely in any other tongue.[47]

As works of art, icons have been communicating in their distinctive language for well over a millennium. John Baggley writes:

> In approaching icons we are entering a world where a different language is used: the non-verbal language of visual semantics, the symbolic language of forms and color. To people accustomed to naturalistic art the learning of this different language of silence can be a hard task; it is a task where we must look and listen, a task in which silence, stillness and attentiveness are our greatest assets.[48]

Through artistic means, the icon presents its theological vision of the person restored to the divine beauty with which that person was first endowed. An Orthodox funeral hymn states,

> Of old You created me from nothing and honored me with Your divine image. But when I disobeyed Your commandment, O Lord, You cast me down to the earth from where I was taken. *Lead me back again to Your likeness, and renew my original beauty.*[49]

In the icon the whole person, restored by the power of God, is depicted and becomes beautiful.

The icon thus expresses a form of wisdom that engages the whole person. It speaks, through beauty, to the full potential of human knowledge. When we come to "know in our hearts," every aspect of our personal existence is involved. Thus, "iconic knowing" is very tightly coupled to "knowledge of the heart" and includes the various dimensions we will now discuss.

Iconic Knowing is Rational/Cognitive

The Gospel of John opens with "In the beginning was the Word (Logos)" (Jn. 1.1). A human being is a (λογικόν ζῷον) – a logical and rational being – because God is logical and rational. St Gregory of Nyssa writes, "The godhead is wisdom and logos (reason, meaning); in yourself too you see intelligence and thought, images of the original intelligence and thought."[50] In the Orthodox Tradition, the rational capabilities of persons, their intellect, intelligence, and reason, are frequently considered the highest aspect of the image of God in humanity. The rational capabilities of humanity are emphasized because, through reason, persons are capable of learning of and about God and entering into fellowship with him. "Knowledge is necessary if man is to reach any degree of similarity to God."[51] In the patristic viewpoint, it is reason, the ability to think – and particularly the ability to discern meaning and morality – that separates humans from other creatures. This is what enabled civilization and culture to develop.[52] Humans are not enslaved to physical and emotional desires – or animal instincts – since they can be controlled through the use of reason.

The encounter with an icon can be an intensely intellectual experience. Icons are capable of stimulating deep thought and serious mental activity in the sensitized viewer. They can spark questions, tell stories, connect events one to another. Beholding icons can stimulate us to want to know more about the identities of the person depicted, their life stories, the significance of their lives. Liturgical experience can enrich our appreciation of an icon's message through hymn, ritual, and symbol – all capable of stimulating the intellect. Related educational endeavors can provide further enrichment by providing additional information and background for even deeper understanding and by stimulating increased appreciation of the personal implications of icons on the lives of the student.

In one icon, the vision of Constantine at the Milvian Bridge and Helen discovering the cross of Jesus are depicted (Figure 5). Two disparate events related to the cross – and to the significance of Constantine and Helen to the Christian Church – are depicted in one icon. In an encounter with this icon, the icon tells its story in its entirety. However, with related information and cognitive activity – regarding names, circumstances, dates, etc. – a fuller appreciation develops, both of the story and of its profound significance to the life of the community.

An icon can depict individuals whose lives might otherwise be considered separate and distinct and stimulate the viewer to formulate the concept that associates them. For example, the icon of the American Saints (Figure 6) challenges the beholder to learn who these people were. Depicted are St Herman of Alaska, St Tikhon the Patriarch of Moscow, St Innocent the Apostle to America, St Peter the Aleut, and the Hieromartyr Juvenaly. Each life has a different story, but a common thread runs through them all – the struggle for initial establishment of the Church in America.

At a deeper level, through the engagement of human reason, this icon can stimulate a personal search for the meaning of the Incarnation. The so-called distortions of figures in icons can engage personal rationality and cognition in a different aspect of iconic knowing. Achieving an understanding of this phenomenon helps one grasp the significance of an art that depicts transfiguration and stimulates reflection on the meaning of transfiguration for one's self and for others.

Iconic Knowing Includes the Memory and Imagination

According to St John of Damascus: "Memory is an image (φαντασία) which has been left behind by some sensory or mental impression that has actually been received. In other words, it is the retention of sensation and thought."[53] Ideally, the icon-filled environment in which Orthodox Christians live stimulates the formation of images and impressions that are retained in memory. The icons depict historical events and people. When we gaze upon an icon, our memories are engaged in a search for experiences that fit with the visual perception. Because we have not had historical contact with the events and people being depicted, our memories seek to retrieve related information that has been learned. Our way of knowing involves continual references to our memories where we store our knowledge and experience.

Imagination is clearly related to our ability to remember. Unfortunately, in the Hebraic, Hellenic, and Medieval Christian understandings, with few exceptions, imagination was seen as a negative faculty of the human mind.[54] The Orthodox Tradition has been no exception. St John of Damascus, the defender of icons, defines imagination as "the faculty belonging to the irrational part of the soul" (φανταστικόν ἐστι δύναμις τῆς ἀλόγου ψυχῆς) that arises out of sensory experience and no object.[55] Stigmatized by this connection to irrationality and the notion that what is imagined is fantasy, it is not surprising that imagination has been traditionally seen negatively, even though in reality there is no substantial basis for this view.

Contemporary thought helps us rehabilitate this issue. A view of imagination that assists us to see this power of the mind in a more positive way is offered by Mary Warnock. She characterizes imagination as:

> an active combining power which *brings* ideas together, and which is at work to create the forms of things which seem to speak to us of the universal, and which at the same time necessarily cause in us feelings of love and awe.[56]

Without imagination, she argues, persons would be unable to "apply concepts to sense experience," thus regulating it, and "purely intellectual life would be without any real content," thereby we would not "experience the world as we do."[57] Imagination is the faculty that unites sensory and intellectual considerations. Imagination empowers the mind to unite di-

verse concepts and experiences and to combine them with what
has been learned and what has been felt. The imagination, then,
by reference to memory and cognition, connects what is re-
trieved with other sensory experiences and assembles our view
of the world.

Archbishop Iakovos offers an affirming personal insight on
this close connection between memory and imagination. He
writes:

> I find, when I think deeply about it, that I can't really sepa-
> rate memory from imagination. They're on a kind of
> continuum in my mind. I remember important events and
> facts, words of principle and promise, from the liturgy and
> from Scripture. These thoughts flow from my past into the
> present and they trigger ideas and visions that help me plan
> for the future. As human beings, our ability to remember
> important things and then use those memories in our imagi-
> nations enables us to live simultaneously in the past, the
> present, and the future.[58]

Iconic Knowing is Bodily

The encounter with an icon is, first and foremost, a visual,
and therefore a bodily experience; an embodied person faces
the icon and the eyes of the person are the means by which
consciousness is engaged. Second, the images viewed by the beholder are of incarnate men and women. Third, in Orthodox
religious piety, the acts of veneration directed toward icons involve the body. The ritual practices of kissing, bowing,
prostrations, kneeling, and processions are all physical bodily
actions.

In the Orthodox Tradition, the body is seen as essentially
good, even as it bears the marks of sin. God himself confirmed
the goodness of the human form by blessing it and endowing it
with the breath of life – a soul. After creating man and woman,
God "blessed them" (Gen. 1.28), and after forming humanity
from the "dust of the ground," God breathed the "breath of

life" into his creation (Gen. 2.7). Sin marred or tarnished human bodily existence, making humanity more keenly aware of and bound to biological considerations. Yet, the Incarnation of Christ is evidence of the goodness of the human body. To paraphrase St Gregory the Theologian, by taking on human flesh Christ healed it.[59] The icons themselves testify to the positive nature of the body in Orthodox thought. If the body were evil in some way, why would there be icons? In reaction to those who would separate humanity from its bodily existence, Philip Sherrard writes:

> It is quite clear that from the Christian point of view man's reality, now or hereafter, is his incarnate self, not any bodiless entity of spirit or pure soul. To view man as a bodiless entity that has fallen into a body for this transient life and in order to expiate a sin, is to commit the deepest kind of evasion, to embrace the deepest kind of lie. Man's reality is an embodied reality, and so much is this the case that for him to think or attempt to act as though he possesses a soul apart from body is to cripple his nature at its roots.[60]

To know, then, must include and involve the body. The movement from image to likeness in the human experience is and must be a bodily experience – no other option is available for a person. In the encounter with the icon, the viewer beholds an embodied individual who has lived the Christian life and experienced fellowship with the divine. The icon, through its art, presents the beholder with the proposition that an embodied individual can attain the likeness of God. In other words, the *beholder* can attain this state in life.[61] This understanding is reflected in the beauty of the human figure in the icon. This beautiful style depicts the God-like person.

However, to some the figures in icons are not beautiful but have been distorted. The Orthodox Tradition does not see the depiction of the human form in icons this way. Rather, the art of the icon depicts a body that has been transfigured, has been filled with the Holy Spirit, and radiates a new life.

> The essence of what is being communicated in icons of the
> saints, for example, is their participation in the divine life;
> their faces are turned toward the beholder, to enter into com-
> munion with them (faces turned sideways often indicates the
> absence of enlightenment and sanctification, as in the repre-
> sentation of Judas Iscariot); the face and head may be
> disproportionately large in relation to the rest of the body;
> eyes and ears are enlarged, while the mouth may be very small
> and the lips tightly closed, thus conveying a sense of inner
> watchfulness and attention; eyes often seem to be inward-
> looking, turned away from the external world of the senses.[62]

In the icon of the Transfiguration (Figure 7), Jesus reveals his
divinity to Peter, James, and John, who are overwhelmed by the
sight. Artistically, even as Jesus radiates the divine light, his bodily
presence is not diminished. In the icon it is fully present, recognizable, and beautiful.

The pious practices of Orthodox Christians provide examples
of the reality that our bodies are a means of fellowship and communion. Orthodox Christians regularly pray before icons, bow
before icons, kneel before icons, prostrate themselves before
icons, kiss icons, place candles and offer incense before icons,
and process through their churches and towns with icons. As
was pointed out in Chapter Two, these practices do not constitute worship of the icon, but veneration of it. This distinction
was explained there and shall not be repeated. However, it is
worth noting that each of these ritual activities involves the use
of the body in some way.

Through ritual acts of veneration, the person engages the icon
and enters into a relationship with the person depicted. The
interaction is not with the icon. Rather, it proceeds through it
toward the person depicted. Ritual, pious practices, are embodied, incarnate acts. A person sees the icon and responds to it
with a bodily act that occurs in space and time. When people

see one another, they wave, shake hands, or embrace. But in an encounter with a person who reflects the radiance of God, the behavior is different. Kissing an icon, bowing, offering incense and candles incarnates a way of being before the holy person depicted in the icon.

Not incidental is the fact that Orthodox behave in many of the same ways toward living persons in liturgy. Incense is offered to the people; there are ritual bows between celebrants and congregation. Through these ritual acts, people show honor and respect to one another. While the person performing the acts would certainly recognize that there is a difference between offering incense toward the members of the congregation and the icon of a saint, both actions honor the presence of the bearer of the image of God. Neither is an abstract act.

Iconic Knowing is Emotional

The icon making its argument through its artistic presentation and beauty can generate an emotional response in the beholder. St. Gregory of Nyssa once wrote that upon seeing a particular painting of the sacrifice of Isaac, he "could not walk by the sight of it without shedding tears."[63] The icon, like all art forms, presents its message for others to contemplate and respond. When a person gazes at a Monet landscape, a certain feeling is generated. When an artist paints, he or she wishes to represent a personal feeling or experience for another to share. The philosopher Susanne Langer argues that "the primary function of art is to objectify feeling so that we can contemplate and understand it."[64] Emotional states and the "inner life" cannot be presented or represented discursively, because as John Dewey stated so succinctly, "If all meaning could be adequately expressed by words, the arts of painting and music would not exist."[65] The inner "emotional" experience that is generated by the icon is the deep awe and personal reverence for the mystery of the divine.

Vladimir Lossky writes, "If the mystical experience is a personal working out of the content of the common faith, theology is an expression, for the profit of all, of that which can be experienced by everyone."[66] The icon is an expression of the experience of God whose purpose is that others may also participate in that experience. The icon is a painted expression of faith, making objective the experience of the interaction of the divine and human – "the point where spirit and visible form meet."[67] Thus, the icon is also a theology, a theology in color, expressing the experience of God with lines and paints rather than with discursive language. The goal of the icon and that of written theology are the same – to lead others to the mystical experience of God. The icon artistically depicts the experience so that others may approach the mystery and be invited to share in it. In the encounter of an icon-filled environment, one can become aware of joy, dread, awe; one can feel the mysterious presence of God.

Iconic Knowing Includes the Soul

When God created humanity, he breathed the breath of life into his creation (Gen. 2.7). The soul of each person is "the life given to each man by God" and "the guarantee that human life is not just health or wealth, but is life that is constantly given by God, that cannot then be limited by death, but is life as God intended it."[68]

Given to humanity by God – for life as he intends it – the soul is the part of human life that is ultimately drawn to God. The soul best explains our eternal connection with God. Its quest is to lead the us to the original God-intended fullness of life, to the restoration of the likeness of God. God intends us to be in fellowship – communion – with him. Let us return to a statement of St Gregory of Nyssa from the beginning of the chapter. "If ... man came into being ... to participate in the divine goodness, he had to be fashioned in such a way as to fit him to share in this goodness."[69] The soul is what fashions humanity, for the sanctification, holiness, and goodness that comes from being in fellowship with God. Placed there by God, the desire to seek God-likeness becomes innate in humanity.[70] Human nature is to desire to become holy, to recapture the divine likeness within each person.

The encounter with the icon is an encounter with something familiar, yet radically other. Kathleen Fischer links such encounters to the religious imagination: "It is on the level of the imagination that we first encounter the divine in this world, for revelation is always given through the material; it is always symbolic, pointing to the ultimate through the finite."[71] Icons speak to the part of the person that seeks to move toward the divine by speaking to the soul (*psyche*, ψυχή) of the person.

The icon invites a personal encounter with holiness that can touch the beholder in the depths of his or her soul. It is knowledge "face to face" (1 Cor. 13.12), an experience of the sacred presence of God. The beauty of the icon is an awesome beauty. It fills us with awe as the sensation of beauty engages the soul with the mystery of holiness, seeking to establish communion. The icon depicts the holy person filled with the Spirit of God and transformed by this fellowship. As John Dewey notes about all artistic encounters:

> we are, as it were, introduced into a world beyond this world which is nevertheless the deeper reality of the world in which we live in our ordinary experiences. We are carried out beyond ourselves to find ourselves.[72]

In the encounter with the icon, the encounter with holiness, the powers of the soul and its longing for God can be energized. John of Damascus points out that "proper to the soul are religion and understanding."[73] The soul desires to read the icon, to know and understand what is seen, to enter into a relationship with the icon, to see the Other. Through such encounter the beholder can come to see and understand that his or her personhood depends on God, that he or she is to live as God lives. The person can come to see that the goal is to become an icon.

Iconic Living and Knowing

The Orthodox Tradition has a maximal vision of humanity. This vision is rooted in the Resurrection of Jesus Christ and the descent of the Holy Spirit at Pentecost. In these events, the ministry of Jesus is fulfilled. The fall of Adam and Eve separated humanity from God and led to physical and spiritual death, decay, and alienation.[74] In the Resurrection, the power of death is destroyed, and humanity is liberated from its subjugation. "Christ is risen from the dead, trampling death by death and bestowing life to those in the tombs" is the hymn of Pascha (Easter). At Pentecost, the Spirit unites all, "the promise is fulfilled, and hope is completed" according to one hymn. The kingdom of God is manifest by the presence of the Holy Spirit.

This vision of humanity is soteriological and pneumatological, but equally important, it is Christological since it is in the person of Christ that salvation is achieved in the kingdom that the Spirit makes present. This vision is depicted through the art of the icon. By beholding icons, we are led to see Christ by the power of the Holy Spirit. According to St Basil the Great: "When we see Christ, the Brightness of God's glory, it is always through the illumination of the Spirit."[75] The Holy Spirit empowers us in fellowship with the risen Christ that we may thus manifest the divine image in our lives.

Theosis is the term most frequently used to describe the union, communion, or fellowship of the human with the divine – the attaining of God-likeness. It signifies human participation in the divine way of being – a life as a free, concrete person, loving and being loved in a communion of persons. *Theosis* is understood Christologically, for in the person of Jesus the union of divinity and humanity is manifest, without change, division, or confusion. The model for Christians is the life, ministry, passion, death, and Resurrection of Jesus of Nazareth, the Christ. His person provides the model for our relation to God as well as to one another, so that through imitating Christ we may become "partakers of divine nature" (2 Pet. 1.4). In the person of Christ, the greatest expression of humanity, the new beginning – the re-creation – of humanity can be seen. Thus, the way of *theosis* is Christological, through Christification. *Theosis* signifies both the already achieved way of existence that Christ's example has made possible for each person and the ultimate goal of human existence. *Theosis* is possible in human life now but reaches its fulfillment in the "not yet" of the kingdom to come. *Theosis* is living the way God lives, revealed to humanity through Christ.

The icons make the abstract concept of *theosis* a personal reality by presenting the vision of divine life in their art. They offer an ever-present model of what it means to be a person, without resort to theological manuals, essays, or patristic texts. By being depicted artistically, *theosis* takes on practical application and becomes iconic knowing and living.

In the icons, the beholder sees persons who have attained divine likeness. The model *par excellence* is Jesus Christ, for he incarnates the divine-human union in his person. The saints are also models of this fellowship. Icons of saints depict persons who have achieved *theosis* according to the discernment and wisdom of the Church. Before they died – to subsequently be depicted in icons – the saints lived a particular lifestyle through which they came to know God "in their hearts." During their time here on earth, the saints were living icons. Their lives reflect their personal fellowship with God through the Holy Spirit. They call on us to imitate them, to acquire similar lifestyles.

Iconic catechesis attempts to inform, form, and transform the multi-faceted image of God in each person to bring all to know God in their hearts, so that each person can manifest the divine presence in his or her life. To know God through an icon is to know through the heart: the whole person encounters a holy person and sees that God intends holiness for all. The icon becomes a means of communication with God – of engaging the Good News – requiring an openness and receptivity to the message. When received and engaged, the encounter with the icon can generate knowledge and wisdom in the heart – the deep core of personal existence. It is no accident that "to know in the heart" has such a physical and intimate denotation. When we know in our hearts, when we personally involve ourselves with others and allow others to involve themselves with us, we come to know and we come to be known. When the heart becomes engaged with the holiness of the icon, it comes to know and experience the mystery of God's love for humanity – which makes it possible for persons to manifest the presence of God in their lives and to live according to this wisdom. Iconic knowing does not mean merely copying or imitating some predetermined patterns of behavior, but making "what is known" an integral dimension of one's being. To know is to become and be – to live iconically.[76] In short, if you do not try to "be" or "become" what you know, then you never knew it in the first place.

At the practical level, *theosis*, iconic living and knowing, is about holiness, the journey and struggle to live as God lives, to practice godliness. St John Chrysostom advises parents: "This, then, is our task: to educate ourselves and our children in godliness."[77]

Holiness, unfortunately, is sometimes mistranslated and misapplied as piety and pietism. Holiness is not about isolated religiosity, but about living a God-like life. It means being fully human, experiencing and living life in its fullness. As Jesus said, "I came that they may have life and life in abundance" (Jn 10.10). And as St Irenaeus wrote, "The glory of God is man fully alive and the life of man is the vision of God."[78] Religiosity or piety, properly applied, is intended to orient our lives, in all of its aspects, toward God. As Nellas writes, "faith, keeping the sacraments, askesis, the whole ecclesiastical and spiritual life" are "the means of realizing that goal."[79] However, he argues that religiosity should not be an escape from our daily business. Rather, "all the dimensions of life – professional, artistic, intellectual … can and should be grafted onto the sacramental life."[80]

Pious practices are beneficial because they are the means and actions that orient us toward God-like living. Our piety toward icons – respect, devotion, veneration that passes toward the holy person depicted – ought to govern both our external and internal disposition, and our behavior toward all persons, and indeed, all creation. Likewise, the icon "testifies to the basic realities of Christian faith – to the reality of the divine penetration of the human and natural world, and to the reality of that sanctification which results from this."[81] In other words, piety intends to bring out the holiness within us so that it may penetrate all aspects of our lives, just as the icon bears witness to the reality that holiness – God – has penetrated our world.

Therefore, to live and know iconically involves much more than pious religious practices, beneficial as they are. Iconic catechesis is much more than teaching these meaningful expressions of religious conviction. Iconic living and knowing and iconic catechesis involve engaging the whole person's being – the intellect, the heart, the body – and nurturing godliness, holiness, *theosis*. They involve reaching for the deepest core of existence – the image of God already present – and leading one to manifest, express, and *live* the likeness of God.

To live iconically calls for each person to strive to become his or her unique, unrepeatable self, to see oneself and others as infinitely precious – endangered species – without whom the world would be diminished. The icon points to the richness of a single life and the unique qualities that this person possesses. In the icon, the Church has engraved this person, no matter his or her station or contribution, in its memory. No one is forgotten in the kingdom of God.

Educationally, this implies valuing and nurturing the contribution of each person. His or her sum of experiences and knowledge is worthwhile; it is unique and can contribute to the learning and enrichment of all. Belittling a student's questions or insights will not help that student learn or grow, but neither will merely agreeing with everything a student says. Assisting learners to see themselves honestly, challenging their questions with additional questions, offering diverse insights and perspectives to their insights and perspectives – these can serve to recognize the unique worth of each learner while still being faithful to the rigor of the classroom.

We choose to live iconically in freedom, freely entering into relationships with and for others that empower us to grow in our uniqueness. The icons of martyrs, perhaps, are the most dramatic example of freedom. St Ignatius of Antioch wrote about his impending martyrdom: "I bid all men know, that of my own free will I die for God … Now am I beginning to be a disciple."[82]

Less dramatically, in living freely a person must be able to choose a direction for one's life out of the myriad of possibilities that exist and carry it out in keeping with one's unique self. The only real limitation ought to be the sum of the characteristics and capabilities given that person by God. However, involvement in a relationship with another – frequently a teacher – is often needed for a realistic assessment of one's abilities, or for assistance in the development of those gifts. If God has not granted a beautiful singing voice, then all aspirations to become an opera singer will likely be fruitless, despite the "freedom" to pursue such a path. The freedom to pursue a talent, in and of itself, usually is not enough; the involvement of others is often required.

In educational practice, no one should feel compelled or fearful. Yet, it is not individualism that should be promoted, but freedom to engage with others in the meaningful "work" of learning. Students should be free to express themselves even as they learn to respect others who are likewise free. Freedom in the educational environment should include personal time for thought, reflection, and action. Engagement with others is made more meaningful when there is time for being alone with oneself.

Each of us is innately creative, seeking to fashion beauty and order out of the chaotic world that seems to surround us. Daily we make hundreds of decisions on how to organize our lives and make it as "beautiful" as possible. Iconic catechesis recognizes this desire for beauty in human life, allowing persons to express themselves creatively, while seeking to orient their creative energies towards the divine beauty, who is God.

A great deal of energy has been spent critiquing the arts, especially in religious education. Well-meaning community leaders bemoan and do not want the proverbial "coloring book" Sunday school or catechetical program. However, this can result in unnecessarily and undesirably limiting the educational program to the cognitive. Through the arts we express our longing for beauty and exercise our ability to order and form beauty in our lives. The icon points to beauty and art as a means of experiencing God. The opportunity to be artistically creative can provide us with a sense of control over aspects of reality that can bolster feelings of competence. Creativity can open up new avenues to the many ways of experiencing God.

The icon invites each person to continually reach beyond his or her present state, to grow in grace and wisdom, in a never ending spiral of ascent, from "glory to glory" (2 Cor. 3.18). Growth is potentially endless in this life. There is always something more to know, and learning should be continual through all phases of life. Our physical and emotional lives can be sources of frustration, and our bodily existence must grow to face the challenges and opportunities that each new stage of development brings. Similarly, our relationship with God is a dynamic experience of the soul, and we must reach out again to God in that never-ending spiral of ascent, with each new level of physical, emotional, and intellectual life.

The sad irony of having to point out that education is for growth reflects the state of education in our churches today. How much of our teaching is static, with little or no dynamism? How much of our teaching boils down to vanquishing foes who were defeated centuries ago and focuses largely on insights that emphasize pride in the past? Do we really expect our students to grow in wisdom? Can we conceive of the possibility that their wisdom could surpass our own – and that it is our duty to help make this happen?

To state that we might educate people to love may seem odd. Love is part of our human nature; we are conceived in love and born to love and be loved. Love, nevertheless, does need to be taught – the awareness of love, the possibilities and challenges of love, the skills of being a loving person. Because love frequently is equated to mere "romance," the term and concept of *caring* as discussed by Nel Noddings appears to be a useful replacement, particularly in the educational environment. She discusses caring in a myriad of expressions – caring for the self, caring for others, caring for ideas, caring for the created order of animals and plants, caring for the created world of objects, machines, and art. As she expresses it, "Caring is a way of being in relation, not a set of specific behaviors."[83] Our experience of love and our expression of love closely resemble our experience of being cared for and our caring for others. To encourage caring in the educational setting of the Church will hopefully lead to a new experience and expression of love among persons in community.

Iconic knowing ought to be intellectual, open, honest, clear-headed thinking and feeling that comes about by being "face to face" and engaging what or whom is to be known. In our experience, we are often filled with ideas that serve more to confuse than to reveal the reality of our lives with God. God and life are ultimately mysteries, filled with paradox and unanswerable questions. Pat answers, pious aphorisms and theories, devotion and nostalgia for earlier centuries can offer insight, but they can, just as often, lead one to divorce from God, especially when they are blind and slavish. We must strive to avoid limiting ourselves to rational, logical thinking, divorced from the soul, the body, the emotions, and memory. The lived experience must condition the intellectual experience and vice versa. For this reason, we must focus on the heart – the faculty that unites the two.

The heart of each person must be educated and come to knowledge and wisdom using all the faculties. The mind and intellect should be stimulated and challenged to think and think clearly, logically, and rationally. Only providing information is not feeding the heart. Learning and education should not be a liability in society or in the Church. Yet, how often have the educated been oppressed, feared, or threatened with annihilation by one or the other? Memory and imagination are critical. Without memory there is no rootedness in the kingdom that has been established by Christ. Without imagination there can be no vision of the kingdom that Christ promises to bring. The emotions must be involved. "Passionless" learning is lifeless; all the possibilities for human emotion need to be accommodated and experienced in the learning environment, if it is to lead to fullness of life. Who has not been emotionally moved by the power of a new idea or the struggle to learn a new skill or concept – and the feelings that were generated upon its successful acquisition or failure? These emotions are felt in our bodies. Our feelings, our hopes, our intellects belong to our bodies. When "we know" something profoundly, it is more than an intellectual experience; "we know it in our guts." Our souls must also know. Knowledge in our souls is not only a "religious" knowledge, but the knowledge that may be experienced through the small or grand encounter that makes the divine, the transcendent, the holy, a reality in our lives.

Conclusion

The icons point us toward a way of living and being, not a set of specific behaviors that one must follow in order to attain holiness.[84] Iconic catechesis strives to nurture the image of God within each person through the religious community and its worldview, ethos, and commitments, so that each person may attain God-likeness. The example of Jesus and the saints provides a vision of being in the world, an ethos of being – a *phronema* – wherein one's humanity is a manifestation of the divine. It involves a deep personal ethic where persons love without boundaries by caring for the self, the other, and the created world, opening up in hospitality to see the stranger as a manifestation of Christ. This ethic is marked by communion or "right relationship," meaning that we are to live "at one" with self, others, and the world.

Iconic living and knowing may appear to be impossible. The icons, however, continually herald the possibility of this vision. They point to saints, men and women who have lived God-like lives according to their unique abilities in their historical context. The icons call each person not to become the Basil, George, Irene, or Katherine who lived centuries ago. They call each person, when and where they find themselves, to become who God already knows them to be – to become who they already are.

NOTES

[1] Paul Evdokimov, *The Art of the Icon: A Theology of Beauty*, trans. Fr. Steven Bigham (Redondo Beach, CA: Oakwood Publications, 1990), p. 50. Emphasis added.

[2] St Athanasius, *On the Incarnation*, ch. 54, trans. "A religious of CSMV" (Crestwood, NY: SVS Press, 1982), p. 93.

[3] John D. Zizioulas, *Being as Communion: Studies in Personhood and the Church* (Crestwood, NY: SVS Press, 1985), pp. 27-30.

[4] Gregory of Nyssa, *An Address on Religious Instruction* (*Catechetical Oration*) 5 in *Christology of the Later Fathers*, ed. Edward Hardy, (Philadelphia: Westminster Press, 1954), p. 276. The reader will notice that many of the works cited do not utilize inclusive language for God or humanity. Among Orthodox writers, inclusive language is not utilized for God and is considered a diminution of the personhood of the members of the Trinity. As far as humanity is concerned, the patristic texts cited tend to have been translated generations before inclusivity was an issue. In most cases, humanity would be an appropriate translation of the texts that utilize *anthropos* in their original.

For contemporary writers, inclusive terminology has become more widespread, and the time when the work was first written or translated would determine whether inclusive terminology would have been used. From contacts with some of the authors cited, despite use of the term "man" in their published works or translations of their works, there is little evidence of any conscious sexism or patriarchy in their theological understandings of humanity. In this work, quoted texts will appear in their published forms. However, this author will utilize inclusive terminology for men and women, while remaining consistent with the Orthodox practice of referring to God with male pronouns.

[5] *The Lenten Triodion*, trans., Mother Mary and Kallistos Ware (London: Faber and Faber, 1978), p. 184.

[6] Kallistos Ware, "'In the Image and Likeness': The Uniqueness of the Human Person" in *Personhood*, ed. John T. Chirban (Westport, CT: Bergin and Garvey, 1996), p. 1.

[7] Leonid Ouspensky, "The Meaning and Language of Icons" in Leonid Ouspensky and Vladimir Lossky, *The Meaning of Icons* (Crestwood, NY: SVS Press, 1982), p. 37.

[8] Leonid Ouspensky and Vladimir Lossky, *The Meaning of Icons* (Crestwood, NY: SVS Press, 1982), p. 119.

[9] Kallistos Ware, *The Orthodox Way* (Crestwood, NY: SVS Press, 1979), p. 65.

[10] Ron Miller, "Freedom in a Holistic Context," *Holistic Education Review* 8:3 (Fall 1995), p. 5.

[11] John Macmurray, *Persons in Relation* (New Jersey: Humanities Press International, Inc., 1991), p. 211.

[12] K. Ware, "Image and Likeness," p. 7.

[13] Ibid.

[14] *Divine Liturgy of St John Chrysostom.*, trans. The Faculty of Holy Cross Greek Orthodox School of Theology (Brookline: Holy Cross Orthodox Press, 1985), p. 20.

[15] Irenaeus of Lyons, *Against Heresies*, IV, 39, 2 in Olivier Clément, *The Roots of Christian Mysticism* (New York: New City Press, 1995) p. 87.

[16] Panagiotis Nellas, *Deification in Christ* (Crestwood, NY: SVS Press, 1987), p. 27.

[17] K. Ware, "Image and Likeness," p. 7.

[18] K. Ware, *The Orthodox Way*, pp. 34-35.

[19] J. Zizioulas, *Being as Communion*, p. 58.

[20] P. Nellas, *Deification in Christ*, p. 127.

[21] Stanley S. Harakas, *Toward Transfigured Life* (Minneapolis: Light and Life Publishing Co., 1983), p. 248.

[22] Apart from monastics and some clergy, the reality is that few Orthodox Christians follow this rule completely. Much more typical is the abstinence from meat at the prescribed times, although during the fast periods, this too is infrequently observed.

[23] Christos Yannaras, *Freedom of Morality* (Crestwood, NY: SVS Press, 1984), p. 111.

[24] Evagrius Ponticus, *The 153 Chapters on Prayer*, 3 in *Evagrius Ponticus The Praktikos and the Chapters on Prayer*, trans. John Eudes Bamberger (Kalamazoo, MI: Cistercian Publications, 1981), p. 56.

[25] See O. Clément, *Roots of Christian Mysticism*, p. 181.

[26] Dumitru Staniloae, *Prayer and Holiness: The Icon of Man Renewed in God* (Fairacres, Oxford: SLG Press, 1982), p. 10.

[27] Anthony Bloom, *Beginning to Pray* (New York: Paulist Press, 1970), pp. 50-51.

[28] Ibid., p. 26.

[29] O. Clément, *Roots of Christian Mysticism*, p. 212.

[30] J. Zizioulas, *Being as Communion*, p. 224.

[31] Ibid.

[32] *The Ieratikon* (Athens: Apostolike Diakonia, 1987), p. 180.

[33] Zachary Xintaras, "Man, The Image of God," *The Greek Orthodox Theological Review* 1 (1954): 1, p. 57.

[34] Tad Guzie, *The Book of Sacramental Basics* (New York: Paulist Press, 1981), p. 72.

[35] Z. Xintaras, "Man, The Image of God," p. 57.

[36] Dumitru Staniloae, "The Holy Trinity: Structure of Supreme Love" in *Theology and the Church*, trans. R. Barringer (Crestwood, NY: SVS Press, 1980), p. 76.

[37] Alkiviadis C. Calivas, "The Sacramental Life of the Church." In *A Companion to the Greek Orthodox Church*, 2nd edition, ed. by F. Litsas (New York: Greek Orthodox Archdiocese, 1988), p. 280.

[38] Ibid., p. 281.

[39] J. Zizioulas, *Being as Communion*, p. 56.

[40] Ibid., pp. 53-59.

[41] *Sayings of the Desert Fathers*, Anthony, 9 (PG 65,77) in Clément, *Roots of Christian Mysticism*, p. 274.

[42] Abba Dorotheus of Gaza, *Directions on Spiritual Training*, 42 in *Early Fathers from the Philokalia*, trans. E. Kadloubovsky and G.E.H. Palmer (London: Faber and Faber, 1954), pp. 164-165.

[43] O. Clément, *Roots of Christian Mysticism*, p. 272.

[44] Ibid., pp. 273-274.

[45] K. Ware, "Image and Likeness," p. 9.

[46] Palmer, Ware, Sherrard, *The Philokalia* 2, pp. 383-384.

[47] John Dewey, *Art as Experience* (New York: Perigee Books, 1980), p. 106.

[48] John Baggley, *Doors of Perception: Icons and their Spiritual Significance* (Crestwood, NY: SVS Press, 1988), p. 78.

[49] From the "Memorial Service" in *The Divine Liturgy of St. John Chrysostom*, p. 164. Emphasis added.

[50] Gregory of Nyssa, *On the Creation of Man* (PG 44, 136-7) in Clément, *Roots of Christian Mysticism*, p. 80.

[51] Z. Xintaras, "Man, The Image of God," p. 53.

[52] Xintaras cites the following Fathers: Athanasios PG 25:101b; Basil the Great PG 44:273B; John Chrysostom PG 56:443C.

[53] St John of Damascus, "An Exact Exposition of the Orthodox Faith" (*De fide orthodoxa*) 2.20 (PG 94.937D) in *Fathers of the Church* Vol. 37, p. 243. I believe it is significant that in the definition for imagination and memory the terms φανταστικόν and its cognate φαντασία are operative, lending credence to the proposal that the two are related.

[54] See Richard Kearney, *The Wake of Imagination* (Minneapolis: University of Minnesota Press, 1988), chs. 1-3.

[55] St John of Damascus, "An Exact Exposition of the Orthodox Faith" (*De fide orthodoxa*) 2.17 (PG 94.933B) in *Fathers of the Church Vol. 37, St. John of Damascus, Writings*, trans. Frederic Chase, Jr. (New York: fathers of the Church, 1958), p. 241.

[56] Mary Warnock, *Imagination* (London: Faber and Faber, 1976), p. 84.

[57] Ibid. p. 30.

[58] Archbishop Iakovos, *Faith for a Lifetime: A Spiritual Journey* (New York: Doubleday, 1988), p. 80.

[59] Gregory writes, "that which is not assumed is not healed." St.

Gregory the Theologian, *Epistle 101, To Cledonius Against Apollinaris* in *Christology of the Later Fathers*, ed. Edward Hardy (Philadelphia: Westminster Press, 1954), p. 218.

[60] Philip Sherrard, *Christianity and Eros* (London: SPCK, 1975), p. 41.

[61] See Margaret Miles, *Image as Insight* (Boston: Beacon Press, 1985), p. 143.

[62] J. Baggley, *Doors of Perception*, p. 83.

[63] St Gregory of Nyssa, *De deitate Filii et Spiritus Sancti* (PG 46, 572 C). In *The Art of the Byzantine Empire 312-1453*, ed. Cyril Mango (Toronto: University of Toronto Press, 1986), p. 34.

[64] S. Langer, *Philosophical Sketches*, (Baltimore: John Hopkins Press, 1962), p. 90.

[65] J. Dewey, *Art as Experience*, p. 74.

[66] Vladimir Lossky, *The Mystical Theology of the Eastern Church* (Crestwood, NY: SVS Press, 1976), p. 9.

[67] Dumitru Staniloae, "Revelation through Acts, Words, and Images" in *Theology and the Church*, trans. Robert Barringer (Crestwood, NY: SVS Press, 1980), p. 131.

[68] Eduard Schweizer, "Ψυχή" in *Theological Dictionary of the New Testament*, vol. 9, trans. G. W. Bromiley, ed. G. Friedrich (Grand Rapids, MI: Eerdmans, 1974), p. 644.

[69] Gregory of Nyssa, *An Address on Religious Instruction* (*Catechetical Oration*) 5. See note 4.

[70] G. Mantzarides, *Orthodox Spiritual Life*, trans. K. Schram (Brookline, MA: Holy Cross Orthodox Press, 1994), pp. 149-50.

[71] Kathleen Fischer, *The Inner Rainbow: The Imagination in Christian Life* (New York: Paulist Press, 1983), p. 10.

[72] J. Dewey, *Art as Experience*, p. 195.

[73] St John of Damascus "An Exact Exposition of the Orthodox Faith" (*De fide orthodoxa*) 2.12, in *Fathers of the Church Vol. 37.* p. 238.

[74] See Maximos Aghiorgoussis, *In the Image of God: Studies in Scripture, Theology, and Community* (Brookline, MA: Holy Cross Orthodox Press, 1999), p. 117.

[75] St Basil the Great, *On the Holy Spirit* 26.64, trans. David Anderson (Crestwood: SVS Press, 1980), p. 97.

[76] See Georges Florovsky, "Human Wisdom and the Great Wisdom of God," in *The Collected Works of Georges Florovsky*, vol. 12 (Vaduz: Buchervertriebsanstalt, 1989), p. 119.

[77] St John Chrysostom, *Hom. 21 on Ephesians*, in *On Marriage and Family Life*, p. 71

[78] St. Irenaeus, *Against the Heresies*, 4, 20, 6.

[79] Panagiotis Nellas, *Deification in Christ*, p. 40.

[80] Ibid. p. 149.

[81] P. Sherrard, *The Sacred in Life and Art*, p. 74.

[82] St Ignatius, *To the Romans* 4-5 in *The Apostolic fathers*, trans. J. B. Lightfoot and ed. J. R. Harmer (Grand Rapids, MI: Baker Book House, 1983), pp. 76-77.

[83] Nel Noddings, *The Challenge to Care in Schools: An Alternative Approach to Education* (New York: Teachers College Press, 1992), p. 17.

[84] See Stanley S. Harakas, "Icon and Ethics," *Orthodoxes Forum* 4:2 (1990): 195-214.

Chapter Four

✳

The Curriculum of Iconic Catechesis:
Sacred Place, Time, Presence, and Communion

In addressing the educational potential of icons, we need to consider their pedagogical approach, style, and method as we ask "How do icons educate a person in faith?" and "What can we do to enhance that learning process?" Chapter Two provided a historical perspective to this question; in the mainline thinking of the seventh and eighth centuries, the icons were books for the illiterate. For those who could not read the scriptural texts, the icons told the story of God's action in history through artistic depiction. The beholder saw the icon, apprehended the story and, hopefully, was influenced to live a more Christian life. "Look, learn, and respond" seems a reasonable way to characterize the general understanding of how the icons taught in that historical period.

Yet, even then, there was a deeper appreciation of icons and how they functioned in the fullness of their potential. Two ancient examples make this point. St John of Damascus understood icons as radiating a divine grace that influenced how people responded to them:

Suppose I have few books, or little leisure for reading, but walk into the spiritual hospital – that is to say, a church – with my soul choking from the prickles of thorny thoughts, and thus afflicted I see before me the brilliance of the icon. I

106

am refreshed as if in a verdant meadow, and thus my soul is led to glorify God. I marvel at the martyr's endurance, and the crown he won, and inflamed with burning zeal I fall down to worship God through His martyr, and so receive salvation.[1]

According to the *Primary Russian Chronicle*, the emissaries of Prince Vladimir of Kiev in the tenth century, after witnessing liturgical services at Hagia Sophia in Constantinople, reported to the prince:

> We knew not whether we were in heaven or on earth, for surely there is no such splendor or beauty anywhere upon earth. We cannot describe it to you: only this we know, that God dwells there among men … For we cannot forget that beauty.[2]

This report secured the conversion of Prince Vladimir and Kievan Rus' to Orthodox Christianity. More recently, Robert Taft described the experience of the icon-filled Byzantine church: "Whoever visits a Byzantine church feels at once in a place of mystery, a holy place, detached from the world and flooded with the presence of God."[3]

Through these observations we can see beauty, brilliance, and a mystical environment leading visitors as well as believers to experience the holy presence of God. In such experiences, the beholder realizes that he is "on sacred ground," as Moses found himself when he encountered the burning bush on Horeb (Ex 3.2-5). For a place to be sacred, God must be present. St John of Damascus wrote that "the space of God is the place where His energy becomes manifest."[4] Philip Sherrard broadens this view by noting that "The sacred is something in which the Divine is present or which is charged with divine energies … Without the Divine – without God – there can be no holiness, nothing sacred."[5] In the above examples, the beholders entered a church, the primary locus of the icon. However, holiness can be found – and lived – wherever the spirit of the icon may be located: home, school, the natural world, workplace, as well as church and monastery.

The Divine is present in all these places – they are already sacred – yet the presence of icons helps us focus on God. They provide the lenses that open up our ability to visually communicate with him in our space and time, to experience his presence, and to enter into communion. The presence of and encounter with icons can create an "epiphany of the sacred."[6] The icons can create communion between the viewer and God, sacred presence, sacred space, and sacred time, for "every icon is ontologically 'miraculous,' filled with the life-giving energy of the Spirit of Christ."[7]

Iconic catechesis recognizes the awesome potential of the sacred as educator. In this chapter, we shall explore sacred place, time, presence, and communion from an iconic perspective. The elements of place, time, presence, and communion interweave and overlap with one another. For example, a "presence" of person to person is experienced in space and time and can lead to communion, while to be in communion with or in relation to another, one must necessarily already be present. Nevertheless, for purposes of discussion, the attempt will be made to address these elements separately, apropos the icon.

Our direction in this discussion is from the icons toward catechesis. The goal is to uncover how the icons function for the purpose of shaping the curriculum for faith education in the Orthodox Tradition. From the icons we can discern two curricula: the visible and the invisible. These are related to the explicit and the implicit curricula that Elliot Eisner has proposed,[8] but the terminology, visible and invisible, is rooted in the Christian Tradition. St John Chrysostom instructed catechumens "to see the invisible as if it were visible" with the "eyes of faith."[9] The visible curriculum consists of the icons themselves, the sacred persons they depict, the sacred stories they convey, and the respect Orthodox Christians give them. The invisible curriculum is the sacred "value system" that guides iconic catechesis in filling place, time, and the interpersonal – presence and communion – with the divine. "Seeing the invisible as if it were visible" invites teacher and learner to intentionally "make sacred," or sacramentalize, the educational enterprise.

Sacred Place

From the introductory examples above, the sense of sacred place or space as educator should be emerging. Belden Lane writes that our experience of God is "inescapably contextual," causing us "to gather up every thread of meaning from the context in which (it) occur(s). In our memories, therefore, we return first of all to the place 'where it happened.'"[10] In each of the above, the place was an icon-filled church. As Evdokimov describes it, "every visit to a church is ... a pilgrimage to a sacred place."[11] A sacred place or space is a place where God has acted, revealing his love to humanity and inviting us to respond. God has initiated and continues to initiate his kingdom on earth by acting in space, making space his dwelling place. All places are sacred because God has acted in space from before creation, inasmuch as "the Spirit of God was moving over the face of the waters" (Gen 1.2). The place where humanity dwells, normally thought of as "our world" was the place of God's presence before ours. God has been present and active in "our" world from before we began. Ultimately, God transcends the boundaries of place, as God is "everywhere present and filling all things," according to a prayer in the Orthodox Tradition. God is "in" space; God is in the boundary of space; God is even beyond the boundary.

Lane points out that a "sacred place is ordinary place, ritually made extraordinary."[12] A church is a sacred place because in it, God's people join God, worship him and relate to him in fellowship and love, manifesting the power of the reign of God in their lives by relating in a new, holy way. A church thus recalls the cosmic space where God has acted, acts, and will continue to act on behalf of human existence – for "our" space.

This space recalls Paradise – the Garden of Eden – the place where humanity, creation, and God first lived in harmony and communion (Gen. 2.8, 15). In one of his hymns on paradise, St Ephraim the Syrian (fourth century) describes the connection between the Church and Paradise in this manner: "The Creator saw the Church and was pleased; He resided in that Paradise which she had planted for His honor, just as He had planted the Garden for her delight."[13] Paradise, the garden that God planted for humanity has become the Church and the Church reconstitutes paradise.

While Ephraim hymns "the Church" as the ecclesial, communal, interrelational place of God's presence, to think of the church space – the architecture – in the same manner is also plausible. In Byzantine thought the church structure is a microcosm.[14] The church embraces the whole created order and integrates it within its walls.[15] Lane notes that "the impulse of the sacred place is both ... local and universal."[16] A sixth century hymn to the newly constructed Cathedral of St Sophia in Edessa states:

> Clearly portrayed in it are the mysteries of both Your Essence and Your Dispensation.
> He who looks closely will be filled with wonder.
> For it truly is a wonder that its smallness is like the wide world, Not in size but in type...[17]

God fills the architectural space, as he fills the cosmos and makes his presence known.

In Orthodox monasteries, the church is traditionally placed in the center of the monastery complex. The church thus becomes not only the spiritual center of the community, but the physical center as well, orienting and ordering the entire life of the community around it. As microcosm, reflection of Paradise, and the center of communal life, one can see how Evdokimov could write that "each church ... is an *omphalos* (navel), a cosmic center."[18] From this center, the whole earth is sanctified. On the Feast of the Elevation of the Cross, celebrated on September 14, there is the moment when the celebrant blesses the four corners of the church and through it the cosmos – north, south, east, and west – with the elevated cross. A hymn for the day states, "The four ends of the earth, O Christ our God, are sanctified today by the Exaltation of Thy Cross with its four arms."[19] The entire cosmos is redeemed, renewed, and restored to its proper relationship with God.

Filled with iconography, an Orthodox church becomes a place where God is present, revealing himself through artistic beauty and the sacred space that the icons delineate. It is a "world" made real by the presence of the icons. The icon of Christ the Pantocrator (Ruler of All) in the dome envelops the church structure and reaches toward the beholders. Christ is surrounded by the heavenly seraphim and cherubim, then the prophets of the Old Testament.[20] At the next level are the evangelists and apostles, the Virgin Mary; closer to the ground are the other saints, both the universally known (Stephen, Athanasios, Katherine, or Basil) and the local (Gerasimos of Cephalonia, Dionysios of Zakynthos, or Herman of Alaska), known by the community. In the church structure itself, God's energy is manifest through his presence and through the presence of saints, who radiate God's energy. The beholders of the icons, the worshipping members of the community, are continually invited to join this sacred cosmos of saints and angels, fully integrating themselves within the divine.[21] The beauty of the sacred environment within the church has the potential to invigorate the heart of the beholder, opening the possibility for communion and relationship. By touching the heart of each, the icons lead the beholder to contemplate the transcendent beauty and awesome mystery of God and his saints. As they radiate the presence of God, the icons usher the heart of the beholder to a sacred, holy dimension in the search for fellowship with the divine.

As bearers of the grace of God, icons can create sacred space wherever they are found. The icons radiate the presence of God in any setting, marking that space as sacred – a place where God manifests himself. Thus, not only can the home become a church (κατ' οἶκον ἐκκλησίαν – Rom 16.5), but the classroom and workplace as well. In each setting, the presence of icons results in an environment in which persons can better relate to one another in ways that reflect God's presence. Through the icon, God acts in "our" space so that we might live more fully – more like him – in his. Yet, there is no guarantee of sanctity by merely placing an icon somewhere. Lane correctly points out that "sacred place can be tread upon without being entered."[22] One must "learn to see" the sacred.

The icons point to God's presence in all places and spaces. The depiction of natural phenomena – mountains, trees, water, etc. – is altered in icons to reflect the presence of God in nature. In icons, the natural world conforms itself to the divine reality depicted. In the icon of the Nativity (Figure 8), the mountain envelops the cave that holds the child, and in the icon of the Transfiguration (Figure 7), the mountain provides the three pedestals on which Christ, Moses, and Elijah stand.

Architectural space also reflects divine realities. Icons of events that occurred indoors (e.g., Figure 1) are depicted with a background that denotes an interior setting. As Ouspensky explains it, "the action is not enclosed in or limited to a particular place."[23] In many icons, a drape, usually red, stretches across the background as a visual clue to the beholder that the event took place in an interior locale. Often architectural space is not depicted in its "natural" manner. Buildings can appear quite unnatural. The intent is not to confuse the viewer, but to

> help … show that the event and its significance are not confined to a precise historical moment of time and space; they belong to the world of the spirit, to a world of human consciousness that is richer and more mysterious than the ordinary everyday world…[24]

Despite the historical locale of the occurrence, it is our space and time that are being addressed by the icon. Our contemporary space becomes the place of the event; it is taking place in our time. The words of Christ to Zacchaeus, "Today salvation has come to this house" (Lk 19.9) are words that can apply to any house at any time. Iconic events that constitute salvation have occurred historically in a different place and at a different time, but these events also occur in the sacred place and time of the believer.

Sacred Time

St Paul writes, "But when the time had fully come (τὸ πλήρωμα τοῦ χρόνου), God sent forth his Son ... to redeem those who were under the law, so that we might receive adoption as sons." (Gal. 4.4). In time God has acted to achieve the salvation of humanity. In the fullness of time, humanity was redeemed by the presence of Jesus Christ in history – in time and space – and restored to fellowship with his Father. Evdokimov, reflecting on the presence of Christ in historical time, concludes, "Christ does not destroy time but fulfills it, renews its value, and redeems it."[25]

Time is analogous to space in that it is a locus of human action. Time is part of our existence as creatures. We measure ourselves by time; we are limited by time in that we live and die within time. Yet, paradoxically, time is the locus of *theosis:* living in fellowship with the uncreated, timeless God. Alkiviadis Calivas writes,

> Time is the framework within which all people are called to salvation, and the body of Christ, the Church, is being built up. The ultimate purpose and meaning of life have been revealed by the incursion of God's action in the historical process. God is calling all, who will hear and respond, to partake of his divine nature. The purpose of time is to allow free persons to come to God.[26]

In the icons, the invisible dimension of time becomes visible.

Through their art and their liturgical use, the icons influence the way time can be perceived. In the icons, time becomes sacred time: a fullness of time, the eighth day, the moment of salvation, an *anamnesis* – the past and future made present.

In the Orthodox Tradition, time is typically considered in two forms. First, there is *chronos* (χρόνος) or chronological time. It is "the time in which we live,"[27] the time of seasons, the calendar, and the clock. The second is *kairos* (καιρός). The *kairos* is the time of opportunity, the time of harvest (Mt. 13.30), the time of fulfillment, and the arrival of the kingdom of God (Mk. 1.15). As St Paul writes, "Behold, now is the acceptable time (*kairos*); behold, now is the day of salvation" (2 Cor 6.2). *Kairos* is "the time of our salvation."[28]

The liturgical cycle of the Orthodox Church merges *chronos* and *kairos*. The cycle commemorates the events of God's activity in time chronologically, and each event provides opportunities for our return to God. A major characteristic of this feature is the language used in the hymns of the feast. Hymns for a feast typically begin with "today," and the language is frequently in the present tense. For example, the *kontakion* for Christmas asserts that:

Today the Virgin *gives* birth to Him who *is* above all being, and the earth *offers* a cave to Him whom no man can approach. Angels with shepherds *give* glory, and Magi journey with a star. *For unto us is born* a young Child, the pre-eternal God.[29]

During Holy (Good) Friday matins, commemorating the Passion of Christ, this hymn is sung:

Today He who suspended the earth amid the waters *is* suspended on the Tree. The king of the heavenly hosts *wears* a crown of thorns. The One who clothed the heavens in clouds, *is* wrapped in mock purple. He who freed Adam in the Jordan *is* buffeted with blows. The bridegroom of the Church *is* transfixed with nails. The virgin's Son *is* pierced with a lance.

We worship Your Passion O Christ. *Show us now* your glorious Resurrection.[30]

Sherrard writes that the icon "assists in delivering the individual worshipper from the constraints and illusions of clock-measured time and profane history by initiating him directly into the dimension of liturgical time and sacred history."[31] On feast days the icons of the day are very prominent and, in the integration of image and word, time is transformed to the sacred time of the kingdom. *Chronos* becomes *kairos*. The hymn of Holy Friday matins, (as cited above), is sung while the cross is carried through the church. The language of the hymns and the appearance of the icons make the depicted events "present" in the sense that the participant is there. Even though these events occurred centuries ago, in the liturgical rendition they are present to the worshipping community. They are not reenactment drama. In the terminology of television, the liturgical encounter with the icon is "live." Through the presence of Christ in history and his commemoration in liturgy, time is opened up to a new, sacred dimension.

By remembering events of human salvation liturgically, time has been sanctified and transformed to a new reality – the incorporation of eternity within time. Georges Florovsky writes:

> The Christian remembrance is much more than just a memory or reminiscence. Indeed, Christians are bound to look back to the mighty events which are the foundation of their faith and hope: Incarnation, Cross and Resurrection, Pentecost. But these individual events of the past are, at the same time, paradoxically present in the Church here and now. The Incarnation of the Word is at once an historic event of the past which can and should be "remembered" in the ordinary way, and also *an abiding presence* of the Lord which can be directly perceived and recognized at all times and at any particular time by the eye of faith, in the Church.[32]

In the liturgical memorial of icon and word, the past is continuously present. An ordinary memory may be forgotten, but the liturgical memory of the great deeds of God for our sake is continuous. As Evdokimov states so succinctly, echoing Florovsky, "We become their contemporaries."[33]

Beyond making the event present, what is remembered is the hope of the Christian, that is, the future that is longed for by the believer. The term *anamnesis* is used to denote this particular vision of remembrance. Not just a historical memorial, *anamnesis* radically alters the perspective, enlarging it, opening it up, bringing the memorial to the present, and simultaneously orienting it toward the future as well. The most decisive moment of *anamnesis* takes place within the Divine Liturgy. At the moment when the eucharistic gifts are offered, the priest exclaims:

> Remembering, therefore, this command of the Savior, and all that came to pass for our sake, the cross, the tomb, the Resurrection on the third day, the ascension into heaven, the enthronement at the right hand of the Father, *and the second, glorious, coming.*[34]

In the gesture of offering the gifts, the community is called to remember the past events of human salvation in Christ and the future event of the return of Christ to fulfill his reign on earth. In the liturgical memorial, the future expectation of the kingdom of God becomes present.

In the icon, the depiction of the person reflects the new time of the Lord. The saint is depicted in his or her deified form, the form that has been transfigured by fellowship with the divine. To achieve *theosis* is to transcend time and history. This is why saints from differing time periods may be placed side by side within an icon or series of icons without any concern for historical anachronism. They have transcended time and space, the marks of history. Their garb is "classical," that is, timeless, not appearing out of place no matter where they are encountered. The art of the icon aids in making the events a "continu-

Figure 1. The Annunciation.
Athanasios Clark, iconographer. St. Basil Greek Orthodox Church, Chicago.

Ο ΑΓ   ΒΑΣΙΛΕΙ

Figure 2. St. Basil the Great.
Athanasios Clark, iconographer. St. Basil Greek Orthodox Church, Chicago.

Figure 3. St. Gregory Palamas.
From V. Lossky and L. Ouspensky, The Meaning of Icons
(Crestwood, NY: SVS Press, 1982), p. 118. Used with permission.

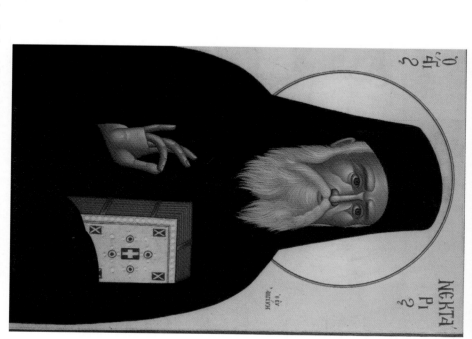

Figure 4. St. Nektarios. A photo of the saint.
Icon from St. Nektarios Greek Orthodox Church, Roslindale, MA.
Photo from a postcard sold at the Holy Trinity Monastery, Aegina, Greece.

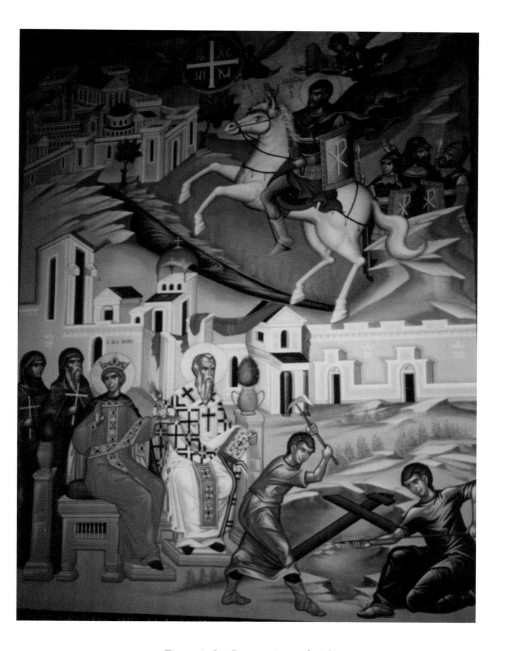

Figure 5. Ss. Constantine and Helen.
Athanasios Clark, iconographer. St. Basil Greek Orthodox Church, Chicago.

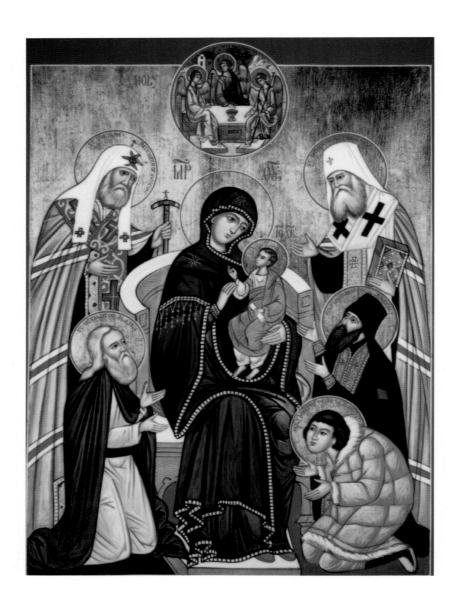

*Figure 6. The American Saints surround the Virgin and Child.
Clockwise from top right: St. Innocent of Alaska, St Juvenaly,
St. Peter the Aleut, St. Herman of Alaska, St. Tikhon of Moscow.
Orthodox Christian Publications Center, Wayne, NJ. Used with permission.*

Figure 7. The Tranfiguration.
From V. Lossky and L. Ouspensky, The Meaning of Icons
(Crestwood, NY: SVS Press, 1982), p. 210. Used with permission.

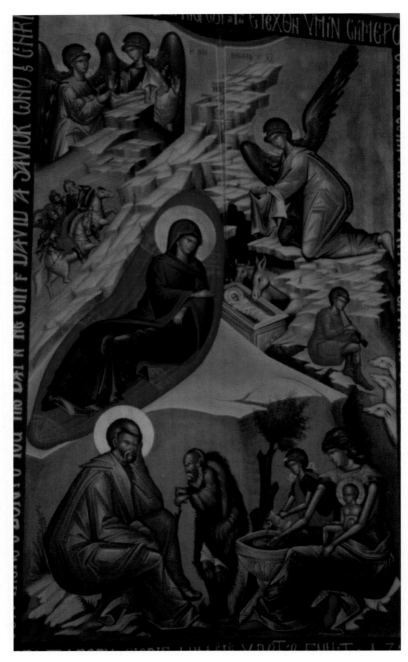

Figure 8. The Nativity of Christ.
Athanasios Clark, iconographer. St. Basil Greek Orthodox Church, Chicago.

Figure 9. top, The Epitaphios Threnos.
Holy Transfiguration Monastery, Brookline, MA. Used with permission.
bottom, The decorated kouvouklion.
St. Basil Greek Orthodox Church, Chicago.

Figure 10. The Holy Trinity by Andrei Rublev.
From V. Lossky and L. Ouspensky, The Meaning of Icons
(Crestwood, NY: SVS Press, 1982), p. 198. Reprinted with permission.

Figure 11. Pentecost.
Athanasios Clark, iconographer. St. Basil Greek Orthodox Church, Chicago.

Figure 12. The Baptism of Christ.
Monastery of St. Dionysiou, 1547, Mt. Athos, Greece. Used with permission.

ous present." In the encounter with the icon, the beholder is invited to engage in an *anamnesis*, that is, to recall the past and envision the future reality of the saint simultaneously.[35]

Sacred Presence

On the Feast of the Transfiguration, the Old Testament readings at vespers retell the encounters of Moses and Elijah with the presence of God. In the second reading, from the Book of Exodus, Moses and God speak "face to face, as a man speaks to a friend" (Ex 33.11). During their conversation, God says to Moses, "My presence shall go with you and I will give you rest." (Ex 33.14). To assure Moses of his presence, God agrees to reveal his goodness and glory to him, although he places Moses in the cleft of a rock to protect him. In the third reading, the prophet Elijah encounters the presence of God, neither in a strong wind nor an earthquake nor a fire, but in a "still small voice" (1 Kings 19.13). Moses and Elijah both experience the presence of God; yet neither sees God.

In the person of Jesus Christ, however, it became possible to see God in his glory, and the feast day recalls this possibility. In the readings of the Divine Liturgy, a pericope from the Second Epistle of Peter states "we were eyewitnesses of his majesty" (2 Pet 1.16). At the Transfiguration, Jesus reveals his glory, and his divinity to Peter, James, and John (Mt 17.1-9; Lk 9.28-36; Mk 9.2-8). With their eyes, Peter, James, and John experience the full presence of God in the person of the transfigured Jesus. Peter wants to remain within that sacred presence, which explains his request to build tents for Jesus, Moses, and Elijah.[36]

All icons make the experience of the presence of God a reality, whether of historical events like the Transfiguration (see Figure 7) when God reveals his divinity to the disciples and allows it to be seen, or of the saints who reveal God's glory through their lives and personal examples. The icon of the Transfiguration, by re-presenting this event for all times and places, offers beholders the opportunity to become eyewitnesses of the sacred presence of God in Christ. According to Evdokimov, "the icon is a witness to the saint's presence and expresses his ministry of intercession and communion."[37] To be face to face with an icon is to be face to face with the sacred presence of the divine.

Icons witness to the presence of Christ and to the saints and events known to the beholder. This witness can be seen in the reverence directed to them when they are carried in liturgical processions. For example, at the vespers service marking the feast day of a saint, the icon of the saint is processed around the church. On the Feast of the Elevation of the Cross, a cross is carried. On Holy (Good) Friday, an icon of the dead Christ (the *Epitaphios Threnos*, Figure 9) is carried. In towns and villages with predominantly Orthodox populations, these processions may take place in the streets, and the entire population will gather. Whether in a church or a town, it is not uncommon to see people kneel during the procession or as the icon approaches them. The presentation of the icon witnesses to the presence of the saint or the event depicted among the congregation. The presentation of the icon becomes a moment for *anamnesis*, recollection and experience of the past and future in the present.

The beholder of the icon, like Peter at the Transfiguration, may wish to remain in the presence of the divine. The beauty radiated by the saint attracts the beholder and invites participation in fellowship with the divine. Three stories from the ascetic literature relate experiences of the sacred presence that the holy person evokes. The first relates the attractive nature of the divine presence through which God radiates, even in silence.

> Three brothers were in the habit of going to see the blessed Anthony every year. The first two would ask him questions about their thoughts and the salvation of the soul. But the third brother would keep silence without asking anything. Eventually Abba Anthony said to him, "You have been coming here to see me for a long time now and you never ask me

any questions." The other replied, "One thing is enough for me, Father, to see you."[38]

Holiness has a magnetic power of attraction. When encountered, the soul becomes restless and is drawn toward the sacred presence as a growing flower turns toward the light to bask in its radiant energy.

Light is a continual theme in the ascetic literature and is recognized as a sign of the presence of holiness. The second story explains that holiness is not achieved simply by obeying rules of discipline, but through total immersion of the person in the divine, which bursts forth in light.

> Abba Lot came one day to see Abba Joseph and said to him, "Father, I keep my little rule to the best of my ability. I observe my modest fast and my contemplative silence. I say my prayers and do my meditation. I endeavor as far as I can to drive useless thoughts out of my heart. What more can I do?" The elder rose to answer and lifted his hands to heaven. His fingers looked like lighted candles and he said, "Why not become wholly fire?"[39]

This fire is the energy of God radiated by the person in fellowship with the divine. *Theosis* involves full participation in the divine way of life, which is the light of the world and has the potential to make its presence felt in the lives of all persons. The third story relates the palpability of this presence. It is told by Evdokimov about St Seraphim of Sarov, the great nineteenth century Russian ascetic:

> Motovilov (one of St Seraphim's disciples) asked St Seraphim to explain to him the meaning of the state of grace. St. Seraphim then told Motovilov to look at him. "I looked at him and was seized with fear" because he appeared to be clothed with the sun. St Seraphim then asked Motovilov what he felt: "an unspeakable joy, calm, and peace," answered the disciple. Motovilov not only felt something in his soul, but his senses also participated in the experience: he saw a blinding

light and felt an unusual heat, and smelled perfume. The conversation ended with this exhortation: "It is not only for you to understand these things but through you, to the whole world."[40]

Through the experience of the sacred presence, a person may be empowered to live in fellowship with God. One monastic writer describes the experience of the presence of the saint thus:

> And yet to have lived and died in such a way that your presence, discretely and from a distance as if a fragrance from someone absent, can give others the possibility to breathe divine fragrance! To grant someone else the possibility of living, of being invigorated ... to give another the ability to love life, to acquire self-confidence and stand on his own two feet, so that from within him there arises spontaneously a "Glory to Thee, O God!"[41]

Yet, to be in the presence of the divine is not only a moment for personal affirmation, even if it leads to glorification of God – to face God is to face the inevitability of judgment. Staniloae writes:

> Penetrated by the holiness of God as supreme conscience, man becomes a burning bush; or again, in the presence of a holy man he feels that he is standing before a burning bush. The shame, the awe, experienced in the presence of holiness exceeds any that can arise in response to human beings; it is of another order, because the divine reality of the supreme conscience made visible to us in the conscience of a saint shows us ourselves exactly as we are, and reveals itself as supremely urgent, judging our sinful condition. And yet, at the same time, holiness attracts us.[42]

Icons make the sacred presence known and felt through their light. Icons radiate light. The gold or neutral backgrounds not only reflect natural light or candlelight, but they radiate their own light, the light of the presence of God. According to Egon Sendler, icons are "perpetually irrupting, radiant energy, reflections of the light of God."[43] Artistically this is achieved through the backgrounds; within the image itself there is no light source creating shadows, "for light is their (the icons) very subject and we can never enlighten the sun."[44] Halos around the heads of persons indicate their sanctity and the light of God that they have made present in their lives.

> For the saints, the saying, "you are the light of the world" is *ontologically* normative. The halos which encircle the heads of the saints on their icons are not simply distinctive signs of their holiness, but the shining forth of their bodies' luminosity.[45]

Sacred Communion

In the previous chapter, communion or relationship was named as a characteristic or quality of the human person striving to achieve God-likeness or *theosis*. The icons create the possibility for communion with the divine and with one another in their art. Sacred communion is necessarily achieved in time, space, and with the presence of persons. Thus, the sacredness of communion includes everything that has already been presented. However, since God is the source and model of relationship and communion, reflecting separately on this theme and the icons' role in it is warranted.

By way of introduction, the relationship between communion and communication through a work of art should be briefly highlighted. Communication is necessary in order to achieve any form of communion in a relationship. Icons are a form of communication. As with all works of art, a discourse can be established between the icon and the viewer.[46] Since there is a sender and a receiver, the communication process requires that the receiver be able to perceive and correctly interpret the transmitted messages. Michael Baxandall insightfully notes that a viewer's mind is not a blank screen, or *tabula rasa*, but possesses knowledge on which the viewer will draw in seeking to understand the communication from the artwork. Therefore, the communication techniques used by the artist must be recognizable and meaningful to the viewer. Consequently, a reservoir of knowledge that is common to the iconographer and to the viewer must exist in order that meaningful communication take place.[47]

Icons draw upon the reservoir of the Tradition, fusing their subject matter, that is, *what* is depicted, with their expressive content, that is, *how* it is depicted, in order to communicate – establish communion – with the viewer.[48] The icon, through its visual language, is able to communicate meaningfully and uniquely with the viewer.

Prayer is the form of communication that is distinctive to the icon. Rooted in its liturgical context, the icon invites the beholder to engage in communication with God through prayer – corporate or personal – and acts of reverence toward the icon. Prayer is an expression and manifestation of communion with God. In prayer aided by an icon, a person engages and enters into discourse with God, Father, Son, and Holy Spirit, who are in engaged in a continual discourse of love. The personal reality of the three persons of the Trinity, their presence to and communion among one another, is the primary model of communion for all persons.

In the icon of the Holy Trinity, this model of communion is depicted. The icon, entitled The Hospitality of Abraham, is based on the story of Genesis 18. Abraham's three visitors are seen in the Orthodox Tradition as a manifestation of the Trinity. In some icons, Abraham and Sarah can be seen. In probably the most famous depiction of this moment, the icon of St Andrei Rublev (fifteenth century Russia, see Figure 10), Abraham an Sarah are absent. In all depictions, however, the beholder's focus is on the three angels seated at the table in conversation.

The three figures are seated in a circular arrangement. No one dominates, and all are equally sized. According to Evdokimov, the central figure is considered to be the Father, seated to the Father's right (viewer's left) is the Son, and to the

Father's left is the Spirit.[49] The circularity of the image recalls the *perichoresis* of the Trinity. Ware discusses the term *perichoresis* and offers a number of terms that can help explain it: "cyclical movement" "reciprocity," "interchange," "mutual indwelling," and "round dance."[50] He continues that "it signifies that each person 'contains' the other two and 'moves' within them."[51] In their continual dance of interrelation, the three share love. As Ware describes:

> By virtue of this *perichoresis*, Father, Son and Holy Spirit 'coinhere' in one another, each dwelling in the other two through an unceasing movement of mutual love – the 'round dance' of the Trinity. There is between them a timeless dialogue … From all eternity the first person is saying to the second, 'You are my beloved Son' (Mark 1.11); from all eternity the second replies, 'Abba, Father; Abba, Father' (Rom. 8.15; Gal. 4.6); from all eternity the Spirit sets his seal upon the interchange.[52]

The circular nature of the image guides the eyes of the beholder in a continual manner from one figure to the next, engaging the beholder in the round dance of the three and inviting the beholder to enter the dance as well.

In the icon, the three persons face one another, and all three are depicted full face. This recalls the literary root of the term person – *prosopon:*

> *Prosopon* in Greek is formed from *pros*, "towards," and *opsis*, "face," or "aspect," and so it means literally "facing towards." The Latin equivalent persona has the literal sense of "sounding through" (*per + sonare*). A *prosopon* or *persona*, then, means a discrete entity with which one enters into contact by looking at him or her, or by hearing him or her speak.[53]

The term suggests presence, encounter, communion, and relationship. All the saints depicted in icons are depicted in full face or at least three quarters. They are never in profile. "Profile interrupts communion, inaugurates a fading away, a flight, and quickly becomes absence. Face to face eye contact plunges the saint's gaze into the spectator's, welcomes it, and immediately establishes a bond of communion."[54] Sinners and evil are typically depicted in profile. Representations of Judas Iscariot are perhaps the most common. In icons of the Last Supper, Judas Iscariot is almost always depicted in profile; he turned away from Christ. To enter into relationship with a person, the full person must be engaged; iconographically this is achieved through full face-to-face contact.

A final element of the icon that establishes communion is the perspective used by the iconographer. Since the Renaissance, artists have traditionally used perspective to designate the relative positions of objects, buildings, and persons to one another. Perspective provides the realism for most artwork. However, in iconography, perspective is used very differently; it is inversed.[55] "The principle of inversed perspective is simple. The lines of this perspective do not meet at a vanishing-point situated behind the canvas, but at a point in front of the canvas."[56] The lines of movement in an icon are not from the viewer toward or beyond the painting, but rather from within the icon toward the viewer. The figures in an icon "leap out" from their painted space, projecting themselves toward the viewer. In the icon of the Trinity, the three angels are "much too large" for their space. "Inversed perspective abolishes distance and depth in which everything disappears at the horizon. The opposite effect is of course to bring the figures close up and to show that God is here and everywhere."[57] Thus, while we may, for convenience, say that we are looking at the icon, from this inverse perspective it is the one depicted who is looking at us!

From this it is possible to note that the icon generates communion in that the icon is not complete without a beholder.

In front of the icon in the eyes of the beholder; one is left feeling that the beholder is essential to the completion of the icon. The essence of the exercise has been to establish a communion between the event or persons represented in the icon and those who stand before it, to "make present" to another person what is presented in the icon.[58]

The icon itself draws the beholder into a relationship with it and thus through it toward the divine, toward God.

THE SACRED AS CURRICULUM

To many people, curriculum merely means textbooks and prescribed programs of instruction. The work of Elliot Eisner has helped educators to significantly broaden this understanding of curriculum. Eisner defines curriculum as "a series of planned events that are intended to have an educational consequence for one or more students."[59] The Latin root of curriculum is *currere,* which means the course to be run. In practice a curriculum consists of much more that merely textbooks and programs for learning a specific topic. It includes the events intended to yield a learned outcome, which may vary from student to student.

Eisner points out that all schools teach three curricula: the explicit, the null, and the implicit.[60] The explicit curriculum is the course of study that is made public – the school's proclaimed goals. All schools tend to have more or less the same explicit curriculum. All elementary schools explicitly teach the "three R's" – reading, writing, and arithmetic – as well as other subjects. Colleges and universities generally teach the liberal arts by focusing on the same areas in the humanities and the sciences. Somewhat of a paradox is the null curriculum. It is what is not taught in a school, yet this too teaches. For Eisner, the null curriculum exposes two dimensions that are not articulated: the "intellectual processes that schools emphasize and neglect" and "content or subject areas that are present or absent."[61] Relative to the first, Eisner notes that cognitive processes are emphasized, while aesthetic processes are neglected. With respect to the second, he reflects on how decisions to emphasize certain subjects, such as years of advanced math, may accrue to the overall detriment of the students because study in another beneficial area, such as economics, may be preempted. The implicit curriculum or hidden curriculum is "that (which the school) teaches because of the kind of place it is."[62] The implicit curriculum can be positive or negative as well as unintentional. It involves elements of school "atmosphere," such as the social structure, reward structure, the organization of the school day, and other aspects of its value system. For example, the timetable for the day can emphasize punctuality and diligence in solving a problem in a defined time period, or it may teach detachment because time is allowed to run out before problems are solved. Does the school value social revolution and transformation or does it value maintenance of the status quo? To reflect on such matters is to reflect on the implicit curriculum of a school.

The Visible and Invisible Curriculum

In iconic catechesis, as in Eisner's principles, the sacred fills the curriculum with visible and invisible elements. From the icons we can discern a visible and an invisible curriculum for catechesis. There are three visible elements. The first is that the icons teach the history of the community, informing the viewer who apprehends the story. They provide a visual means of accessing and recalling the foundational stories of the community. This was their primary educational significance during the iconoclastic controversy. The sacred history of the acts of God in the lives of his people that have brought about their salvation are depicted for the entire community to behold and remember. To behold the icons is to have an experience with the history of the Christian people. Through their artistic style, the icons contemporize the stories for the community, making them a continual present tense, in effect stating that these stories are as much a part of the present of the community as they are of its past.

The second element of the visible curriculum is the sacred person, the divine-human fellowship. The icons invite their beholders to allow the sacred to fill their lives and to become holy. In Jesus Christ, the model of human existence, which is the fellowship of the divine and human, is united in his person. In his icon we see his person, his *hypostasis* that is both human and divine "without confusion, change, division, or separation" as defined by the Council of Chalcedon (451).[63] For the saints, the icons provide a visual expression of divine-human *synergy*. In the saints, holiness is achieved through the power of the Holy Spirit in cooperation with human effort. The icons depict the human transformed by the divine, while maintaining and fulfilling the freedom, uniqueness, growth, relationality, and knowledge of the person. In the icons, the sacred radiates and invites the beholders to enter into this relationship and be transformed through the engagement.

The third element of the visible curriculum is the experience of sacred place, time, presence, and communion. These components can be seen because they are depicted in the icons. The respect that Orthodox Christians pay to the icons bears witness to the sacred reality they see in them: the icons "create reverence."[64] Young and old may enter a church or place where icons are prominent and see the reverential behavior of the beholders. Even in museum displays of icons, the sense of awe and sanctity can often be perceived.[65] As we shall see, this sacred milieu, especially when expressed through liturgy, is the context for forming persons in faith.

The invisible curriculum of the icons is multifaceted, and the longer the icons are reflected upon, the more elements may be revealed. Yet, the four key points discussed in this chapter – sacred space, time, presence, and communion – comprise the primary elements of the invisible curriculum, teaching through the sacred environment they foster. From this statement may be tempted to conclude that iconic catechesis means placing an icon in every classroom and somehow, magically, this sacred environment appears. Icons certainly belong within the faith education classroom. In a corner of a classroom, they can become a place for veneration, contemplation, and prayer. They are aids in instruction. Teachers will often use an icon as "the picture" of a story they are telling to their students.

Yet, to claim the sacred as the invisible curriculum means that the educational environment must be guided by the sacred. The visible curriculum should lead to the invisible curriculum. Because the icons depict transfigured life, the curriculum itself can also be transfigured.[66] The invisible needs to become visible in the teaching-learning experience.

The intention of catechesis should not be merely study *about* God, but the *experience of* God through the place, time, presence, and communion of the catechetical curriculum. The place of learning needs to become a sacred place, a context where God is encountered and the center of one's being is touched, much like a church. If classrooms or any places where learning occurs are to become "sacred places" they must be arranged in a way that welcomes God. God is already present in this space. The initiative is God's, but the space itself can make the divine presence felt and welcome to the occupants. The space of catechesis should strive to be a place where God is accessible to learner and teacher and where each may reveal God to the other.

The time of teaching and learning needs to become sacred time, full and filled with opportunities to come to personal knowledge of Christ. The way time is utilized must reflect God's presence in time, both *chronos* and *kairos*. There is a *chronos* for catechesis – a time and sequence for learning and teaching the sacred story of God's ongoing relationship with his people. There is also a sequence to learning, and there are certain times for learning certain things. Yet, there are moments that appear and make themselves available for decisive action and learning – a moment of insight or a time of intensive activity. This is a catechetical *kairos*, when an opportunity ought to be seized. Also, the time of catechesis must reflect a time of fulfillment, both from the perspective that time is used well and productively, and also when time is used to celebrate and refresh after one's labor. "This is the day that the Lord has made, let us rejoice and be glad in it" (Ps 118.24). Joy should fill the time of learning.

The sacred presence and communion that icons depict and create turns the attention to the personal attributes of teachers and learners and the way both interact and relate with one another. While more will be presented in the next chapters, a few initial comments should be made. First, iconic catechesis mantains that each learner and teacher is striving to become an icon, reflecting God-likeness in his or her life. The teacher plays a special role in this dynamic because the teacher is responsible for leading the learners – a responsibility that should not be taken lightly: "Let not many of you become teachers ... for you know that we who teach shall be judged with greater strictness" (Jas 3.1). Teachers are icons, bearing the Tradition in themselves, with the potential to become models of iconic living and knowing. Each learner, too, is responsible for his or her learning, and is called to grow in grace and knowledge. From the variety of persons depicted in icons, we can discern that all persons are capable of coming to the knowledge of Christ, no matter what age or status in life. Indeed, growth and acquisition of knowledge are aspects of personhood. Because God has created humanity for growth, all persons can learn. The learning dynamic involves *synergy*, reaching out through the icon toward God and allowing God's grace to fulfill the desire for "heart knowledge" in the learner. Thus, the iconic curriculum expects learners and teachers to work together to create a milieu where all may learn.

Michael Schiro presents curriculum from three viewpoints: curriculum as object; curriculum as interaction; and curriculum as intent.[67] Each one of these can be seen in the iconic curriculum. Curriculum as object focuses mainly on the idea that a curriculum is made up of books. As objects, the icons themselves become a major textbook of the life of the Church.

They contain the elements of study needed to learn to be an Orthodox Christian. In the icons we discern the story and Tradition of the community. We can see its doctrines of the persons of the Trinity and the teachings about humanity and the saints. We can discern a praxis for Orthodox Christians, that is, a way of life, through the customs, piety, and ethos or *phronema* that make up the Orthodox way.

Curriculum as interaction refers to the experiences that teach in an educational experience. First and foremost, icons can create interaction through their ability to draw persons into prayer, that is, into an interaction with God. Icons also create interaction through the pious practices and liturgical rites associated with them, from veneration to grand solemn processions. Orthodox Christians are continually interacting with icons in their parish liturgical life, chiefly through feast days and the liturgical year. In their homes or other places, they can also interact with icons as part of their personal lives of prayer and celebration of significant days in the liturgical calendar. This interactive curriculum can become a significant opportunity for teaching and learning.

Finally, there is the curriculum as intent, which refers to the goals of a planned sequence. Here, as we have seen, the icon makes itself fully present in both inward and outward manifestations for the person. The inward intent is to make the invisible, that is, the *phronema* of the Church, a reality in persons lives in order to lead to the outward intent. The outward intent of the icon is iconic living and knowing, to live and know as God lives and knows.

Through the iconic curriculum – a curriculum of objects, interaction, and intent – the educational environment can become a microcosm, becoming a place where the divine and the human may engage one another. This microcosm becomes a sacred course to be run, a sacred curriculum of visible and invisible elements, mutually reinforcing one another. Through this vision of curriculum iconic living and knowing can becom possible.

NOTES

[1] John of Damascus, *On the Divine Images*, First Apology, Ancient Documentation, trans. D. Anderson (Crestwood, NY: SVS Press, 1980), p. 39.

[2] As cited in T. Ware, *The Orthodox Church* (London: Penguin Books, 1963), p. 269.

[3] Robert Taft, S.J., *Beyond East and West: Problems in Liturgical Understanding* (Washington, D.C.: The Pastoral Press, 1984), p. 121.

[4] John of Damascus, *An exact exposition on the orthodox faith*, 1.13 (PG 94.852A).

[5] Philip Sherrard, *The Sacred in Life and Art* (Ipswich, UK: Golgonooza Press, 1990), p. 1.

[6] Paul Evdokimov, *The Art of the Icon: A Theology of Beauty*, trans. S. Bigham (Redondo Beach, CA: Oakwood Publications, 1990), p. 125.

[7] Boris Bobrinskoy, "The Icon: Sacrament of the Kingdom," *St. Vladimir's Theological Quarterly* 31 (1987): p. 294.

[8] Elliot Eisner, *The Educational Imagination: On the Design and Evaluation of School Programs* (New York: Macmillan Publishing Co., 1979).

[9] St John Chrysostom, *Baptismal Instructions* 2.9, Ancient Christian Writers, vol. 31, trans. Paul Harkins (New York: Newman Press, 1963), p. 46. Of course, the Nicene-Constantinopolitan Creed also refers to these elements when it states that God created all things visible and invisible.

[10] Belden Lane, *Landscapes of the Sacred: Geography and Narrative in American Spirituality* (New York: Paulist Press, 1988), p. 5.

[11] P. Evdokimov, *Art of the Icon*, p. 139.

[12] B. Lane, *Landscapes of the Sacred*, p. 15.

[13] Ephraim the Syrian, *Hymns on Paradise* 6.10, trans. Sebastian Brock (Crestwood, NY: SVS Press, 1990), p. 112.

[14] Kathleen McVey, "The Domed Church as Microcosm: Literary Roots of an Architectural Symbol," *Dumbarton Oaks Papers* 37 (1983), p. 91.

[15] In some of the churches of Ravenna, Italy the ceilings are decorated with stars, becoming a visual reminder of the integration of the cosmos.

[16] B. Lane, *Landscapes of the Sacred*, p. 15.

[17] K. McVey, "The Domed Church," p. 95.

[18] Evdokimov, *Art of the Icon*, p. 145.

[19] Hymn of Matins in *The Festal Menaion*, trans. Kallistos Ware and Mother Mary (London: Faber and Faber, 1969), p. 157.

[20] Often, the icon of the Pantocrator or the dome itself is ringed with a rainbow, reminding the community of the heavens. In a photo of a dome that I have seen, the constellations of the zodiac were depicted as the symbols of the heavenly constellations.

[21] See John Baggley, *Doors of Perception: Icons and Their Spiritual Significance* (Crestwood, NY: SVS Press, 1988), p. 92. See also, Alexis Vinogradov, "The Orthodox Christian Experience of Liturgical Space," *Ecumenism* No. 123 (September, 1996): p. 34-35.

[22] B. Lane, *Landscapes of the Sacred*, p. 15.

[23] Leonid Ouspensky, "The Meaning and Language of Icons," in Leonid Ouspensky and Vladimir Lossky, *The Meaning of Icons* (Crestwood, NY: SVS Press, 1982), p. 40.

[24] J. Baggley, *Doors of Perception*, p. 82.

[25] P. Evdokimov, *Art of the Icon*, p. 131.

[26] Alkiviadis C. Calivas, *Come Before God in Prayer and Solemn Feast* (Brookline, MA: Holy Cross Orthodox Press, 1986), pp. 3-4.

[27] Ibid., p. 7.

[28] Ibid.

[29] *The Festal Menaion*, p. 277. Emphases added.

[30] *The Services for Holy Week and Easter*, trans. Leonidas Contos (Northridge, CA: Narthex Press, 1994), p. 207. Emphases added.

[31] P. Sherrard, *The Sacred in Life and Art*, p. 83.

[32] Georges Florovsky, "The Worshipping Church" in *The Festal Menaion*, p. 28.

[33] P. Evdokimov, *Art of the Icon*, p. 133.

[34] *The Divine Liturgy of St John Chrysostom*, trans. the Faculty of Holy Cross Greek Orthodox School of Theology (Brookline, MA: Holy Cross Orthodox Press, 1984), pp. 21-22. Emphases added.

[35] See Constantine Kalokyris, *The Essence of Orthodox Iconography* (Brookline, MA: Holy Cross Orthodox Press, 1985), p. 85ff.

[36] This is the interpretation of A Monk of the Eastern Church, *The Year of Grace of the Lord: A Scriptural and Liturgical Commentary on the Calendar of the Orthodox Church* (Crestwood, NY: SVS Press, 1980), p. 241.

[37] P. Evdokimov, *Art of the Icon*, p. 179.

[38] *Sayings of the Desert Fathers*, Anthony, 27 (PG 65.84) as cited in Olivier Clément, *The Roots of Christian Mysticism* (New York: New City, 1995), p. 146.

[39] *Sayings of the Desert Fathers*, Jospeh of Panepho, 7 (PG 65.229) as cited in Olivier Clément, *The Roots of Christian Mysticism* (New York: New City, 1995), p. 144.

[40] P. Evdokimov, *Art of the Icon*, p. 27.

[41] Archimandrite Vasileios, *Beauty and Hesychia in Athonite Life*, trans. C. Kokenes (Montreal: Alexander Press, 1996), p. 9.

[42] Dumitru Staniloae, *Prayer and Holiness: The Icon of Man Renewed in God* (Fairacres, SLG Press, 1982), p. 13.

[43] Egon Sendler, *The Icon: Image of the Invisible*, trans. S. Bigham (Redondo Beach, CA: Oakwood Publications, 1988), p. 169.

[44] P. Evdokimov, *Art of the Icon*, p. 186.

[45] Ibid., p. 188.

[46] See Whitney Davis, "Communication theory" in *Grove Dictionary of Art*, vol. 7, ed. Jane Turner (New York: Macmillan, 1996), pp. 659-662.

[47] Michael Baxandall, *Painting and Experience in 15th Century Italy*, 2nd edition (Oxford: Oxford University Press, 1988), see ch. 2.

[48] See Joshua Taylor, *Learning to Look: A Handbook for the Visual Arts*, 2nd edition (Chicago: University of Chicago Press, 1981), pp. 51-52.

[49] P. Evdokimov, *Art of the Icon*, p. 248-249. Evdokimov provides an extensive study of the icon in Chapter 24 of the text (pp. 243-257), from which this is cited. Kallistos Ware reflects on the icon and utilizes material from Evdokimov's study in "The Human Person as an Icon of the Trinity" *Sobornost* 8:2 (1986), pp. 6-24. See also, Leonid Ouspensky and Vladimir Lossky, *The Meaning of Icons* (Crestwood: SVS Press, 1982), pp. 200-205. Their interpretation of the icon is similar, although they place the Son in the center.

[50] K. Ware, "The Human Person as an Icon of the Trinity," *Sobornost* 8:2 (1986), p. 11.

[51] Ibid.

[52] Ibid., pp. 11-12.

[53] Ibid., p. 14.

54 P. Evdokimov, *The Art of the Icon*, p. 226.

55 E. Sendler has presented the various theories of inversed perspective in *The Icon: Image of the Invisible*, chapter 9.

56 E. Sendler, *The Icon*, p. 127.

57 P. Evdokimov, *Art of the Icon*, p. 246-247.

58 J. Baggley, *Doors of Perception*, pp. 80-81.

59 E. Eisner, *The Educational Imagination*, p. 39.

60 Ibid., ch. 5.

61 Ibid., p. 83.

62 Ibid., p. 82.

63 See J.N.D. Kelly, *Early Christian Doctrines*, rev. ed. (San Francisco: Harper Collins, 1978) p. 339-340.

64 Anthony Coniaris, *Introducing the Orthodox Church: Its Faith and Life* (Minneapolis: Light and Life Publishing, 1982), p. 171.

65 I recall in 1985 visiting the Tretyakov Museum in Moscow, where the famous Virgin of Vladimir and Rublev Trinity are displayed as well as other icons. The museum personnel expected "church like" behavior from all in the galleries of icons. Even considering their sharp looks, the general atmosphere in the gallery was hushed. Using my broken Russian, when I told the monitors, mostly elderly women, that I was an Orthodox Christian from America, their eyes lit up with the shared sense that, despite the museum setting, we knew we were in a sacred place. More recently I recall my visit to monasteries on Mt Athos, which house magnificent examples of iconography and compare it to my visit to the museum exhibition of the Treasures of Mt. Athos in Thessalonike about one week later. The experience of the icons in the monastery, their home, was quite moving. There was something missing from the museum experience that I cannot fully put into words.

66 Eisner, recall, also speaks about a null curriculum. In light of the icon, a pious paradox emerges on this topic, consistent with the maximalist and triumphalistic viewpoint of many Orthodox perspectives. There is no null sacred curriculum. The null curriculum cannot exist when the sacred fills it. God is fullness and can leave nothing wanting. Making a "curricular" exclamation, a psalm states, "You show me the path of life; in your presence there is fullness of joy, in your right hand are pleasures for evermore" (Ps 16.11). When God reveals the curriculum, the path of life, and makes himself known, there is

fullness in the educational endeavor, and nothing is to be left out. The full range of human experience and knowledge are to be both explored and utilized in the process of learning. The sacred fills all things, and thus all things are subjects to be studied and subject to the divine.

[67] Michael Schiro, *Curriculum for Better Schools: The Great Ideological Debate* (Englewood Cliffs, NJ: Prentice Hall, 1978), pp. 24-26.

Chapter Five

*

Informed, Formed, and Transformed
Through Iconic Catechesis

In the preceding chapters, the aims and pedagogical style of iconic catechesis have been discussed by pointing to the icons and their theological rationale and discerning educational principles. The direction was from the icons to catechesis. In this chapter, our direction is from education to the icons, that is identifying catechetical commitments and bringing them to the icons. The three commitments constituting the overarching theme of this chapter are from the catchy, alliterative phrase – "inform, form, and transform."[1]

The concepts of formation and transformation are very much at the heart of the Orthodox Tradition and its Hellenistic roots. In Greek, education is μόρφωσις (*morphosis*) – formation – and an educated person is μορφωμένος (*morphomenos*) – formed. In the early Church, education was seen as a plastic, formative process analogous to the work of the sculptor, with deification as its goal.[2] Deification involves transformation, which is, of course, very much a Christian concept. The Church celebrates the Transfiguration of Christ – Ἡ Μεταμόρφωσις τοῦ Χριστοῦ – that is, his transformation. St Paul called the Roman Christians to be transformed (μεταμορφοῦσθε) by the renewal of their minds (Rom. 12.2). Patristic writings present and discuss

136

the new life in Christ as an ongoing μετάνοια (*metanoia*) – conversion or repentance. As John Chryssavgis explains it, *metanoia* "denotes a change of mind, a reorientation, a fundamental *transformation* of outlook, of man's vision of the world and of himself, and a new way of loving others and God."[3] *Metanoia* is an ongoing process of formation and transformation. It involves not only a change of mind but also a change of the heart. Thus, the three dimensions of religious education being addressed – information, formation and transformation – are firmly rooted in the Tradition and are clearly applicable to Orthodox educational practice today. Furthermore, I believe they can be discerned through study of the icons themselves and, thus, are eminently suitable to iconic catechesis.

The commitment to inform, form, and transform may appear to distinguish my position from that of other Orthodox religious educators, most notably John Boojamra. He recently wrote: "Any education program ... must have built into it two fundamental principles – education is growing and changing and is rooted in knowledge (information) and the building of a community of learners (formation)."[4] I agree with Boojamra on the importance of information and formation but, I would note, his statement only implies the necessity for transformation through catechesis. I believe that transformation should be an explicit dimension of the catechetical process.

Identification of transformation as an explicit goal of education in the Church is of first-order importance for at least three reasons. First, at the most basic level, it is evident that providing information results in transformation – the change from "ignorance" to "knowledge." To believe that teachers are value-free providers of information and that learners remain neutral in the educational process diminishes both. Recognizing that information is both formative and transformative relates to the question: "What information has been, is being, and should be provided?" The answers to this question clearly affect the learners. The educational process shapes people, contributing in a major way to the formation of both character and worldviews.

The icons depict persons transformed through Christian living. Since the potential in education exists to lead learners into a deeper, transformative relationship with self, others, God, and the world – and with iconic living as an aim of catechesis – the personal transformative dimension must be present. Simply stated, Orthodox education is about transforming lives; let it be explicit. Second, without transformation as an objective, education for community could be reduced to a mere maintenance of the status quo. Religious educators of many faith traditions frequently wring their hands at the poor state of community life, and the Orthodox are not exempt from this plight. There is no benefit in perpetuating the existing situation. Including the transformative dimension in catechesis offers the potential for the needed renewal of the community. Third, the transformative dimension expressed in the concept of *theosis* is a distinctively Orthodox contribution to catechesis. The commitment to emphasize transformation as an explicit goal of religious education, along with information and formation, reaches for the fullness of the Orthodox way.

One final introductory point needs to be made. In viewing iconic catechesis as an "artistic approach" to education, we cannot help but notice that the term "form" is the root of all three dimensions, in two ways. "Form" is both a verb and a noun. We use "form" to refer to something we do, and we use "form" to refer to the result of something we have done or made.[5] Thus, we can think of iconic catechizing – the verb – and ask, "What does it mean to inform, form, and transform learners through education?" – that is, "What is the process?" We can also think about iconic catechesis – the noun – and ask "what does it mean to have become informed, formed, and transformed through education?" – that is, "what is the product?"

INFORMED THROUGH ICONIC CATECHESIS

Of the three dimensions to be discussed in this chapter, to be informed through iconic catechesis appears, at first glance, to be fairly straightforward. By observing icons, viewers receive information that relates the stories of the community to them. While it has been stated several times, the following statement bears repeating in this context. The icons historically were considered books for the illiterate, informing the beholder of the Gospel with information equal to that of the written word. As "books" the icons are story-laden "texts" that can be "read" – indeed studied – by believers. It has been noted that in speaking and writing about icons the terminology used is often more closely associated with literature than with art. One can hear iconographers speak about "writing" an icon rather than "painting" one. Also, a catechist can "read the story" from the icon to another person. In the previous chapter, we saw how the icon can communicate with a viewer, which is integral to our understanding of the potential of the icon to inform. As we ask about the content of these texts and how they might influence those who engage them, the issue of information becomes more complex. The discussion that follows begins with the content of icons – the depicted story – and how it may inform persons in faith.

Depicting the Story of the Community

As expressed by James Fowler:

> Our characters and faith orientations are shaped by the master stories that we tell ourselves and by which we interpret and respond to the events that impinge upon our lives. Our master stories are the characterizations of the patterns of power-in-action that disclose the ultimate meanings of our lives.[6]

Education in Orthodox Christian faith involves the telling, repeating, and learning of the community's master stories, the stories of the Orthodox Church. These stories are comprised of the most ancient ones, from the Old and New Testament, the Early Church, and the Byzantine period. Depending on comprehensiveness and cultural or geographic orientation, they may include stories from post-Byzantine times and from the

Greek, Slavic, Syrian, Coptic, or Oriental (non-Chalcedonian) traditions.

For the Orthodox, as for all Christians, the dominant story is the life, ministry, Passion, death, and Resurrection of Jesus Christ. Other stories of significance include the life of the Virgin Mary, important events in Church history (Constantine's vision, the finding of the Cross, the seven councils, and the lives of the saints). Adhering to these stories and living according to the wisdom they impart are at the core of what it means to be an Orthodox Christian. To be a member of the community, one must share the stories of the community and embrace them fully, accepting them as foundational for doctrine, sacrament, and normative lifestyle.

To step into an Orthodox church is to be engulfed by the master stories of the community, both at a universal and local level, as they are depicted by the icons. At the universal level, we have the stories known to all Orthodox Christians. The dominant iconographic program relates to the life of Christ as recorded in Scripture, typically depicted on the walls above the congregation. Second is the Virgin Mary; in the Greek Byzantine Tradition her icon dominates the apse above the sanctuary, but she also appears in many icons of the life of her son. Then one might also see the prophets, apostles, martyrs, teachers, hierarchs, and other saints known throughout the Church. Among the icons of the universal saints, or set apart, will be the local saints, those recognized by the national churches – Greece, Russia, Romania, etc. – who are usually less well known outside their local contexts.[7] Depicted on the walls of the churches iconically, the stories of the community are present for all to see. The visitor to the church as well as the member of the community has access to the stories and can read the texts and come to know their content.

As the content of the stories begins to be uncovered, a significant realization begins to emerge. The icons depict the story through the interpretive lens of the community and its Tradition. The information content of the icons is not limited to scriptural texts but encompasses the wider level of the Tradition of the Church. As Staniloae writes,

> Tradition has two meanings: a) the totality of the various ways by which Christ passes over into the reality of human lives under the form of the Church and all his works of sanctification and preaching; b) the transmission of these ways from generation to generation.[8]

The story has been interpreted by the iconographer for the viewer, in keeping with the Tradition of the Church. The information included and the visual language of the icon present the values of the Church, and the Church's interpretation of the story, which has also been transmitted through texts, homilies, hymns, and customs. For example, in the icon of the *Epitaphios Threnos*, the Lamentation of Christ, the elements of the icon depict a particular way of considering the moment after the body of Christ was removed from the cross (see Figure 9). In the center of the icon is the cross. Instead of the typical inscription INBI (Greek) or INRI (Latin) for "Jesus of Nazareth, King of the Jews," found in the Synoptic Gospels, the inscription is "King of Glory" (Ὁ Βασιλεὺς τῆς Δόξης) in abbreviated form. The icon is not incorrect; it is expressing an interpretation of the kingship of Christ found in Christ's dialogue with Pontius Pilate in the Gospel of John (Jn 18.33-38): "My kingship is not from the world" (v. 36). Set near the cross is the lance that pierced the side of Christ, which is mentioned only in John's Gospel (Jn 19.34). The artist has interpreted the event, artistically informing the viewer about the paradox of the kingship of Christ, which is achieved through his suffering and death.[9]

The interpreted story in this icon has an even broader base. All the elements depicted are not found in Scripture. The Gospels do not describe a moment when the Virgin Mary, Mary Magdalene, Joseph of Arimathea, Nicodemus, John the Beloved Disciple, and other women lament over the body of Christ. In

the scriptural narratives, the crowds leave the scene of the crucifixion in a lament (Lk 23.48). There are only brief references to
the deposition of the body of Christ and his entombment (Mt
27.59, Mk. 15.46, Lk 23.53, Jn 19.40), and except for John's
Gospel, which mentions Nicodemus, only Joseph of Arimathea
is involved in the burial. The sources of the story of the lamentation appear to be apocryphal texts.

Other icons also are rooted more in the Tradition than in the
Gospel narrative. The typical icon of the Resurrection used by
Orthodox is not the angel at the empty tomb as described in
the Synoptics (of which there is an icon) but the "Descent into
Hades," an event the Gospels do not describe.

The icon of the Nativity (see Figure 8) typically contains two
scenes in the lower corners. In one corner, a disheveled figure
stands in front of Joseph, and in the other, midwives bathe the
infant Jesus. The standard interpretation of the first scene is
that the figure in front of Joseph is the devil, tempting him with
doubts about the virgin birth. The other scene depicts ordinary
events of birth that emphasize the human nature of the Christ-
child. Both scenes are rooted in apocryphal texts.[10] Although
they are present in the icon, the Gospels do not mention an ox
or an ass. These would appear to based on Isaiah 1.3: "The ox
knows its owner and the ass its master's crib." Other icons depicting scenes in the early life of the Virgin Mary are rooted in
the *Protevangelium* of James.[11]

The breadth of the information base can be best understood
through the perspective of the living Tradition of the Church.
As Staniloae pointed out, the Tradition consists of the totality
of ways by which the reality of Christ and his message have
been and are being transmitted. The Tradition includes not only
Scripture, but much more, and the totality is considered to be a
valid witness to Divine Revelation.[12] Through the icons, the
Tradition is inherited from previous generations, articulated artistically for the present, and passed on to future generations.
The master stories, unchanged from generation to generation,

are expressed anew. Teachers – here understood in the broadest sense – guide the process of appropriating the canonical and non-canonical expressions of *the* master story, the message of redemption, justification, salvation, and sanctification through Christ. Faithful to the past and in prayerful openness, the teacher guides the learner to a personal appropriation and expression of the story, situated in the Church and in the reality of that community.

The Truth of the Information

This discussion of information conveyed by icons raises the challenging topic of truth. It is particularly challenging because in our "post-modern" era, to claim truth about anything may seem foolish. However, we can open the door with a discussion of the living Tradition, which includes canonical and non-canonical texts as information sources. This topic is extensive, but a few words about truth in iconic catechesis seem in order.

Iconic catechesis ought to be about the pursuit of and personal conviction regarding religious truth that gives rise to and sustains the identity and agency of the person in community. Religious truth is often contrasted with scientific truth, for the purpose of pointing out that the latter is objective and true, while the former is subjective and not true. The insights of Andrew Louth and Parker Palmer offer a convincing corrective to this perspective. Louth writes that:

> Real truth, truth that a man would lay down his life for, was essentially subjective: a truth passionately apprehended by the subject. To say, then, that truth is subjective is to say that its significance lies in the subject's engagement with it; it does not mean that it is not objective in any sense: indeed if it were objective in no sense, if it were simply a collection of subjective impressions, there would be no engagement, and consequently no question of truth at all.[13]

The information provided by the icons is true because it speaks to the heart of the viewer and engages the viewer in a relationship of faith. Iconic knowing involves having – at the personal intersection of mind, body, emotions, and soul – what we have called "heart knowledge." Even as icons depict the master stories of the community, they engage the persons who interact with them in a highly personal manner. Through interaction with the icons, questions of faith are raised by the viewer and brought to the icons, and the stories they depict lead to a new or renewed personal commitment.

Parker Palmer points out that in the Christian tradition truth is "personal, not propositional." That is, those who seek truth are called to enter into a relationship with the one who calls himself truth – Jesus Christ.[14] Interacting with the stories of the icons can lead one to deepen one's relationship with God and, in turn, deepen one's identity and agency in the world as an Orthodox Christian. The stories depicted in icons, whether from the canonical Scriptures or non-canonical writings, have the same intent – to lead one to God. As Palmer writes, "Learning the truth requires that we enter into personal relationship with what the words reveal. To know truth we must follow it with our lives."[15] Icons are often called "windows to heaven." They do not mirror the gaze of beholders back onto themselves. Rather, they open windows to new, transcendent realities that exceed the domain of scientific truth. The icons point to the divine reality – Jesus Christ – and invite the viewer to enter into a relationship of faith with that reality. Thus, the icons are true because of the commitments and fidelity they foster in the heart of each person who seeks their wisdom and strives to live by the norms they reflect, that is, when the icons lead the believer to iconic knowing and living.

Individual members of the community and the community as a body should be engaged in a search for truth. Based on the nature of Orthodox understanding of person rather than individual, the necessity for the engagement of both person and community is self-evident. Even though the community and its tradition have existed for centuries, the contemporary community must be concerned with pursuing and maintaining that truth. For while members have joined the community long after this truth has been established, each member is responsible for acquiring it, protecting it, and advancing it by bearing witness to it.

Information will always be a significant part of catechetical instruction. Because we cannot assume that families still remember it, the Orthodox Tradition needs to be told; the narratives and the doctrine that are based upon it must be related to young and old. Thus, each Orthodox Christian must be well-informed, having come to know the "heart knowledge" and the scriptural and traditional stories of the community that mark it as an Orthodox community distinct from other Christian communities of faith or other religious traditions. This means that each member of the community becomes part of the living Tradition of the Church, able to share the knowledge with another generation.

In addition, Orthodox Christians should know primary doctrinal concepts of the Church, including but not restricted to the Nicene-Constantinopolitan Creed, that Jesus Christ is both God and human, Mary is Theotokos, and icons are not worshipped as idols, but venerated. They should be able to participate in the liturgical life of the Church, knowing prayers and practices. Efforts at informing Orthodox Christians should include basic positions of the community on ethical issues, and more significantly, help in forming and making moral and ethical decisions that are consistent with the Orthodox way.

To become informed, each member needs to be taught, and given access to the information. The icons offer direct access to the information in that they are constantly present for the community to view. This simple fact points out that each Christian can have direct access to the sources of information in the Church, the texts as well as the icons. While the icons can communicate the information, one must "learn to read" the visual information contained within them and be guided in their sources and interpretation. This requires the guidance of a catechist, someone who can call the various elements of the icon to the learner's attention. Without a catechist, one may grasp the broad outline of the story from the icon, but a teacher can help the learner notice and come to understand the details and subtleties of the icon's message. Catechists, then, need to immerse themselves in the Tradition and be able to draw from the same reservoir of knowledge as the iconographer, so that the information of the icon can be more fully communicated.

FORMED THROUGH ICONIC CATECHESIS

At the beginning of the chapter, formation was identified as a classical Christian understanding of education. Iconic catechesis shares this understanding and sees the socialization of the person in the community with icons as formative. Boojamra writes:

> The process of ... socialization (characterized as the interaction of symbol and person) gives rise to enhanced self-awareness and to awareness of the self as Orthodox. Through systematic interaction in the community, home, or parish with the symbol system and practices of the Church, the child comes to perceive himself as a member of the Orthodox Church.[16]

Socialization with icons is one of the ways in which a person learns to live iconically, ideally beginning at a young age and continuing throughout life. The socialization process includes the learning of various ritual practices, which help to actualize the religious feelings of the person interacting with the symbols. As Margaret Miles points out about the place of religious practice in the early Church:

> The aim of religious practices was thus not to "act out" previously held ideas or beliefs, but to realize – to make real – in a person's body the strong experience that, together with the

religious community's interpretation of that experience, produced a countercultural religious self.[17]

Through the icons and the practices surrounding them, Orthodox Christians can experience what others have experienced and thus begin to be formed as living icons.

By exploring individual icons and the liturgical and pious practices that relate to them, we can begin to see the cultural framework in which an Orthodox Christian is socialized and formed.

The anthropologist Clifford Geertz argues that "meanings can only be 'stored' in symbols." Sacred symbols "sum up, for those for whom they are resonant what is known about the way the world is, the quality of emotional life it supports, and the way one ought to behave while in it."[18] Icons are symbols, artistically presenting their sacred stories and their interpretations of those stories for the community to behold. The icons seek to communicate the Christian Gospel to people's hearts, handing down the reality of Christ through their visual language.

Geertz also points out that works of art are "primary documents, not illustrations of conceptions already in force, but conceptions that seek – or for which people seek – a meaningful place in a repertoire of other documents, equally primary."[19] This assertion, calling the icons "books," echoes once again the language of the ancient Church. The icons depict the world and the way it ought to be when the presence of God is recognized. This vision is depicted in an artistic "shorthand," which when read, understood, and accepted directs the beholder to respond.

According to Geertz, a religious system or culture is "a cluster of sacred symbols, woven into some sort of ordered whole."[20] The iconic decoration of Orthodox churches reflects this understanding; it incorporates the sacred curriculum described in the previous chapter. When one steps into an Orthodox church, one cannot help but notice that icons dominate the environment. In older churches especially, icons fill every available space.

As has been pointed out, there is an order to the icons; their placement is not happenstance. This system of symbols is an orderly reflection of the worldview established and perceived by the community. Geertz points out that such a systematic presentation offers both "a model of reality" and a "model for reality."[21]

It is not accidental that the icon of Christ the Pantocrator (the Ruler of All) is placed in the dome of Orthodox churches, and the icons of saints surround the people. The people are linked to the saints as part of the cosmos unified and ruled over by Christ.[22] As a model for reality, this arrangement offers a visual expression of how each member of the community ought to perceive himself or herself. Each should live in the reality that Christ rules the universe, not just a "spiritual" kingdom, but also the earthly domain that includes the viewer.

Perceiving and being formed by the reality presented by the sacred order of the symbols involves interacting with them through ritual and pious practices. From childhood, Orthodox Christians interact with icons through kissing, bowing, making the sign of the cross before them, prostration, lighting candles, offering incense, etc. To see a parent hold a small child before an icon of Christ, the Virgin Mary, or a saint and instruct the child to make the sign of the cross and kiss Jesus, *Panagia* (a term for the Virgin Mary meaning "all holy"), or the saint is very common. In some churches, stands for panel icons are made "child height" to assist the smaller members of the community perform these actions on their own.

Furthermore, the Orthodox Church uses icons extensively in its liturgical practices. This use of icons also becomes a means of socialization as the entire community of faithful gathers to participate in the service and engage in the relevant rituals. On a feast day, an icon will be carried in procession through a church. This action bears witness to the presence of the person or event being remembered and invites the community to respond appropriately. The members of the congregation will bless themselves, and some may kneel as the icon passes before them. In the liturgical service, whether vespers, orthros (matins), or the Divine Liturgy, the congregation will also engage with the icon through the hymns for the feast. Through the integration of visual and verbal, in the sacred environment of the church and its ritual acts of veneration, the icon is personally engaged, and a new reality emerges for the assembled believers. Liturgical services in an icon-filled environment can provide this intense ordering of experience, directing the heart to respond to its understanding of the event – a powerfully formative experience.

To fully grasp this understanding, one would necessarily need to experience this interaction personally. "Thick description" as Geertz calls it, is a task of the anthropologist and ethnographer, a process of describing and analyzing the structures or layers of meaning within a particular culture so that the culture can be understood. In his easy-to-understand analogy, through thick description, we can perceive and analyze the rapid contraction of a single eyelid and determine whether it is an involuntary twitch or an intentional wink.[23] Thick description can help us understand the formative power of the icons in the Orthodox liturgical tradition. Through thick description we can begin to unravel the threads of the visual, verbal, and ritual that weave together as Orthodox Christians gather to remember liturgically – in an *anamnesis* – an event or person. The death of Jesus Christ commemorated on Great (Good) Friday provides an excellent example.

On Great Friday in the Orthodox Church, the dominant icon in the liturgical services of the day is the *Epitaphios Threnos*, mentioned above (see Figure 9). In the icon, Christ is being lamented by a group of men and women after his body is removed from the cross. Photios Kontoglou describes the icon as follows:

> The Cross is in the middle of two mountains. And below it lies a large marble slab, covered with a sheet. Christ is lying

on the slab, dead and naked. Panagia [the Virgin Mary] is kneeling or is seated at his head; crying, she is embracing her son and kissing his face. Opposite her is the Noble Joseph [of Arimathea], old and with a medium beard, kneeling; he kisses the pure foot of the Lord. John, bent and lamenting with a grievous expression, kisses the hand of the Lord. And behind Joseph, stands Nicodemus, with a black and rounded beard, leaning on a ladder, with his hand on his cheek, beholding the Lord with tear-filled eyes. Also the holy women lament, pulling the hair on their heads, and Mary Magdalene is stretching her arms toward heaven, and cries out loud. Laying on the ground, in front of the slab, is the basket with the nails, the pliers, the hammer, and the vessel with water and wine, with which the wounds of the Lord were washed (Mt 27.59, Lk 23.53, Jn 19.40). The title of the icon is The Lamentation at the Tomb.[24]

In the Greek tradition, during the afternoon vespers service that recalls the removal of Christ from the cross, this icon is carried in procession and placed in the *kouvouklion* (κουβούκλιον), an elaborate canopied bier that has been decorated with flowers by members of the community earlier in the day. At the end of the vespers, the congregation approaches and venerates the *Epitaphios*. In the evening, the community gathers again to sing the orthros (matins),[25] whose hymns are an interlace of lamentation for the death of Christ and anticipation of the coming Resurrection and the salvation it brings.

The icon and the hymns direct the congregation to contemplate this central event in the passion narrative. Like a verse-by-verse scriptural exegesis, each figure and detail of the icon can be explained. A few highlights illustrate the point.[26] The icon depicts at least six different emotional responses to the event. The women in the icon are in various poses of grief: holding their hands to their faces; holding their veils tightly around their face to stifle cries; generally, their hair and garments are loose, an expression of having pulled at them as a sign of grief. Mary Magdalene has her hands uplifted; her hair and garments are loose. Dark triangular lines, the marks of crying, appear under the eyes of nearly everyone.

John the beloved disciple is depicted in a posture of deep reverence, an act of veneration before the body of Christ. Joseph of Arimathea and Nicodemus appear rather stoic, but a hymn of the day expresses Joseph's profound grief:

> Joseph with Nicodemus took Thee down from the Tree, who deckest Thyself with light as with a garment; and looking upon Thee dead, stripped, and without burial, in his grief and tender compassion he lamented, saying: "Woe is me, my sweetest Jesus! When but a little while ago the sun saw Thee hanging on the Cross, it wrapped itself in darkness; the earth quaked with fear and the veil of the temple was rent in twain. And now I see Thee for my sake submitting of Thine own will to death. How shall I bury Thee, my God? How shall I wrap Thee in a winding sheet? How shall I touch Thy most pure body with my hands? What songs at Thy departure shall I sing to Thee, O compassionate Saviour? I magnify Thy sufferings; I sing praises of Thy burial and Thy Resurrection, crying: O Lord, glory to Thee."[27]

The Virgin Mary is the most composed of the individuals. She shows that she has been crying, but the veil of her head covering, the *maphorion,* is undisturbed. While the task of the group is to prepare the body of Christ for burial, it will be Mary's task to wash and cover his face. Thus, she cradles the head of Christ in her lap, bending down to kiss him. A Byzantine oration for the day expresses Mary's thoughts at that moment:

> Behold, [Lord], your benign dispensation [of the Incarnation] has taken its end. ... For now you, the bestower of all breath, recline in bodily form, without breath. I am now holding and embracing the body without breath of the maker of the universe, the controller of my own breath.... I am now kissing the motionless and wounded limbs of him who cures the incurable wounds of nature .... I am now embracing the

voiceless mouth and silent lips of the maker of every natural power of speech .... I am kissing the closed eyes of him who invented the operation of sight.[28]

Mary's lamentation is a major theme of the hymnology for the day, perhaps eclipsed only by doctrinal concepts about the meaning of the death of Christ. The hymns repeat many of the ideas already mentioned and include dialogue, which adds to the poignancy and intimacy.

Seeing her own Lamb led to the slaughter, Mary His Mother followed Him with the other women and in her grief she cried: "Where dost Thou go, my Child? Why dost Thou run so swiftly? Is there another wedding in Cana, and art Thou hastening there, to turn the water into wine? Shall I go with Thee, my Child, or shall I wait for Thee? Speak some word to me, O Word; do not pass me by in silence. Thou hast preserved my virginity, and Thou art my Son and God."[29]

As part of the orthros service, the congregation participates in the singing of "The Lamentations." The full text of this hymn contains 188 short, one-line verses (most parishes sing only a selection of sixty or seventy) alternating with verses of Psalm 119, in three sections (or stanzas), each with its own distinct, extremely well-known, easy-to-sing melody. Verses from the lamentations direct the Virgin's grief directly to her Son: "When the most pure Virgin saw Thee prone, O Logos, a mother's dirge she sang Thee." The very next stanza offers the dirge: "O, my most sweet Springtime! O, my Son beloved, whither doth fade Thy beauty?"[30] During the singing, various verses are "acted out." For example, during the verse, "Women, bringing spices, came with loving forethought, Thy due of myrrh to give Thee,"[31] a group of young girls will come forward and scatter flower petals on the icon. During the verse, "Myrrh the women sprinkled, bearing stores of spices, to grace They tomb ere dawning"[32] the priest will sprinkle rose water on the icon, the bier, and the entire church and congregation.

Clearly this is no ordinary depiction of people lamenting a death. The liturgical context of the icon, which includes hymn and narrative, informs us that this is more than the everyday drama of death. The liturgy is the catechist, recreating, retelling, and expanding the story the icon encapsulates and symbolizes. The icon, as a bearer of meaning for the community, is educational and formative. The icon quizzes the viewer about the death, the mystery of the Incarnation, and the Passion of Christ and its connection to the salvation of the world. The intellect, memory, and imagination of the worshiper are engaged by the story being told. The body and the spirit are engaged through the sensory nature of Orthodox worship; in the worshiper's imagination the totality of the experience merges. The experience is a pedagogical moment with an expected outcome. The response expected by the icon is more than the acquisition of information and intellectual assent. It is the re-orientation of the individual, through lamentation for the death of Christ on the Cross, to the salvation of the cosmos. While the person may feel grief about the death, in some of the lamentations, Christ expresses the significance of his sacrifice and the expected reaction from the faithful. For example, in direct response to Mary's lament, Christ says, "Lament not, O my Mother, I endure the Passion to set free Eve and Adam."[33] In another verse, he states, "That I may renew man's corrupted and subverted nature, gladly in my flesh do I now take death on Me. Wherefore, Mother, be not stricken with lament."[34]

The symbol of the icon and the liturgical context it inhabits places the "ordinary" event of death in an "ultimate context." As Geertz states:

> It is this placing of proximate acts in ultimate contexts that makes religion, frequently at least, socially so powerful. It alters, often radically, the whole landscape presented to common sense, alters it in such a way that the moods and motivations induced by religious practice seem themselves supremely practical, the only sensible ones to adopt given the way things "really are."[35]

The historic reality of the death of Jesus made present for the congregation and its meaning is expressed ritually, dramatically, and powerfully. The event is established as the ultimate event, leading to the salvation of the cosmos and the transformation of human existence.

In the liturgical context, the congregation is led to contemplate this event and respond with motivations and moods to respond in a fitting and appropriate manner. The emotional responses possible are varied but directed. Our attitude, ideally, should be like Mary's, but the icon recognizes that other reactions are possible, from the stoic to the histrionic. The hymns, however, continually point to the mystery of Christ's death and the Resurrection that will be proclaimed. Thus, the mood of the day is one of *harmolype* – χαρμολύπη – translated as "joyful sadness" or "bright sadness." The tone is both sad, on account of Christ's death, but joyous and bright because of the certainty of the Resurrection that follows.

As John Dewey states, "Continuity of culture in passage from one civilization to another as well as within the culture, is conditioned by art more than by any other one thing."[36] In the last century, Leo Tolstoy wrote: "Art, all art, has this characteristic, that it unites people."[37] Orthodox Christians have commemorated the death of Christ in this manner for centuries. From childhood, a member of the community would have been involved in the commemoration, whether decorating the bier, throwing petals on the icon, participating in the procession, venerating the icon, or singing the hymns. The focus of the congregation is uniform for the day: it is a day of strict fasting, and the churches are generally overflowing Great Friday evening. Through participation in the life of the community, and the sacred curriculum with its visible and invisible elements, the worshiper interiorizes the whole experience and comes "to know" the Tradition. The vision of the event was formed by the ancient community and succeeding generations are formed by participating in it.

Thus, to be formed in Orthodox Christian faith is to see with the eyes of the Tradition, and as much as anything else, the icons symbolize the depth, richness, and vitality of the Tradition. One is socialized with Orthodox Christians, begins to see oneself as Orthodox, and is "formed" as an Orthodox Christian through participation in the liturgical life and the religious practices of the community both in the parish and in one's home.

Ideally, then, communities and families ought to participate in the liturgical life as fully as possible for it to have its desired outcome. However, as neither parent nor priest, I want to restrain my zeal on this topic because I do not have enough direct personal experience in these domains to make sweeping recommendations to others. And I am not suggesting that the present efforts of well-intentioned parents and clergy are in vain. Nor do I wish to idealize home or parish life; it is very difficult to prepare a family to attend church on a Sunday morning or to observe the rhythms of the liturgical year. However, a question needs to be asked: How might parents who "want the best for their child" include the religious in that desire? Parents do need to see themselves as agents of religious, spiritual, and ethical formation in their home life as much as they see themselves as providing material needs for their children. The home is often called a "little church," a sacred place where God could be encountered. Parents, one might say, are the "ministers" of that church, responsible for the religious life of the home just as the clergy are responsible for the religious life of the parish. As a result, the types of activities that a parish would or should perform – worship and prayer, building fellowship among the members, service to the poor, learning and witnessing to the faith – should also extend into the life of a family.

Engaging in religious practices at home and connecting them to the narrative and living Tradition of the wider Orthodox community can become a first step in the formation of Orthodox Christians, upon which parish life can then build. An icon in the home can be a witness of God's presence, particularly when it becomes part of the family's "prayer corner" or "worship center," where a vigil lamp, home censer, and incense are used.[38] The icons point to a transformed way of living, and icons in the home can be powerful witnesses to the new life. An icon (along with a couple's wedding crowns from their marriage ceremony) can be a powerful reminder of the sacramental nature of marriage, encouraging and enabling spouses to relate to one another in ways that are consistent with the icon's sacred witness, that is, in love, respect, and mutuality. An icon can be a source of faith in God's protection of the small child, comforting the child who, thinking himself or herself to be alone, fears the darkness.

The sacramental life of the Church can extend into the life and rhythm of a family. Practices that a family might begin include: blessing the home and its residents with holy water and the sign of the cross (that a parent can do as well as a priest); observing the fasting periods of the Church; prayer in the home before daily or festive meals, certainly, but also at other times; religious conversation, not just church gossip; and religious reading. Each of these practices can become a formative example of faith in the life of a family. The danger is in extreme and inappropriate use of any of these practices. I can recall stories of parents who were proud of the fact that their toddler performed twelve prostrations before bedtime and punished their children with prayer time for wrong doing. Even religious practices that have been handed down from one generation to the next continue to need the guidance and support of a formative community.

Through catechesis, each member can come to interact with the symbols, stories, and traditions, learning from them and learning their significance. This interaction leads to acquiring what Baxandall calls a "period eye," that is, the ability to fill in what one's vision perceives with acquired knowledge in order to comprehend the image.[39] In catechesis, a formative aspect of the classroom is to "train" learners in the acquisition and development of an "ecclesial eye," that is, to learn to see what the Church sees in the icons, the stories of the Church, and the whole of life.

Learning to "read" the icons is an ideal example. Without a teacher, many might not have the opportunity to know what or who is being depicted in an icon. While a learner, without much assistance, may be able to discern the broad outline of the story depicted, a teacher is necessary for a fuller appreciation of the details and subtleties of an icon, many of which are outside our present literary, cultural, or even religious experience. For example, in the icon of Pentecost (Figure 11), how would someone know that the old man depicted at the bottom of the icon represents the world, or that in the icon of the Baptism of Christ (Figure 12), the figures in the Jordan River are personifications of the waters? Unless one is well-versed in Scripture, how would one understand the presence of an ox and ass in the Nativity icon (Figure 8) as a reference to the book of Isaiah? In each instance, a teacher is necessary to focus the gaze of the learner more intently on the icon, to tell the story, and to explore the Tradition, seeking the additional, and less obvious resources that explicate the icon more fully. The act of teaching becomes an act of re-membering, putting the pieces back together so the original experience of the icon can be experienced anew. This re-membering can be quite rigorous and challenging, involving the study of philosophical, mythical, scriptural, patristic, and liturgical texts and connecting aspects of them to the various elements of an icon (a glimpse of this was provided with the *Epitaphios* icon). Teaching "forms the eyes" of the learners so that they may look more purposefully at the icon, and thus, at the Tradition, and begin to see more clearly what has always been there.

This effort does not replace following the way of life envisioned in the icons. To study an icon and learn to read it is not a substitute for living iconically. A strictly informational approach is dangerous. Information is a stepping-stone to fuller participation in the way of life depicted in the icons and enacted in the liturgical expression of the Church.

Transformation is at the heart of the Christian message. Both St John the Baptist and Jesus proclaimed a call to transformation through conversion, "Repent, for the kingdom of heaven is at hand" (Mt 3.2. cf. Mk 1.14). The call of the Gospel is to a new personal life and a new social and cosmic reality achieved by following, in discipleship, the commands of Jesus. Discipleship is about responding to the call of Jesus to "follow me," that is, to follow the way of the Master. Discipleship is characterized by acquiring knowledge of Christ by engaging him, learning from him, and growing into a deeper relationship with him in the Church, a relationship marked by lifelong *metanoia*. Discipleship includes information and formation but is incomplete without transformation. As Demetrios Trakatellis writes: "Discipleship as a deep understanding of Christ is a dynamic and alive state of existence in continuous progress and in continuous alertness and vigilance."[40]

Icons depict persons who have become disciples of Christ to the fullest extent recognizable by the Church. These persons have attained God-likeness, having been transfigured or transformed into "christs," that is, "anointed ones," through the power of the Holy Spirit working in their lives.

The call of the Gospel to the kingdom of God highlights the social and cosmic reality of the new life that Christ has initiated for the world. Many have reflected on the meaning and nature of the kingdom. Briefly, the kingdom of God has been realized in the salvific ministry of Jesus Christ and the coming of the Holy Spirit but is yet to be fully realized and is the expectation of all Christians. The kingdom is a personal reality in that it signifies life with God, but it is also a social and cosmic reality through the presence of the Trinity experienced in the Church. In the Orthodox Tradition, the historical reality of the kingdom is expressed at every Divine Liturgy, which begins with, "Blessed is the kingdom of the Father and the Son and the Holy Spirit now and forever and to the ages of ages." As an experience, or sacrament of the kingdom, the Church is a community in which members may participate in, as Georgios Mantzaridis calls it, "a veritable 'communion of deification.'"[41] Transformation thus has a personal, social, and cosmic manifestation.

The icons bear witness to the kingdom of God and the transformation it invites because the icons are visions of what persons are to become when they, in love, freely permit God to penetrate every aspect of their lives. As human persons are social beings and creatures, this transformation extends to the social and created order. The icons bear witness to this transformation because all things depicted in the icons – architecture, nature, persons, relationships – are transfigured by of the presence of God within them. From the icons, then, transformation is personal, social, and cosmic; iconic catechesis embraces them all.

Personal Transformation

Recalling the maximalist anthropology of the Orthodox Tradition, the statement of St Athanasios reflects the radical nature of the personal transformation sought in iconic catechesis: "God became human so that humans could become like god."[42] *Theosis*, attaining God-likeness, is to be transformed or transfigured. The characteristics of *theosis*, iconic living, were discussed in an earlier chapter. The reality of the transformation is expressed artistically in a feature characteristic of icons. The features of the person are depicted, not according to their natural state, but according to their new, transfigured existence in the kingdom of God.[43] The totality of the person – eyes, ears, mouth, etc. – has been transformed by the power of God, and the new reality is expressed artistically, typically by enlarging the eyes, raising the forehead, thinning the nose, diminishing the mouth, and interiorizing the ears. Each of these transformations has been accorded symbolic meaning by Orthodox theologians.

Michael Quenot's analysis of the symbolism of each artistic device is representative. Relative to the eyes he points out that: "The eyes are both animated and large, witnessing to the Scripture verse of Ps 25.15, 'My eyes gaze continually at the Lord,' 'because my eyes have seen Thy salvation' (Lk 2.30). They have been opened to marvel at the sublime and at the vision of the works of our Creator." The raised forehead reflects the "power of the Spirit and ... wisdom." The nose is thin because it "no longer detects the scents of this world, but only the sweet odor of Christ and the life-giving breath of the Spirit gushing from a throat and neck that are disproportionately large." The lips are drawn shut, reflecting the silence required for contemplation. Quenot points out that the mouth is small because, as Cyril of Jerusalem notes, "the body no longer needs earthly nourishment because it has become a spiritual wonder." The ears have been drawn in close to the head because they do not hear the sounds of the world, but hear the commandments of the Lord, "attentive only to the interior voice."[44]

The transformed physical features depicted in the icon reflect the transformed personal life of the saint. They reflect a heightened awareness of the presence of God in all things. To say that the eyes of the saint have "seen salvation," see the face of Christ in all people, or see God in ways that most people do not see is particularly evocative. The wide open eyes of the persons in the icon recall the five wise maidens of the parable who were vigilant and prepared for the bridegroom to arrive to the banquet (Mt 25.1-13). The Orthodox Tradition sees the quality of vigilance as preparation for the coming of the kingdom – the definitive moment of transformation – a time that will come in the middle of the night, when sleep is the norm. The Tradition refers to this characteristic as "watchfulness" (*nepsis*, νῆψις), and it has multiple meanings. Generally, to be watchful means to guard the intellect and heart to prevent evil from overtaking oneself, to keep one's perspective clearly on things from God.[45] The discipline of watchfulness is cultivated among monastics by praying through the night, in anticipation of the kingdom of God. A hymn during Holy Week states:

> Behold, the Bridegroom cometh in the middle of the night, and blessed is that servant whom He shall find watching; and again unworthy is he whom He shall find heedless. Beware, therefore, O my soul, lest thou be borne down with sleep, lest thou be given up to death, and be shut out from the Kingdom. But rather rouse thyself and cry: "Holy, holy, holy art Thou, O God…"[46]

Shaking off sleep, keeping eyes wide open to see the surrounding reality, and expecting the kingdom of God to arrive describe the transformation that is sought by the hymn and the icons.

The quality of watchfulness or vigilance is noted by others, outside the Orthodox Tradition as well. Maxine Greene notes that "wide-awakeness" is a quality of moral life. She comments on the serious issues that society faces and the feelings of powerlessness and domination that are experienced by many. Then she suggests

> that such feelings can to a large degree be overcome through conscious endeavor on the part of individuals to keep themselves awake, to think about their condition in the world, to inquire into the forces that appear to dominate them, to interpret the experiences they are having day by day … Only then can they develop the sense of agency required for living a moral life.[47]

Greene points out that certain works of art were intended to "move people to critical awareness, to a sense of moral agency, and to a conscious engagement with the world."[48] The icons point to a state of being wide awake and seeing oneself in the critical light of the Christian message, the arrival of the kingdom of God. While the Orthodox concept of watchfulness may have its origins in the monastic and ascetic disciplines, the concept has value for all persons in that it becomes a reminder of the need for personal critical awareness and vigilance in one's moral and ethical conduct.

This personal critical awareness is most fully expressed in the Orthodox Tradition through the concept of *metanoia,* or repentance. In order to repent and be transformed, one must become like the icon, with eyes wide open to recognize one's separation from God and others and to strive for restoration of communion. "*Metanoia* is the gateway to oneself, to one's fellow man, and to heaven. It leads inwards, but it also leads outwards by leading inwards. The world ceases to rotate round the self and begins to gravitate toward the other – the divine and human other."[49]

Recall that to be a person, a *prosopon,* is to be face to face with the other. Before an icon, the inclination is to turn away, an act of recognition of the sinful state in which humanity lives. The icons are often called "mirrors" because by looking in them viewers can see their true selves. In the encounter with the icons, the viewer is faced with the realization that the relationship is broken and in need of restoration. Through *metanoia* the potential for restoration is offered. The icons create the possibility for *metanoia* through the communion they establish with the viewer. They depict persons in communion with the divine. The sacred presence of the icon fosters a new vision, that of living in relationship with the divine and of being able to face God again. This vision is powerfully attractive, and the icon, through the device of inverse perspective, but more significantly through the attraction of divine beauty itself, draws the beholder into it.

The invitation to transformation comes through the icon from God who, in the words of the Divine Liturgy, "did not cease doing everything until (He) led us to heaven and granted us (His) kingdom to come."[50] The call to repentance, a change of mind, is continual, and like the father in the parable of the Prodigal Son (Lk 15.11-32), God searches and runs out after his lost child (v. 20) in order to embrace him. Despite human frailty and weakness, repentance is accepted, even as one falls again and again. Each time God receives the person, restores the relationship, and lovingly invites him or her to his kingdom.

Social Transformation

Whenever one encounters an icon, one is gazing at a world and cosmos that has been transformed by the presence and power of God's Holy Spirit – an encounter with the kingdom of God. Alexander Schmemann writes that the icon is "a symbol of the kingdom, the 'epiphany' of the new and transfigured creation, of heaven and earth full of God's glory."[51] In the Lord's Prayer, we say, "Your kingdom come; your will be done on *earth* as in heaven." The Church is the first experience of the kingdom on earth – a new ordering of relationships under the rule of Christ.

The icon of the Descent of the Holy Spirit at Pentecost (see Figure 11) reflects the qualities of that kingdom. Twelve Apostles are seated in a semi-circular arrangement, with Sts Peter and Paul at the top of the circle. St Paul is included in the icon, despite not being present at Pentecost, because he was destined to become one of the greatest Apostles.[52] They are seated in harmony and order, an indication of the "unity of the body of the Church, with all the multiplicity of its members."[53] At the head of the gathering, between St Peter and St Paul, there is an opening, leaving a place for "the invisible Head of the Church, that is Christ."[54] At the bottom of the icon stands an old man holding twelve scrolls in his hands. He represents the "inhabited world (*oikoumene*), while the scrolls symbolize the teaching by each one of the twelve apostles that was to take place in various parts of the world."[55] The old man represents the world waiting to receive the Gospel.

In the Church, as the visible symbol of the kingdom of God, the vastness of God-given creation, including the human and social order, is transformed by being offered to God and waiting to be filled with the Holy Spirit. In the Divine Liturgy, the ultimate act of the Church, gifts of bread and wine are lifted up and offered to God with these words, "We offer to You these gifts from Your own gifts in all and for all." During the consecration of the gifts, the priest prays to the Father that he send down the Holy Spirit upon the congregation and the gifts (in that order), so that by receiving the gifts of communion, the kingdom of heaven is fulfilled.[56] Through the Liturgy, the people enter into communion with God and with one another by sharing in the gifts; through them the kingdom is experienced.

The Church marks a new reality shaped by a new way of being in the world, transforming structures according to the presence of God in history. Through the descent of the Spirit at Pentecost, the decisive inauguration of the Church, a new era has begun because of the presence of the Trinity. The presence of the Trinity in history transforms the social order, and the Church is the first expression of this new reality. Nikos Nissiotis writes, "The institution of the Church is of a different order from that of any human association; for it expresses the life of the Trinity, with no pre-eminence given to any one Person, which would tend to separate the three."[57]

Conciliarity in the structure of the Church has been identified as the approach that best reflects the Trinitarian model. Neither governance by committee, nor democracy, conciliarity recognizes both hierarchy and council. Both are necessary because in the Trinity there is a perfect hierarchy of persons and a perfect council, "so that many are one (and not merely 'united') without ceasing to be many."[58] In the Trinity, conciliarity signifies that the personal gifts and charisms of each person are recognized as unique and contribute to the work of salvation even as the persons are one. In the Church, conciliarity signifies a way of perceiving one's relationship and ministry in the community as contributing to the work of extending the Gospel of salvation in Christ by relating to all in love.

From the experience of the kingdom in the Church – the

experience of salvation – all Orthodox Christians are called to preserve their fellowship with Christ, with one another, and to extend that fellowship and the experience of salvation to all who are captive to sin and suffering. This is done, according to the Divine Liturgy of St Basil the Great, "for the life of the world."[59] The "life of the world" becomes the overarching theme of the social and cosmic dimensions of transformation. In the Divine Liturgy this theme is symbolized in the act of offering the eucharistic gifts to God for sanctification and consumption, achieving communion with God and with all who partake of the gifts and destroying sacramentally the fragmentation and isolation of our existence.

That these actions are "for the life of the world" clearly has implications for the ministry that Christians are called to have in the world. The work of Christians, their responsibility in the world, is to extend the kingdom of God – the presence of the Trinity in history – that they experience in the Church among all people, for the very life of the human, social order. The responsibility of Christians in the world is to relieve suffering wherever it exists, work to end oppression and injustice, and restore and renew systems that depersonalize into systems that empower individuals toward their personhood, restoring the likeness of God within them. Ideally, the Church offers this transformed vision within its own life, thus becoming the "leaven" of society, offering its critique of "the world" by living as a paradigm of the kingdom. As Christos Yannaras writes,

> It is the dynamics of social transformation embodied in the eucharistic community, the diocese or parish. When the diocese and the parish form a true ecclesial communion, this leads dynamically and organically to the transformation of mass existence into a communion of persons. It provides a basis for social justice which is genuine and not merely rationalistic; it liberates work from slavery to need, transforming it into a personal relationship, and it brings out each human being's creative distinctiveness. Through the correct function-

ing of the eucharistic community there is created a form of politics which serves the existential truth and authenticity of man, a form of science which gives reason and meaning to man's relationship with the world, and a form of economics which serves life rather than subjugating it.[60]

The dynamism of social transformation is rooted in humanity working synergistically with the power of the Holy Spirit, who descended upon humanity at Pentecost, filling the Apostles with the boldness to preach the Gospel to all nations, cultures, and races. However, implicit in Yannaras' statement is the recognition that the parish and diocese do not always live up to this vision. Personally, I must confess that Orthodoxy, despite having such a beautiful vision of soteriology and the kingdom, often falls short in the area of social teaching and practice. Orthodox seem content to focus on the liturgy or the theological vision of salvation, seemingly oblivious to the depth of the surrounding human suffering, injustice and oppression, even in their own midst. In a recent article, Daniel Clendenin points to the lack of social teaching and awareness among the Orthodox as one of his reasons for not becoming an Orthodox Christian.[61] While Clendenin's point is well taken, Orthodox have taken some steps toward greater social awareness. Stanley Harakas has pointed to a growing social consciousness among the Orthodox in America, evident in hierarchical encyclicals and resolutions of archdiocesan assemblies. However, he also notes that words have not been generally followed by actions.[62] Also, the Ecumenical Patriarchate of Constantinople has, over the past decade, begun to speak loudly about ecological issues and environmental protection. In 1989 Patriarch Dimitrios declared September 1, "the day of the environment" to be observed annually with appropriate religious services. This particular concern will be discussed below.

Cosmic Transformation
The vision of transformation extends beyond the social. The

kingdom of God revealed by the presence of the Trinity has cosmic implications as well. The appearance of Christ in space and time, and the salvation he brought, chiefly through the Resurrection, has transformed all creation – the cosmos – granting it renewed life. Of course, the consideration of "cosmic realities" is enormous, but I believe that the transformation of the environment and the restoration of humanity's right relationship to nature offers a sufficiently "cosmic perspective." The icon of the Baptism of Christ and the Feast of the Theophany (Epiphany), celebrated January 6, serves as a prime example of the ecological stewardship to which Orthodox Christians are called.

The icon of the Baptism of Christ (see Figure 12) depicts the Gospel account of the Baptism in the Jordan by John (cf. Mt 3.13-17; Mk 1.9-11; Lk 3.21-22). The Gospel description of the Spirit hovering over Jesus in the form of a dove is depicted (Mk 1.10). Symbolizing the voice from heaven that said, "You are my beloved Son, in whom I am well pleased" (Mk 1.11) is a half-circle at the top of the icon. Angels surround the scene, not only providing balance and symmetry to the composition, but since they typically hold towels in their hands, they are present to serve Christ, drying him after he was fully immersed in the waters.[63]

First and foremost, the icon of the Baptism and the Feast of Theophany serves to reveal the presence of the Trinity. The hymn for the feast begins:

> When Thou, O Lord was baptized in the Jordan, the worship of the Trinity was made manifest. For the voice of the Father bore witness to Thee, calling Thee the beloved Son, and the Spirit in the form of a dove confirmed His word as sure and steadfast...[64]

At the Baptism, the three persons of the Trinity reveal themselves together for the first time in human history.

Secondary to the revelation of the Trinity, the Baptism of

Christ speaks to the sanctification of all creation through the descent of Jesus into the Jordan. A hymn for the day says precisely that: "Today, the nature of the waters is sanctified…"[65] In many icons of the Baptism, the waters are personified symbolically through the depiction of a man and a woman each mounted on a fish – the woman symbolizes the oceans, the man the rivers – with expressions of awe on their faces. Their presence is in accordance with Psalm 114:3, "The sea looked and fled, Jordan turned back." This verse is repeated in many of the hymns of the day.[66]

Through the waters, the source of all life, all creation is offered the potential for participation in salvation in Christ and unity with God.[67] A hymn for the day states: "Christ is baptized: He comes up out of the waters, and with Him He carries up the world ($\varkappa \acute{o}\sigma\mu o\varsigma$)."[68] Water is seen as offering the potential for sanctification because it has been sanctified by Christ's Baptism in the Jordan. Consistent with this understanding of the event, the Orthodox Church blesses water on the feast and offers it to the faithful. Holy Water is drunk, sprinkled on the people, and used to bless homes and places of business. According to custom, water is blessed twice, in the church and, if one is nearby, at a body of water – a river, stream, lake, sea, or ocean.[69] The prayer for the blessing of water is lengthy, but two excerpts exemplify the understanding of the Church about the importance of water:

> Today the waters of the Jordan are transformed into healing by the coming of the Lord. Today the whole creation is watered by mystical streams. Today the transgressions of men are washed away by the waters of the Jordan. Today Paradise has been opened to men and the Sun of Righteousness shines down upon us. Today the bitter water, as once with Moses and the people of Israel, is changed to sweetness by the coming of the Lord. Today we have been released from our ancient lamentation, and as the new Israel we have found salvation. Today we have been delivered from darkness and illuminated

with the light of the knowledge of God … Today things above keep feast with things below, and things below commune with things above.[70]

Therefore, O King who loves mankind, do Thou Yourself be present now as then through the descent of Thy Holy Spirit, and sanctify this water. And confer upon it the grace of redemption, the blessing of the Jordan. Make it a source of incorruption, a gift of sanctification, a remission of sins, a protection against disease, a destruction to demons, inaccessible to the adverse powers and filled with angelic strength: that all who draw from it and partake of it may have it for the cleansing of soul and body, for the healing of their passions, for the sanctification of their dwellings, and for every purpose that is expedient. For Thou art our God, who hast renewed through water and Spirit our nature grown old through sin … Grant to all those who touch it, who anoint themselves with it or drink from it, sanctification, blessing, cleansing, and health … So, by the elements, by the angels, and by men, by things visible and invisible, may Thy most holy Name be glorified…[71]

By being blessed and filled with the Holy Spirit, water – the source of all life – has been restored to its proper relationship to humanity, becoming a source for transformed life, marked by healing, remission of sins, and fellowship with the divine.

This extremely positive approach to the created world of matter ought not surprise the reader. It is consistent with the Orthodox defense of the icons. The Incarnation of Christ redeemed the whole of creation; in Christ all matter became filled with the divine, and thus all created matter could be a means of achieving fellowship with God. The words of St John of Damascus echo down:

I do not worship matter; I worship the Creator of matter who became matter for my sake, who willed to take His abode in matter; who worked out my salvation through matter.

Never will I cease honoring matter which wrought my salvation! I honor it.[72]

In 1987 Orthodox theologians drafted a statement on the significance of the created world for humanity and its transformation. The following excerpt points to the icons, placing human transformation firmly on the earth.

> The value of the natural creation is revealed in the fact that it is made for God (something which is beautifully expressed in Orthodox iconography), i.e. to be the context for God's Incarnation and humankind's deification, and as such, the beginning of the Kingdom of God. We may say that the cosmos provides the stage upon which humankind moves from creation to deification.[73]

This understanding guides the Orthodox approach to ecological issues and the necessity of transformation through the restoration of a proper relationship between humanity and the cosmos. The cosmos was created as a gift, and humans were created from its very elements and called by God to "till and keep" (Gen 2.15) the garden where God placed them. Humanity completed God's acts of creation by naming the creatures that God formed (Gen. 2.20) and so accepted responsibility for living in communion with God and all of his creation. In the Fall of humanity, the relationship was broken and not restored until the Incarnation of Christ, "who united in His person the created world with the uncreated God, and who unceasingly refers creation to the Father as an eternal eucharistic Anaphora and offering."[74]

The Fall had disastrous results, not only for humanity, but for creation. The ecological catastrophes that humanity faces are of its own making. Philip Sherrard writes, "We are treating our planet in an inhuman, god-forsaken manner because we see things in an inhuman, god-forsaken way. And we see things this way because that basically is how we see ourselves."[75] According to Patriarch Dimitrios, humanity "has lost the sense of the sacredness of creation and acts as its arbitrary ruler and rude violator," and creation "groans and travails in all its parts" (Rom 8.22).[76] In order to restore the relationship, humanity must experience a *metanoia* and repent, bearing "some of the pain of creation as well as to enjoy and celebrate it."[77]

As members of the Body of Christ who have experienced the kingdom in the Church, Orthodox Christians are called to "restore communion between heaven and earth" through *metanoia*.[78] A necessary step in the process of repentance is developing an ascetic discipline toward creation, hearing and seeing its suffering, striving to live in harmony with it, and adopting a liturgical posture toward it. This final point returns to the icons inasmuch as the icons are material objects that point toward the divine while participating in it. "The use of materials to make icons and the presence of elements of the natural word in most icons – animals, plants, countryside, mountains, rivers – all affirm the God-given nature of creation; its Transfiguration and its place with us in salvation."[79]

Alexander Schmemann understood humanity's fundamental role as one of priesthood.

> He stands in the center of the world and unifies it in his act of blessing God, of both receiving the world from God and offering it to God – and by filling the world with this eucharist, he transforms his life, the one that he receives from the world, into life in God, into communion with Him.[80]

Humanity lives as a steward of creation, using it to satisfy all proper needs and wants, but not exploiting it, learning about it and learning from it, and forming it insofar as humanity completes God's act of creation, so that the material world is an expression of fellowship with the divine. Humanity is responsible for transforming the cosmos, renewing the environment and living in a relationship to creation that offers it to the Creator, once again, for the life of the world.

Iconic catechesis strives to transform each person and, as a result, the social and cosmic realities in which he or she lives. To be personally transformed is to live and know iconically, to have attained *theosis*, which as has been stated, is both process and product, verb and noun. *Theosis* is a noun because achieving communion with God is the aim of Christian life. In the icons, we see that this fellowship has been achieved in the saints. Iconic living is a verb because it is a way of life, a way of being and knowing in the world that is offered by the Church, the manifestation of the kingdom of God on earth. The Church offers this way of life, directing each of us to strive continually to manifest it, and when, because of human frailty, we fall short, it requires us to rise up again after each fall. Yet, because of human capacities for growth, we seem always to "lack one thing" (Mk 10.21). Therefore, progress in iconic living and knowing, of ongoing transformation, is continual.

In the efforts for communion with God, persons strive for fellowship with one another, which involves transforming the social dimensions and structures of life from those of alienation, isolation, and oppression to structures of freedom, unity, and community under the kingship of Christ. The Church is the manifestation of the community united in and to Christ, an expression of the kingdom of God. It has already been transformed by the presence of the Trinity, but as a human institution, it simultaneously stands in need of ongoing transformation. The people of the Church must admit that they frequently fail to express the unity called for by Christ (Jn 17.20-23) and must work to overcome the human brokenness within the Church.

Overcoming brokenness extends to living in right relationship to the earth, and iconic catechesis must intentionally strive to promote ecological renewal because the kingdom of God includes the created, natural order. This means coming to know, through the symbol of water, that the created world sustains human life, yet our brokenness has turned it into an instrument of death. All persons are to know that they are called to live as stewards of the earth, caring for it, protecting it, exercising loving dominion over it, and continually working to renew it, so that it may be offered back to God as a means of our sanctification.

Part of the teaching encounter ought to include making connections to the wider realm of personal and human experience, seeking the transformative dimension or application of what comes to be grasped. Catechesis should engage learners as agents of personal, social, and cosmic transformation at home and within the Church.

Transformation in education can occur when the aims of iconic catechesis become the aims of home and catechetical life. Parents and teachers should strive to see and nurture the qualities of iconic living and knowing in each person and learner they encounter, even as they recognize the inherent challenge and difficulty of achieving these qualities. As was discussed in an earlier chapter, teachers and parents should strive to look at each person in their care as being created "in the image and likeness of God." Each possesses inestimable value and a unique combination of talents – "an endangered species" to recall Ware's story – and despite human limitations and frailty, each is fully capable of iconic living and knowing. The icons of saints do not point to weaknesses or deficiencies, even though on close examination they can be found in their lives. The icons points to their invaluable works, thoughts, or ministries within the Church as exemplars for all Christians to emulate. For example, when we see the icon of St. Basil the Great, we do not lament that he did not write a treatise on a particular subject or that his philanthropic work was limited in some way. We remember Basil as a pillar and beacon of Christian living, and we glorify God for his life and his exemplary achievements.

The environment of the classroom can foster the ongoing transformation and conversion of each person therein by being an experience of the kingdom of God. To begin to experience the kingdom, the life of the Trinity needs to be the model for the classroom. The loving relationship of Father, Son, and Holy

Spirit, the communion of persons, who are in dialogue with one another, freely serving and being served, can become a model for classroom interaction. For example, the teacher as the leader or expert can set the tone of a class, initiate the activity, and be a source for the good ordering of the experience, with the expectation that the learners will respond accordingly. The teacher as a member of that community must relate to the learners, attending and responding to their needs, desires, and wants. There ought to be mutuality among teachers and learners, reflecting the hierarchical and conciliar nature of the Trinity, kingdom, and Church. If in teaching about the hierarchical and conciliar nature of the Church, a teacher is despotic and arbitrary, the lesson will not be learned, no matter how well planned and executed. The classroom dynamic is not one-way, from teacher to learner, but "all ways," from teacher to learner, from learner to teacher, and from learner to learner. As William Ayers writes, "Teachers must understand that even as they teach, they will also be taught; even as they help others develop, they will themselves change and grow."[81]

Through inverse perspective, the icons look at the beholder; they are incomplete without the beholder. In similar fashion, teachers and learners must look at one another and recognize that neither is complete without the other. Teachers and students need one another. The variety of persons depicted in icons helps us to recognize that there is immense variety in the teaching and learning styles that can be encountered and from which we can benefit. A teacher may be active, continually being involved in the activity of learners, or may be more quiet, yet still concerned about the learning taking place. The same holds true for learners. When each person in the educational endeavor genuinely strives toward fellowship with God, the teaching and the learning are empowered through the Holy Spirit.

NOTES

[1] Thomas Groome, *Sharing Faith: A Comprehensive Approach to Religious Education and Pastoral Ministry – The Way of Shared Praxis* (San Francisco: Harper Collins, 1991), p. 2.

[2] Werner Jaeger, *Early Christianity and Greek Paideia* (Cambridge, MA: Belknap Press, 1961), pp. 86-90.

[3] John Chryssavgis, *Repentance and Confession in the Orthodox Church* (Brookline, MA: Holy Cross Orthodox Press, 1990), p. 5. Emphasis added.

[4] John L. Boojamra, "The Goal of Church Education," *The Word* (September, 1996), p. 17. Also, a recent piece by Kyriaki FitzGerald explicitly mentions only formation and information. See Kyriaki Karidoyanes FitzGerald "The Role of the Academy in Ministerial Formation and Theological Education," *Ministerial Formation* (October 1996), p. 17-18.

[5] Elliot Eisner, "Aesthetic Modes of Knowing," in *Learning and Teaching the Ways of Knowing*, Elliot Eisner, ed. Eighty-fourth Yearbook of the National Society for the Study of Education (Chicago: University of Chicago Press, 1985), p. 27.

[6] James Fowler, *Stages of Faith: The Psychology of Human Development and the Quest for Meaning* (San Francisco: Harper San Francisco, 1981), p. 277.

[7] A note about sainthood is warranted here. There is no official process for the recognition of saints in the Orthodox Church, as is found in Roman Catholicism. Saints are proclaimed by the local churches, usually based on popular sentiment. For example, George Bebis reports that Basil the Great was recognized as a saint immediately upon his death by the people. However, this "procedure" can lead to abuses. Recently, the heads of local churches – patriarchs or archbishops – have issued encyclicals in recognition of saints, yet still reflecting the feelings of the local populace. See George Bebis, "The Saints of the Orthodox Church," in *A Companion to the Greek Orthodox Church*, Fotios Litsas, ed. (New York: Greek Orthodox Archdiocese, 1988), p. 90.

[8] Dumitru Staniloae, *The Experience of God*, trans. Ioan Ionita (Brookline, MA: Holy Cross Orthodox Press, 1994), p. 48.

[9] Anton C. Vrame, "An Exegesis of the *Epitaphios Threnos*," *The Greek Orthodox Theological Review* 39:3-4 (1994), p. 302.

[10] L. Ouspensky and V. Lossky, *The Meaning of Icons*, trans. G. E. H. Palmer and E. Kadloubovsky (Crestwood, NY: SVS Press, 1982), p. 160.

[11] "The Protevangelium of James" in *The Other Gospels: Non-canonical Gospel Texts*, pp. 107-121, ed. Ron Cameron, (Philadelphia: Westminster Press, 1982). This text contains the story of Joachim and Anna, Mary's birth, early life, betrothal to Joseph, the Annunciation, the Nativity – including the midwives – and infancy stories about Jesus. Many of these scenes have been depicted iconographically.

[12] St Basil the Great articulated this view centuries earlier when he wrote: "Concerning the teachings of the Church, whether publicly proclaimed (*kerygma*) or reserved to members of the household of faith (*dogmata*), we have received some from written sources, while others have been given to us secretly through apostolic tradition. Both sources have equal force in true religion." St. Basil the Great, *On the Holy Spirit*, 27.66 (Crestwood, NY: SVS Press, 1980), p. 98.

[13] Andrew Louth, *Discerning the Mystery: An Essay on the Nature of Theology* (Oxford, Clarendon Press, 1983), p. 27.

[14] Parker Palmer, *To Know as We Are Known: A Spirituality of Education* (San Francisco: Harper San Francisco, 1983), p. 47.

[15] Ibid., p. 42.

[16] John Boojamra, *Foundations for Christian Education* (Crestwood, NY: SVS Press, 1989), p. 36.

[17] Margaret Miles, *Carnal Knowing* (Kent, UK: Burns and Oates, 1992), p. 24.

[18] Clifford Geertz, *The Interpretation of Cultures* (New York: Basic Books, 1973), p. 127.

[19] C. Geertz, *Local Knowledge* (New York: Basic Books, 1983), pp. 99-100.

[20] C. Geertz, *Interpretation of Cultures*, p. 129.

[21] Ibid., p. 93.

[22] See Alexis Vinogradov, "The Orthodox Christian Experience of Liturgical Space," *Ecumenism* (No. 123, September, 1996), p. 34-35.

[23] C. Geertz, *Interpretation of Cultures,* pp. 6-7.

[24] Photios Kontoglou, *Ekfrasis tis Orthodoxou Eikonografias, tom. 1.* (Athens: Astir Publishing, 1960), p. 178, translation mine.

[25] The order of services during Holy Week in the Orthodox Church are "pushed up" in time, being sung "by anticipation." For this example, the vespers of Friday evening are celebrated in the afternoon, and the Orthros of Saturday morning is celebrated on Friday evening. Alkiviadis Calivas offers a number of possible explanations for the transposition of services in his *Great Week and Pascha in the Greek Orthodox Church* (Brookline, MA: Holy Cross Orthodox Press, 1992), pp. 13-16.

[26] A. Vrame, "An Exegesis of the *Epitaphios Threnos*" contains a more complete explanation of the icon.

[27] *The Lenten Triodion,* trans. Mother Mary and Kallistos Ware (London: Faber and Faber, 1978), p. 615-616.

[28] Henry Maguire, "The Depiction of Sorrow in Middle Byzantine Art," *Dumbarton Oaks Papers* 31 (1977), p. 162. The homily is Oration VIII of George of Nicomedia, PG 100 1488A-B. A later homily also reported by Maguire and written by Symeon Metaphrastes echoes George of Nicomedia's thoughts: "Nicodemus alone ... placed you painfully in my arms, which even lately lifted you joyfully as an infant.... And once I took care of your swaddling-clothes, and now I am troubled with your funerary apparel. I washed you in lukewarm water, now I bathe you in hotter tears. I raised you in a mother's arms, but leaping and jumping as children do. Now I raise you up in the same arms, but without breath, and lying as the dead. Then I dipped my lips in your honey-sweet and dewy lips ... Many times you slept on my breast as an infant, and now you have fallen asleep there as a dead man" (PG 114 261B-C).

[29] *The Lenten Triodion,* pp. 619-620.

[30] *The Lamentations of Matins of Holy and Great Saturday,* trans. Holy Transfiguration Monastery (Boston: Holy Transfiguration Monastery, 1981), p. 27.

[31] Ibid., p. 25.

[32] Ibid., p. 31.

[33] Ibid., p. 29.

[34] Ibid., p. 16.

[35] C. Geertz, *Interpretation of Cultures*, p. 122.

[36] John Dewey, *Art as Experience* (New York: Perigree Books, 1934), p. 327.

[37] Leo Tolstoy, *What is Art?* trans. Aylmer Maude (New York: Liberal Arts Press, 1960), p. 149.

[38] Without interrupting the flow of my above thought, this also raises the concern of the "visual" dimension of home life. What pictures do families see on the walls of their homes? Which television programs, videos, video games, and films are watched? In addition, are they being watched critically and with conversation among the viewers about what is being seen or passively, accepting what is seen as true and acceptable forms of behavior? Each of these in their own way contributes to the formation of the family.

[39] Michael Baxandall, *Painting and Experience in Fifteenth Century Italy*, 2nd ed. (Oxford: Oxford University Press, 1988), esp. pp. 29-50.

[40] Demetrios Trakatellis, "Ακολούθει Μοι/Follow Me" (Mk 2.14): Discipleship and Priesthood," *The Greek Orthodox Theological Review* 30:3 (1985), p. 281.

[41] Georgios I. Mantzaridis, *The Deification of Man* (Crestwood, NY: SVS Press, 1984), p. 41.

[42] St Athanasius, *On the Incarnation*, ch. 54, trans. "A religious of CSMV" (Crestwood, NY: SVS Press, 1982), p. 93.

[43] See Constantine Cavarnos, *Byzantine Sacred Art* (Belmont, MA: Institute for Byzantine and Modern Greek Studies, 1992), p. 89.

[44] Michael Quenot, *The Icon: Window on the Kingdom*, trans. A Carthusian Monk (Crestwood, NY: SVS Press, 1991), p. 97. The statement from Cyril of Jerusalem is from *Catechesis* 18 (PG 33, 613).

[45] See Stanley S. Harakas, *Living the Faith: The Praxis of Eastern Orthodox Ethics* (Minneapolis: Light and Life, 1992), p. 96.

[46] *Selected Byzantine Hymns According to the Tradition of the Great Church of Christ* (Brookline, MA: Holy Transfiguration Monastery, 1981), p. 40.

[47] Maxine Greene, *Landscapes of Learning* (New York: Teacher's College Press, 1978), pp. 43-44.

[48] Ibid., p. 162.

[49] J. Chryssavgis, *Repentance and Confession*, p. 7.

[50] *Divine Liturgy of St John Chrysostom*, trans. the Faculty of Hellenic College and Holy Cross Greek Orthodox School of Theology (Brookline, MA: Holy Cross Orthodox Press, 1985), p. 20.

[51] Alexander Schmemann, *The Eucharist: Sacrament of the Kingdom*, trans. Paul Kachur (Crestwood, NY: SVS Press, 1988), p. 45.

[52] Constantine Cavarnos, *Guide to Byzantine Iconography* (Brookline,

MA: Holy Transfiguration Monastery, 1993), pp. 208-212. See also L. Ouspensky and V. Lossky, *The Meaning of Icons* (Crestwood, NY: SVS Press, 1984), pp. 207-208.

[53] L. Ouspensky and V. Lossky, *Meaning of Icons*, p. 207.

[54] Ibid.

[55] C. Cavarnos, *Guide to Byzantine Iconography*, p. 209.

[56] *The Divine Liturgy of St. John Chrysostom*, p. 22.

[57] Nikos A. Nissiotis, "The Importance of the Doctrine of the Trinity for Church Life and Theology," in *The Orthodox Ethos*, ed., A.J. Philippou, (Oxford: Holywell Press, 1964), p. 64.

[58] Alexander Schmemann, *Church, World, Mission* (Crestwood, NY: SVS Press, 1979), p. 165.

[59] *The Ieratikon* (Athens: Apostolike Diakonia, 1987), p. 180.

[60] Christos Yannaras, *The Freedom of Morality*, trans. Elizabeth Briere (Crestwood, NY: SVS Press, 1984), p. 219.

[61] Daniel Clendenin, "Why I'm Not Orthodox," *Christianity Today*, January 6, 1997, pp. 33-38.

[62] See Stanley S. Harakas, *Let Mercy Abound: Social Concern in the Greek Orthodox Church* (Brokline, MA: Holy Cross Orthodox Press, 1985), esp. pp. 168-170.

[63] See C. Cavarnos, *Guide to Byzantine Iconography*, pp. 152-153.

[64] *The Festal Menaion*, trans. Mother Mary and Kallistos Ware (London: Faber and Faber, 1984), p. 363.

[65] Ibid., p. 348.

[66] C. Cavarnos, *Guide to Byzantine Iconography*, pp. 147-148.

[67] See Stanley Harakas, "The Integrity of Creation: Ethical Issues" in *Justice, Peace and the Integrity of Creation: Insights from Orthodoxy*, ed. G. Limouris, (Geneva: WCC Publications, 1990), p. 72.

[68] *The Festal Menaion*, p. 361.

[69] One can occasionally see photos from Russia of people gathered at a frozen river bank and the clergy blessing the water through a hole cut in the ice. In more tropical climates, the congregation will gather at the banks of a body of water, and the clergy will bless the waters in huge celebrations, often marked by the throwing of a cross into the water and divers racing to retrieve it. In the United States, one such large festival takes place in Tarpon Springs, Florida.

[70] *The Festal Menaion*, pp. 354-355.

[71] Ibid., 357-358.

[72] St John of Damascus, *On the Divine Images*, First Apology 16,

trans. David Anderson (Crestwood, NY: SVS Press, 1980), p. 23.

[73] "Orthodox Perspectives on Creation," in *Justice, Peace and the Integrity of Creation*, p. 3.

[74] Ecumenical Patriarch Dimitrios, Protocol No. 629, "On the Day of the Protection of the Environment, Sept. 1, 1989" in *Orthodoxy and the Ecological Crisis* (Gland, Switzerland, World Wide Fund for Nature, 1990). See also Nicholas P. Constas, "Commentary on the Patriarchal Message on the Day of the Protection of the Environment," *The Greek Orthodox Theological Review* 35:3 (1990), pp, 179-194.

[75] Philip Sherrard, *Human Image: World Imange, The Death and Resurrection of Sacred Cosmology* (Ipswich, UK: Golgonooza Press, 1992), p. 2.

[76] Patriarch Dimitrios, "On the Day of the Protection of the Environment."

[77] The Ecumenical Patriarchate, *Orthodoxy and the Ecological Crisis* (Gland, Switzerland, World Wide Fund for Nature, 1990), p. 11.

[78] *Orthodox Statement on Environmental Principles* (unpublished document, 1996).

[79] Ecumenical Patriarchate, *Orthodoxy and the Ecological Crisis*, p. 7.

[80] Alexander Schmemann, *For the Life of the World* (Crestwood, NY: SVS Press, 1973), p. 15. See also Harakas, "The Integrity of Creation," p. 73.

[81] William Ayers, *To Teach: The Journey of a Teacher* (New York: Teachers College Press, 1993), p. 80.

Chapter Six

✳

The Sacrament of Education:
Catechesis in the Orthodox Way

When the principles of iconic catechesis are applied to educational efforts and processes, education in faith can become a "sacrament." To call an educational enterprise a sacrament, with all of the term's overtones, may seem to overstep the boundaries of good sense, to over-romanticize, to over-idealize what actually transpires in the learning environment with all its shortcomings. Nevertheless, I believe iconic catechesis justifies such consideration based on the aims and processes described thus far: the sacred curriculum, the formative and transformative dimensions of catechesis, *theosis,* and deification. While an addition to the usual list of seven sacraments is not being proposed, the understanding necessary to embrace iconic catechesis has so much in common with the understanding of sacrament that, at minimum, there appears to be no conflict. Perhaps stating it another way makes the assertion more readily acceptable: the understanding of sacrament embraces the view of religious education as sacrament. The Orthodox Tradition has such an understanding.

Thomas Hopko writes, the "practice of the Orthodox Church is to consider everything which is in and of the Church as sacramental or mystical."[1] As prime evidence, the Orthodox Tradition has not fixed dogmatically the number of sacraments at seven.

While the Orthodox have continued to discuss and teach the seven sacraments (Baptism, Chrismation, Eucharist, Matrimony, Penance, Unction, and Ordination),[2] when examined more closely, other acts are also seen as sacraments: the consecration of a church, the blessing of chrism, the blessing of water, the tonsure of a monastic. Icons and the blessing of icons are often included in lists of sacramental practices in the Orthodox Tradition.[3]

The Tradition does not call these acts sacraments; instead it calls them "mysteries," although for convenience Orthodox use the terms interchangeably. Kallistos Ware writes that "a mystery is ... something that is revealed for our understanding, but which we never understand exhaustively, because it leads into the depth or darkness of God."[4] We can begin to understand that God is acting through the sacraments, but because we are led to experience God in the sacraments, we may never fully comprehend the experience. Sacraments use visible means to convey invisible grace and sanctification to their participants, but any explanations that are offered ultimately collapse in inadequacy. How does the Holy Spirit transform the bread and wine of the Eucharist into the body and blood of Christ? How does the sacrament of Chrismation "seal" the Holy Spirit within a person? How do rings and crowns unite two people in matrimony? How does the sacrament of Ordination make someone a deacon, priest, or bishop? Each one of these acts, their texts and rituals, can be studied and explained through various prisms of understanding, but their ultimate meaning will continue to transcend these explanations.

Calling an action a sacrament points our attention toward two agents, God and humanity, and their cooperation (*synergy*) and interaction in the sacrament. Of course, faith helps us realize that God always acts in the sacrament. God is the one who initiates, celebrates, and completes the sacrament, who transforms the bread and wine, makes the candidate a priest, and so forth. While God always acts in the sacrament, human participation is also necessary. Thus, the human dimension must be examined more closely. The sacraments are neither magic nor alchemy. In the sacraments, God invites the human participants to enter into a covenantal relationship. God does not violate our freedom and transform us without our wanting to be transformed. Voluntary human involvement and participation in the sacrament are necessary.

With this understanding, calling education a sacrament may seem less startling and more plausible, perhaps even intriguing. Since icons are considered sacraments, then a catechesis based upon them ought to be sacramental as well. Catechesis is part of the life of the Church, one that we can explore from many angles. Still, education is a mystery in that we must stop short in our explanations of how persons come to know and how teaching facilitates that process. The process of learning and teaching ultimately transcends rational explanation; there is an unknowable, invisible dimension that cannot be fully explained. Education involves the work of parents, teachers, clergy, and learners who strive to cooperate with the power of God's Holy Spirit in order to come to "heart knowledge" and live as God intends humanity to live. God acts when a sacrament is celebrated, and thus God's Spirit is present and active in the educational sacrament.

Iconic catechesis is not a method of instruction. Like the icons that have informed it, which cannot offer concrete proposals for behaving in a particular way, iconic catechesis points to a way of thinking about our educational life in the Orthodox Tradition. Iconic catechesis points to a *phronema,* the Orthodox way, for educators to consider adopting in their praxis. How they will apply this *phronema* ought to be in continuity with the received wisdom of the icon, but the particular expression will be as unique as their personalities.

Six principles of iconic catechesis will be offered in this chapter followed by four "rubrics" of the sacrament of education.

PRINCIPLES OF ICONIC CATECHESIS

Principle 1. The Tradition possesses a wisdom greater and deeper than what is seen at the surface.

Just as one can walk past an icon and barely notice it, one can also view the Tradition at a superficial level. The Orthodox Tradition can be seen as a vast reservoir with many currents and layers from the very ancient to the very contemporary. Typically in our educational practice, we merely skim the surface. We look only for what we want to find, and we absolutize one period of time or one people's experience. Rarely do we look deeply into the Tradition, into its fullness. When we do we cannot escape the realization that our roots are centuries old and that within the Tradition there is a wisdom that continues to nurture and nourish our journey, now and into the future.

Orthodox religious education has been no exception to this superficial vision. Contemporary Orthodox religious educators have typically borrowed from others and then been dissatisfied with the outcome. This exploration of iconic catechesis has been about discovering principles from deep within the Orthodox Tradition that may offer the potential to renew the educational practice of the Church. The icons, I believe, have continually pointed to educational practice – if we were willing to take them seriously and not merely as a peculiar art form that decorates Orthodox churches. I am convinced that the process of looking more closely at the icons, exploring in depth the wisdom they convey, and engaging them in an educational conversation challenges us to look at ourselves honestly as Christians in terms of our efforts toward iconic living and knowing. It challenges us as educators to consider our Tradition seriously and the *praxis* it calls us to implement.

The icons have the potential to teach the Tradition, and the Tradition must be taught. But it must be taught as a living Tradition. It is alive, and to keep it alive, we must live it. The Tradition will not survive if Orthodox Christians do not live it.

Living the Orthodox Tradition does not mean mere re-creations of historic moments and practices. A living Tradition is a growing Tradition. It stretches itself, incorporating new ways of thinking, acting, and feeling, even as the old ways challenge the new, leading to a new synthesis for this time and place, while still in continuity and communion with all other times and places.

Principle 2. Truth and wisdom dwell in the network of relations we call the Body of Christ.

A single icon has the potential to point to the truth and wisdom of the Gospel. The icon-filled church manifests the truth and wisdom of the community of faith, for within it one may finds images of the humblest ascetic and the most powerful patriarch side by side, part of a choir proclaiming the Gospel. The icons should remind each educator that within the most educated to the illiterate members of the Body of Christ there is knowledge, experience, and wisdom about what it means to live the Orthodox way. When the Body of Christ – the Church – gathers to celebrate the liturgy and sacraments, the truth of the good news of Jesus Christ is proclaimed: that all who place their trust in him and live according to his way experience the kingdom of God. When the Body of Christ gathers to decide how it shall live and know as a community, truth is articulated and defined. Neither of these points to some "objective" truth from the scientific paradigm, that is, a hypothesis that is subject to test, retest, and proofs. Both point to the truth of a community of faith, persons in communion with one another and with God. In practice, this community is comprised of hierarchs, priests, deacons, and non-ordained, young and old, men and women, wealthy and poor, educated and uneducated. Each needs the other; truth cannot reside in only one dimension of the Body, even as the distinctive gifts (*charismata*) and talents of each member are recognized.

The received body of knowledge from the past, coupled with

the living experience of the Body of Christ in the present, becomes the source for discerning and living the wisdom and truth of the Church in a given time and place. It implies that through serious reflection, dialogue, prayer, study, and practice, all Christians can come to live and know the Orthodox Tradition. All members of the community have the right as well as the responsibility to learn and study. Styles of educational practice that encourage engaging the past, dialogue among the participants, and commitment, are to be favored over methods that see learning as mere fact retention and learners as passive.

The life of the parish offers many opportunities for nurturing its members in the Orthodox Tradition and its way of life. Many of the insights of Maria Harris' work, *Fashion Me A People*,[5] can be applied in an Orthodox setting. Her paradigm of *koinonia, leiturgia, didache, kerygma,* and *diakonia* is already expressed among Orthodox pastoral workers as *koinonia, leiturgia, martyria* (meaning "witness" and thus incorporates Harris' *kerygma* and *diakonia*). Orthodox religious educators have also added *matheteia*, to include the significance of ongoing learning and discipleship.[6] By extension, *matheteia* could include teaching or *didache*. Harris' statement, "the church does not have an educational program; it is an educational program"[7] should enter Orthodox pastoral consciousness. The challenge for pastoral practitioners is to begin seeing everything that a parish does in the light of how it forms the faith of the people who will engage in that activity, not only forming them for better parish participation, but for other facets of their lives as well. Within the educational ministry of an Orthodox parish, program developers and catechists can begin to see their programs as forming persons in faith for their lives and not just informing them about the Tradition.

Formation extends into the classroom when the classroom experience is seen sacramentally, that is, as an opportunity for God to be encountered and his kingdom to be experienced. The catechetical environment, then, should be organized around the sacred that is mediated through the icons, and also through the narratives and the entire life of the community. The "Catechesis of the Good Shepherd," an approach developed by Sofia Cavalletti based upon the educational principles of Maria Montessori, offers a model worth experimenting with in Orthodox settings. The "Catechesis of the Good Shepherd" sees the classroom as being more like a church because the classroom is "less a place of instruction than a holy ground where Christ is encountered in word and action."[8] This catechetical approach sees the classroom as a place where children learn to live the realities of life as a Christian, not just acquire the information that Christians should acquire.[9] To place these concepts in the terms of an iconic catechesis, the classroom ought to become a sacred place where persons engage the visible and invisible curricula in order to come to live and to know iconically.

Principle 3. Personal and corporate prayer – liturgy – are central to the catechesis of the Church.

The home of the icon is the worshipping community of persons. In liturgy, icons offer their fullest potential for educating Orthodox Christians in iconic living and knowing. There the mystery of God and the Good News of Jesus Christ are encountered in word and ritual, visually and verbally. For the community of faith, these can become informative, formative, and transformative experiences, leading the members to a new or a deeper awareness of their Christian vocation.

The home of the learner is the liturgical and sacramental life of the Church. Long after attendance at any formal educational program has ceased, Christians will still find themselves gathering as a community to worship God and experience his life in the mysteries of the Church. Our lives flow in and through the worshipping community. Rituals and sacraments mark the transitions and passages, the decisions and commitments of each person's existence from birth to and through death. Liturgy celebrates our communal identity – it is one way we know who we are. It is also one way others know who we are as well. Liturgy celebrates our personal identity as Orthodox Christians, both as part of a community and also at home through the practices we engage; like fasting, prayer, acts of charity and service.

Our educational practice, then, should strive to lead to and from worship and prayer, both corporate and personal. Classrooms and homes should strive to become places of prayer and ritual celebration.

Principle 4. We must take our humanity seriously.

As obvious as this seems, it bears repetition: icons are depictions of human persons, men and women, who came to know and lived God-like lives. Lives are lived in time and in places with a context and a particular reality. To come to know what it means to know God and live like God means to deal with one's social and historical context. God reveals himself in our lives today and calls us to discern and commit ourselves to living like him wherever we are. The full range of our human experience has already been, and can continually be, informed, formed, and transformed by God.

Iconic living and knowing involves all aspects of our lives, not just the church-going part. Too often, we compartmentalize or separate the "spiritual" or "religious" as somehow distinct from the "bodily," "intellectual," or "secular." Faith is lived in the whole of our lives, in all of its dimensions: parish and Church, marriage and family, community and nation, work and career, etc. However, our efforts at catechesis have emphasized one's identity and agency *within* parish life, when in fact, most of us spend most of our time in other pursuits. Centuries ago, the lives of Christians may have revolved around the village church, its rhythms and cycles, but today our lives are spent outside that reality. In short, our time is overwhelmingly spent "in the world," with different rhythms. Thus, our mission is to carry the Gospel into that "world."

Our faith is reflected in our lives and is seen in the lives of others. Our Orthodox identity is action based. Litugy, rituals, prayer and fasting, acts of charity and mercy toward others, striving for justice and righteousness are each actions. Without *praxis* we cannot see faith, and "faith without works is dead" (Jas. 2.26). This means getting out of one's chair and doing something Christian, especially on behalf of others: caring for the poor, sick, and oppressed and restoring the damage done to the natural world. Individual teachers, classes, youth groups, Sunday schools, and adult groups can plan and implement programs of service and ministry for a wide variety of local and global concerns. Catechists involved with these efforts should insist that time be included before, during, or after the program for the participants to learn about and reflect on their participation in light of the Orthodox Tradition. Our educational work should lead to actions on the part of learners. The biblical question, "What then must *we do* to be saved?" (cf. Acts 2.37) becomes an educational "So what?" So what difference does knowing something about one's Orthodox Tradition make in the person's life? Can it lead to a new commitment to live iconically?

There are at least three educational implications for taking our humanity seriously. The first is that the way of iconic catechesis is through life. Orthodox often boast that Orthodoxy is not a system of theology; rather, it is a way of life. But we have taught it to those who seek its wisdom as if it were a system. The old way of education in the Orthodox Church has been to fill learners with facts, names, dates, places, memorization, and relying upon socio-cultural conditions to provide the material of life, the rituals, practices, and the wisdom of the Orthodox Tradition as it has been experienced over the generations. Orthodox Christianity has had a relatively insulated American experience, remaining ethnically homogeneous (whether Greek, Arab, or Slavic) and with few exceptions outside of the mainstream and its challenges.[10] Most Orthodox can probably recall Sunday school lessons in which they were taught religious information and rewarded for their ability to simply

play it back to their teachers. Family involvement with parish
life, through its various activities of worship, youth groups, and
the personal example of clergy and other faithful men and
women assured that the young would be formed into the Tradition. Recent generations can recall the centrality of the Church
in their day-to-day lives, spending most of their time outside of
school or work involved with parish activities. Today's and future Orthodox Christians face a more culturally diverse, less
homogeneous Church than before, and one that can and already has been directly confronted with the issues of the
mainstream.[11] As a result, efforts for catechesis must be able to
reach out to a more diverse Orthodox audience as well as deal
with a broader range of topics and interests. Thus, our catechesis
must reach into areas of life – the living reality faced by members of Orthodox parishes and by those who seek to embrace
Orthodoxy. Just as a person's whole life encounters the icon and
the icon encounters the person, our intentional efforts at
catechesis should also be an opportunity for lives to encounter
the Tradition, be engaged with one another, for lives to be informed, formed, and transformed and the Tradition enriched
by the presence of these lives.

Second, all of our ways of being and knowing can be engaged. Iconic catechesis is holistic. Education in faith is more
than an intellectual, cognitive endeavor; it is a matter of the
heart. Iconic knowing is "heart knowing," which in the Orthodox Tradition involves the intellect, emotions, body, and soul of
the person. Thus, efforts at catechesis should continually strive
to touch each of these aspects of the learner.

Discussing the intellect in efforts of faith education may appear superfluous; oftentimes this seems to be the only dimension
catechesis influences. However, educating the intellect is and
should remain an important priority of catechesis. If catechetical
programs are often boring to students, it may be due to the low
level of intellectual stimulation they offer. While Sunday schools
do not need to imitate graduate schools of theology in their

level of intensity, even a Sunday school program should challenge the minds of its learners, and efforts of adult catechesis must stimulate the intellects of more mature learners. Asking questions that may stimulate more than a regurgitated answer, posing challenging ethical or doctrinal questions and situations, or examining fundamental texts of the Tradition with a critical eye may help raise the level of intellectual challenge. Of course, to do this also requires a concomitant raising of the knowledge of the teachers. Given that most catechists are volunteers, often without much formal background in teaching or the Tradition, this will also be a challenge. An obligation of churches is to provide teachers with good catechetical materials and programs. Fortunately, the Orthodox churches have made great strides in developing such resources. Yet, even with excellent program materials, teachers still deserve to be challenged to grow in knowledge of the Tradition and in approaches to greater catechetical effectiveness.

Catechists are often afraid, of the emotional effects that their teaching may have upon their students. There is good reason for a certain amount of dispassion in teaching, and catechesis should not resort to "cheap emotionalism" to make a point or prompt a response from learners. However, "heart knowledge" will involve touching the emotions of students, eliciting their whole range over time. In keeping with the best of the patristic heritage of the Orthodox Tradition, powerful rhetoric can be a persuasive teaching tool among people; teachers should not shy away from its occasional use. Kieran Egan points out that our extremely logical approach to education, divorced from any emotional or affective dimension, is disastrous. Stories are designed to evoke an emotional response, achieving it through the use of opposites, such as good and evil.[12] Sanitizing the story of the crucifixion of Christ to avoid upsetting students may seem good sense – and judgment ought to be used – but the story is horrific, filled with pain and sadness. To avoid the suffering of the Passion narrative also lessens the news of the Resurrection, the story that should fill Christians with overwhelming joy.

Catechesis ought to include the nurture of both the body and the soul. The practices of the Church involving the body still need to be taught by parents and teachers. As a very simple example, the acts of veneration and prostration, the physical engagement with and reverencing of the icon needs to be taught along with making the sign of the cross according to the Orthodox practice. The ascetic discipline of fasting also needs to be taught and encouraged for practice in homes and churches.

In regard to the souls of the learners, our educational efforts should try to help them reach into their innermost selves and reach out toward the transcendent God as they also strive to discern the workings of God in their lives. To work toward this, each educational encounter should include prayer, involving both teaching persons how to pray as well as setting aside times for prayer within the educational gathering. Many classes begin and end with prayer, involving traditional forms of prayer or spontaneous, creative approaches. Also, serious conversations about prayer and helping learners cultivate a rule of prayer outside of church gatherings should also be included in our efforts. In addition, catechists can help nurture the souls of learners by exploring other means of experiencing God's presence, in corporate worship, in nature, and in life events, such as the miracle of birth, the pain of illness, or the mystery of death. Our catechetical efforts should attempt to nurture a sense of awe and reverence toward God. By working to include all dimensions of the person – intellect, emotions, body, and soul – iconic catechesis can educate the whole person.

Principle 5. Theosis is practical.

Theosis as a goal of education has been articulated by others, but to recognize that *theosis* is depicted in the icons makes their vision of life a practical aim. How can *theosis* be called "practical"? It appears far above anyone, too abstract to comprehend, and too distant to achieve. *Theosis* does not mean becoming superhuman, but human or fully human, living life in fellowship with God and others. As St Irenaeus stated, "The glory of God is man most fully alive…"[13] A practical goal does not mean than it can be easily attained. To be practical means to relate to our *praxis* as educators, clergy, and parents alike.

Iconic living and knowing is the goal of iconic catechesis, but in order to achieve the goal, a step must be taken toward it by putting away old practices and beginning new ones. The term *proskynesis,* the act of veneration of an icon, is a combination of the preposition *pros,* (προς) meaning "toward" and the verb *kyneo* (χυνέω, to kiss), meaning "to reverence." Like a kiss, an act directed toward another out of love, devotion, and desire, the act of *proskynesis* is an act of the whole person, body, soul, emotion, and mind toward the icon. Yet the icon, as the symbol of the goal of iconic catechesis, points not merely toward the icon but toward God and toward others. The ritualized action of *proskynesis,* engaging the icon in love, respect, and desire is intended to become a practiced movement toward others and God outside the worship context. In order to live iconically, to live as God intends humanity to live, one must move toward God and others, even in the knowledge that one will likely fall. Stories from the Tradition presented in previous chapters highlighted this. Recall Dorotheus of Gaza's description of the way to attain God: to move toward one's neighbor. In his analogy, the center of the circle is God, and the rays of that circle are the lives of persons. As each person moves closer toward God, he or she moves closer to other persons. To reach God and others, one must move toward them. Thus, each Christian must see himself or herself on that journey toward *theosis.* The act of *proskynesis* toward the icon becomes a symbolic expression of the journey that each ought to be taking in his or her life.

The way of iconic living is the way of *metanoia,* a continual change of heart. It involves one's whole being, moving toward Jesus Christ – the image of the invisible God (Col. 1.15) – knowing that with each step, the person could and will likely fall. A story from the ascetic tradition exemplifies the necessary attitude:

A brother asked Abba Sisoes, saying "What shall I do, father? For I have fallen." And the old man said unto him, "Rise up." And the brother said to him, "I did rise up, but I fell again." The old man said to him, "Rise up again." And the brother said to him, "I did rise up again, many times, and I fell [again]." The old man said to him, "Rise up again." And the brother said to him, "Until when?" The old man said to him, "Until you advance, either in good deeds or in falling; for in the road wherein a man advances he goes, whether it be to death or to life."[14]

Thus, as in the story, our approach to falling in our ongoing efforts for conversion is to "rise up" after each fall. *Metanoia* is an ongoing praxis. Each day a Christian will face new challenges, struggles, or obstacles in the journey toward God, whether placed there by others or himself. An icon can be placed almost anywhere – home, place of business, automobile – as a continual reminder that the journey toward God is not only a journey in church or on Sundays, but a journey that takes place in the ordinary events of each day – in how one treats a child, a parent, a coworker, a customer. The way toward *theosis* is through the daily life each of us leads, and each step taken in life can be a step toward *theosis*.

Principle 6. Teachers are icons of iconic living and knowing.

Just as icons have taught generations of Orthodox Christians, teachers must see themselves as icons of the Tradition for their learners. Students, whether children or adults, will come to imitate their teachers, if the teachers are living or striving to live the Orthodox way of life, they are teaching. Teaching that growth is an aim of iconic living, without providing opportunities for learners to grow in heart knowledge, to explore unexplored territories of inquiry, or to pursue opportunities for ministry to others could stifle the personally transformative dimensions of catechesis. And how can one teach others that freedom is an expression of the image of God within humanity without providing learners the opportunity to make free choices? Is it possible to encourage the development of a sense of community among a group of believers without creating an environment that fosters relationship building? To teach love, justice, and mercy to others without striving to be loving, just, and merciful oneself will be ultimately ineffective. Teaching others to participate in the worship life of the Church, to pray, to read the Scriptures or the fathers, or to become involved with acts of charity and service to others, will go unheeded unless learners see such involvement by their teachers. As John Westerhoff writes, to teach is "to offer an example of that which is possible and necessary for all people."[15] Teachers should reflect the reality that iconic living and knowing is not only possible but is the way that persons are intended to live.

Teachers can imitate the qualities of icons, their openness, their ability to engage believers, and to speak to their hearts, patiently and silently awaiting the response of those who encounter them. Just as the aim of the icon is to lead the viewer to the person depicted and not remain fixed on the icon, so the aim of teachers is not to draw attention to themselves but to point learners to Christ. Modeled after the icons, teachers would become fully present among learners, open about their experiences in living the Orthodox way, sharing their expectations for learners, and inviting the learners to become open with themselves and among one another. As the icons often teach in silence, the teacher can also use stillness and silence. Words should be used with care. Teaching is as much about knowing when not to speak as it is about preparing what will be said or asked. Inasmuch as icons symbolize the Tradition, teachers, clergy, and parents need to begin to see themselves as bearers and stewards of the Orthodox Tradition, responsible for the growth, cultivation, and propagation of the Tradition among the next generation.

A Final "Rubric"

While not a method of instruction, considering iconic

catechesis sacramentally focuses attention on the "ritual" dimension or practices involved in the teaching/learning encounter. Sacraments are usually accompanied by rubrics – instructions and guidelines to direct the practitioner. Some have already been suggested above. I would like to close this work with four additional "rubrics" – guidelines for the practitioner of the sacrament of education.

"In your presence there is fullness of joy" (Ps 16.11)

As the icons bear witness to the sacred presence of God, giving joy to those who experience it, iconic catechesis ought to be marked by joy and happiness in the activity, encounter, and outcome. Education in faith that leads to heart knowledge of Christ should be a joyous pursuit that is deeply satisfying and leads to a sense of fulfillment. However, joy is different from fun and playfulness; education is not necessarily fun and games. Joy is inviting and contagious, filling persons' hearts. A joyous catechesis should also be inviting, drawing learners in order to fill their hearts.

Unus Christianus – nullus Christianus[16]

Iconic catechesis is inherently social and personal. Indeed, to be personal, it must be social! Modeled after the life of the Trinity, iconic catechesis should strive to build a community of persons – the Body of Christ – who gather together to learn from one another through the sharing of their lives of faith. To build a community among the participants, the catechist must strive to create a space for the participants to bring their lives to the educational endeavor. As William Ayers points out, the space of the classroom should be a place where persons are visible to one another, "where students are known and understood, where they feel safe and valued."[17] The icons make the lives of saints visible in a place where they can become known and their memories treasured within the community, to be remembered by another generation. Catechetical efforts should not be isolated, private matters, but a social process of persons interacting to the fullest extent possible. These efforts require that the learners not only receive the wisdom of the community, but also involve themselves, participating in that wisdom as seen in sacramental actions.

Within a sacrament, persons bring their lives to the community, placing significant moments – of birth and death, conversion and commitment – before the assembly for sanctification and direction. For example, in matrimony, the bride and groom stand before the congregation, hear its vision of marriage through prayer and the reading of Scripture, and have their union blessed. Toward the end of the marriage sacrament, the priest, holding the Gospel in one hand and the joined hands of the couple in the other, leads the couple in a procession around the table where the sacrament occurs. This event is referred to as the "Dance of Isaiah," in reference to the first hymn that is sung during this procession. One can see how the words of a sacrament can instruct and sanctify the lives of the newly married couple. Particularly evocative, however, is the liturgical dance as the physical direction of the couple in the way they should walk: led by the Gospel of Christ through the received wisdom of the community.

Modeled on this dance, teachers can begin to arrange their educational practices to engage the lives of students, where they can bring their experience to the community for direction and blessing through interaction with the wisdom of the community. The teacher as a mediator and steward of that wisdom can serve as a valuable partner and guide for student's lives, directing learners on the path they should walk.

The Icon is a Symbol

A great deal of time and effort will go into the ministry of catechesis, but calling the icon a symbol should remind us that education is not the goal but the way, or one way, to the goal of iconic living. While I do not want to undermine the importance and significance of education, there are many ways to achieve the goals of iconic living and knowing, and many people have reached it with little or no education. St Anthony the Great is a notable example. According to his biography, he "could not bear to learn letters" as a young man and, apparently, he had no formal education.[18] Yet, his biographer calls Anthony "extremely wise. It was a marvel that although he had not learned letters, he was a shrewd and intelligent man."[19] In one episode, Anthony was visited by a number of philosophers. After a lengthy conversation, the philosophers marveled at the wisdom of the saint.[20] As indicated by the life of St Anthony, catechists should approach their work with a great deal of humility regarding its outcome. Teaching may be successful with some but not with others. While iconic living and knowing does not depend entirely on catechesis, for most it will be a necessary and desirable experience.

Iconic catechesis is also a symbol because it participates in the reality of the life of the Church. When one steps into a catechetical setting, one is stepping into a microcosm of the Church. The strengths and weaknesses of the Church at that time will impact the educational endeavor. For example, if a strong missionary atmosphere is present, it will translate into receptiveness that enriches the catechetical process. If there is confusion about what it means to be Orthodox in a pluralistic society, this confusion is likely to intrude negatively into the classroom environment. These impacts, positive and negative, apply as well to those who prepare catechetical programs. Catechesis is not isolated from the rest of the life of the Church.

The classroom is also a foretaste of the Church to come. If teaching is bland, confusing, or out of touch with the Orthodox Tradition – whether due to well-meaning but inadequately prepared teachers, nostalgic and fanciful misconceptions of the Tradition, or failure to touch the lives of the learners – the Church that eventually emerges will likely reflect the disabilities of those earlier learning conditions. Also, if learning is not ongoing, extending into adult ways of knowing and being in the world, then the Church of the future may well suffer from a shallow and immature faith. In its educational endeavors, the Church must face the problem of "sandbox Christians,"[21] that is, Orthodox Christians with significant secular educational and professional achievements who seemingly rely in religious matters on lessons from their childhood, when they played in a sandbox. The issue is that education in faith ceases for far too many in adolescence – and adult crises are faced with the faith of children. Boojamra has identified this as one of the dysfunctions of Orthodox educational ministry, and he calls for learning opportunities throughout the life span.[22] I share his concern and his call for increased efforts in adult learning and look to a hopeful future that responds to the critical need for lifelong catechesis with appropriate programs and resources.

Parishes have many opportunities to educate their members, working to provide them with access to the Tradition and explore its meaning for personal life in at least three different avenues. First, there is education for the sake of education. Often there are people who want to know the Tradition, its history, doctrines, and practices. Acquiring information is their goal, and the parish should work to provide it, including opportunities, when appropriate, for reflection upon the information's significance, meaning, and direction to the participants' lives. Second, parishes can develop programs to prepare persons to mark various transitions and passages of life, especially when a sacrament of the Church is involved. For example, pre-marital encounters are becoming more common.[23] There are also other opportunities: before a child is born and baptized, when couples are notoriously craving information and guidance; when rearing children, parents and their adolescents seems an appropriate topic; and dealing with topics of illness and death, facing the loss of a parent, spouse, or one's own mortality. A third opportunity is when someone seeks to join the Orthodox Church from another faith tradition. The number of people embracing

Orthodoxy is increasing, especially with the large percentage of intermarriages. Yet, as a Church we still have no general program of education or guidelines on how to prepare people for reception into Orthodoxy. For the most part, parish clergy devise programs of their own, for example, a "three-meeting" preparation for Chrismation that involves reading a book or two and talking to the priest about any questions the books leave unanswered. Christianity has a very early and long tradition of preparing non-Christian adults to receive baptism and dealing with those from other Christian groups. The practices of the Church from centuries ago could be researched, appropriated, or adapted for present usage.[24] Rather than develop a program that may serve to inform, form, and transform persons' lives through the resources of the Tradition, by doing very little in these areas, the future of the church can be predicted.

Finally, when we feel that our eductional efforts are frustrating or frustrated, we can look to the icon as a visual standard bearer. Recall that the concept of *theosis* was not a logical doctrine, but a vision of life. The icon bears witness to the ideal that education should strive to attain. We may seldom, if ever, reach that ideal. Through its continual presence and witness to the power of the Holy Spirit to transform, the icon provides hope in the possibility of the vision.

"By this we know love" (1 Jn 3.16)

In iconic catechesis, the message that must become actualized is that through Jesus Christ, Orthodox Christians can see God's love for humanity that enables them to have fellowship with God. The icons reveal, in one instant, the truth about God and humanity: that in spite of our fallen state, sinful lives, and the broken world we have fashioned, God has come among us and reunited us with himself, making it possible to live according to the beauty God had originally created within and for humanity. In the sacrament of education, the presence of Christ should be felt among each participant. In practice, the presence of Christ is experienced personally and achieved person by person one at a time. The real program is the ministry of persons for and on behalf of other persons, their lives, their concerns, their hopes, and making God present in and through them. Despite all the concern for an educational program, the program does not give communion but provides the means for persons to discover, reveal, to live and know as God has intended and share this discovery, revelation, life, and knowledge with others. Enacting the sacrament should bring each participant closer to that beauty of being created "in the image and likeness."

NOTES

[1] Thomas Hopko, *The Orthodox Faith, Vol. 2: Worship* (New York: Department of Religious Education – The Orthodox Church in America, 1976), p. 25.

[2] See Alkiviadis C. Calivas, "The Sacramental Life of the Orthodox Church," in *A Companion to the Greek Orthodox Church*, pp. 31-35, ed. Fotios Litsas (New York: Greek Orthodox Archdiocese, 1984).

[3] See for example, Anthony Coniaris, *These Are the Sacraments: The Life-Giving Mysteries of the Orthodox Church* (Minneapolis: Light and Life, 1981), p. 10.

[4] Kallistos Ware, *The Orthodox Way* (Crestwood, NY: SVS Press, 1979), p. 18.

[5] Maria Harris, *Fashion Me a People: Curriculum in the Church* (Louisville: Westminster/John Knox Press, 1989).

[6] "Orthodox Catechesis" (Brookline, MA: Greek Orthodox Archdiocese Department of Religious Education, n.d.), mimeographed.

[7] M. Harris, *Fashion Me a People*, p. 47.

[8] Sofia Cavalletti, *The Religious Potential of the Child*, trans. P. M. Coulter and J. M. Coulter (Chicago: Liturgy Training Publications, 1992), p. 5.

[9] Ibid., p. 56.

[10] See *Report to His Eminence Archbishop Iakovos Concerning the Future Theological Agenda of the Greek Orthodox Archdiocese* (Brookline, MA: Holy Cross Orthodox Press, 1990), pp. 4-5. A notable example of when Orthodoxy engaged mainstream issues was in March, 1965,

when Archbishop Iakovos participated in the march on Selma with Martin Luther King, Jr., gaining the Archbishop much notoriety for his position, as well as being pictured on the cover of *Life* magazine (March 26, 1965).

[11] For example, the problem of clergy sexual misconduct has come to light among parishes and has begun to be discussed in church circles. See John T. Chirban (ed.), *Clergy Sexual Misconduct: Orthodox Christian Perspectives* (Brookline, MA: Hellenic College Press, 1994).

[12] Kieran Egan, *Teaching as Story Telling: An Alternative Approach to Teaching and Curriculum in the Elementary School* (Chicago: The University of Chicago Press, 1986), pp. 27-30.

[13] St Irenaeus of Lyons, *Adversus haereses* 4.20.6.

[14] As reported in John Chryssavgis, *Repentance and Confession in the Orthodox Church* (Brookline, MA: Holy Cross Orthodox Press, 1990), p. 37.

[15] John Westerhoff, *Spiritual Life: The Foundation for Preaching and Teaching* (Louisville, KY: Westminster/John Knox Press, 1994), p. 37.

[16] Georges Florovsky, "The Church: Her Nature and Task," in *The Collected Works of Georges Florovsky Vol. 1: Bible, Church, Tradition* (Vaduz: Buchervertriensanstalt, 1987), p. 59.

[17] William Ayers, *To Teach: The Journey of a Teacher* (New York: Teachers College Press, 1993) p. 60.

[18] Athanasius, *The Life of Antony*, 1, in *Athanasius, The Life of Antony and the Letter to Marcellinus*, trans. Robert C. Gregg (New York: Paulist Press, 1980), p. 30.

[19] Ibid., 72, p. 83.

[20] Ibid., 72-80, pp. 83-89.

[21] I must attribute this phrase to Fr. Laurence, Abbot of the New Skete Monastery in Cambridge, New York.

[22] John Boojamra, *Foundations of Orthodox Christian Education* (Crestwood, NY: SVS Press, 1989), p. 9.

[23] In the Greek Orthodox Diocese of Boston, they are required before couples may marry in the Church.

[24] In the Roman Church, the Rite of Christian Initiation of Adults (RCIA) has been promulgated for more than twenty years. The RCIA is rooted in the baptismal practices described by Hipploytus in the second century but has been adapted for modern usage. A major component of the RCIA program is the educational preparation of the catechumens. The approach of the RCIA should be studied as a model for developing a contemporary Orthodox model for receiving converts.

Works Cited and Consulted

Acts of Pilate (Gesta Pilati). Translated by W. O. Clough. India-napolis: Robert Douglass, 1880.

Adams, Doug and Apostolos-Cappadona, Diane, eds. *Art as Religious Studies*. New York: Crossroads, 1987.

Aghiorgoussis, Maximos. *In the Image of God: Studies in Scripture, Theology and Community*. Brookline, MA: Holy Cross Orthodox Press, 1999.

Alexander, Paul. "The Iconoclastic Council of St. Sophia (815) and its Definition (*Horos*)," *Dumbarton Oaks Papers* No. 7 (1953): 35-66.

———. *The Patriarch Nicephorus of Constantinople*. Oxford: Clarendon Press, 1958.

Allchin, A. M., ed. *Sacrament and Image: Essays in the Understanding of Man*, London: The Fellowship of St. Alban and St. Sergius, 1967.

Anastos, Milton. "The Ethical Theory of Images Formulated by the Iconoclasts in 754 and 815," *Dumbarton Oaks Papers* No. 8 (1954): 151-160.

Apostolos-Cappadona, Diane, ed. *Art, Creativity, and the Sacred: An Anthology in Religion and Art*. New York: Crossroads, 1989.

Arida, Robert. "Second Nicea: The Vision of the New Man and New Creation in the Orthodox Icon," *The Greek Orthodox Theological Review* 32:4 (1987): 417-424.

Arnheim, Rudolf. "The Double-Edged Mind: Intuition and the Intellect." In *Learning and Teaching the Ways of Knowing*. Eighty-fourth Yearbook of the National Society for the Study of Education, pp. 77-96. Edited by Elliott Eisner. Chicago: University of Chicago Press, 1985.

———. "A Plea for Visual Thinking." In *New Essays on the Psychology of Art*, pp. 135-152. Edited by Rudolf Arnheim. Berkeley, CA: University of California Press, 1986.

————. *Thoughts on Art Education*, Occasional Paper 2. Los Angeles: Getty Center for Education in the Arts, 1989.

Athanasius, St. *The Life of Antony and the Letter to Marcellinus.* Translated by Robert G. Gregg. New York: Paulist Press, 1980.

————. *On the Incarnation.* Translated by a religious of CSMV. Crestwood, NY: SVS Press, 1982.

Ayers, William. *To Teach: The Journey of a Teacher.* New York: Teachers College Press, 1993.

Baggley, John. *Doors of Perception: Icons and their Spiritual Significance.* Crestwood, NY: SVS Press, 1988.

Barasch, Mosche. *Icon: Studies in the History of an Idea.* New York: New York University Press, 1982.

Basil the Great, St. *On the Holy Spirit.* Translated by David Anderson. Crestwood, NY: SVS Press, 1980.

Baur, Chrysostomus. *John Chrysostom and His Times, Antioch - the Later Years*, Vol. 1, Part 2. Vaduz: Büchervertriebsanstalt, 1988.

Baxandall, Michael. *Painting and Experience in Fifteenth Century Italy*, 2d ed. Oxford: Oxford University Press, 1988.

Baynes, Norman. "The Icons Before Iconoclasm." *Harvard Theological Review* 44 (1951): 93-106.

Bettenson, Henry, ed. *Documents of the Christian Church.* 2d ed. London: Oxford University Press, 1967.

Bloom, Anthony. *Beginning to Pray.* New York: Paulist Press, 1970.

Bobrinskoy, Boris. "The Icon: Sacrament of the Kingdom," *St. Vladimir's Theological Quarterly* 31:4 (1987): 287-296.

Bondi, Roberta C. *To Love as God Loves: Conversations with the Early Church.* Philadelphia: Fortress Press, 1987.

Boojamra, John, L. "The Goal of Church Education." *The Word* (September 1996): p. 17.

————. "Report of the Department of Christian Education." *The Word* (November, 1995): p. 16.

————. "Socialization as a Historical Model for Christian Integration," *St. Vladimir's Theological Quarterly* 25:4 (1981): 219-237.

————. "The Liberation of Christian Education," *Phronema* 6 (1991): 39-49.

————. *Foundations for Orthodox Christian Education.* Crestwood, NY: SVS Press, 1989.

Boys, Mary C. *Educating in Faith: Maps and Visions.* San Francisco: Harper and Row, 1989.

Calivas, Alkiviadis. *Come Before God in Prayer and Solemn Feast.* Brookline, MA: Holy Cross Orthodox Press, 1986.

———. *Great Week and Pascha in the Greek Orthodox Church.* Brookline, MA: Holy Cross Orthodox Press, 1992.

Cameron, Ron, ed. *The Other Gospels: Non-canonical Gospel Texts.* Philadelphia: Westminster, 1982.

Cavaletti, Sofia. *The Religious Potential of the Child.* Translated by P. M. Coulter and J. M. Coulter. Chicago: Liturgy Training Publications, 1992.

Cavarnos, Constantine. *Byzantine Sacred Art.* Belmont, MA: Institute for Byzantine and Modern Greek Studies, 1992.

———. *Guide to Byzantine Iconography.* Brookline, MA: Holy Transfiguration Monastery, 1993.

———. *Meetings with Kontoglou.* Belmont, MA: Institute for Byzantine and Modern Greek Studies, 1992.

———. *Orthodox Iconography.* Belmont, MA: Institute for Byzantine and Modern Greek Studies, 1992.

Chirban, John T., ed. *Clergy Sexual Misconduct: Orthodox Christian Perspectives.* Brookline, MA: Hellenic College Press, 1994.

Chryssavgis, John. *Love, Sexuality, and the Sacrament of Marriage.* Brookline, MA: Holy Cross Orthodox Press, 1996.

———. *Repentance and Confession in the Orthodox Church.* Brookline, MA: Holy Cross Orthodox Press, 1990.

Clément, Olivier. *The Roots of Christian Mysticism.* New York: New City Press, 1995.

Clendenin, Daniel. "Why I'm Not Orthodox," *Christianity Today,* January 26, 1997, pp. 33-38.

Coniaris, Anthony. *Introducing the Orthodox Church: Its Faith and Life.* Minneapolis: Light and Life Publishing, 1982.

———. *These Are the Sacraments: The Life-Giving Mysteries of the Orthodox Church.* Minneapolis: Light and Life Publishing, 1981.

Constas, Nicholas P. "Commentary on the Patriarchal Message on the Day of the Protection of the Environment," *The Greek Orthodox Theological Review* 35:3 (1990), pp. 179-194.

Coucouzes, Archbishop Iakovos. *Faith for a Lifetime: A Spiritual Journey.* New York: Doubleday, 1988.

Davis, Leo Donald. *The First Seven Ecumenical Councils (325-*

787): Their History and Theology. Wilmington, DE: Michael Glazier, 1987.

Davis, Whitney. "Communication Theory." In *Grove Dictionary of Art, Vol. 7,* pp. 659-662. Edited by Jane Turner. New York: Macmillan, 1996.

Dewey, John. *Art as Experience.* New York: Perigee Books, 1934.

———. *Experience and Education.* New York: Macmillan Publishing Co., 1938.

Divine Liturgy of St. John Chrysostom. Translated by the Faculty of Holy Cross Greek Orthodox School of Theology. Brookline, MA: Holy Cross Orthodox Press, 1985.

Doulis, Thomas, ed. *Toward the Authentic Church: Orthodox Christians Discuss Their Conversion.* Minneapolis: Light and Life Publishing, 1996.

Ecumenical Patriarch Dimitrios, "On the Day of the Protection of the Environment, Sept. 1, 1989." Protocol No. 629. In *Orthodoxy and the Ecological Crisis,* pp. 1-2. Gland, Switzerland, World Wide Fund for Nature, 1990.

Ecumenical Patriarchate, The. *Orthodoxy and the Ecological Crisis.* Gland, Switzerland, World Wide Fund for Nature, 1990.

Egan, Kieran. *Teaching as Story Telling.* Chicago: University of Chicago Press, 1986.

Eisner, Elliot. *The Educational Imagination: On the Design and Evaluation of School Programs.* New York: Macmillan Publishing Co., 1979.

———. "Aesthetic Modes of Knowing." In *Learning and Teaching the Ways of Knowing.* Eighty-fourth Yearbook of the National Society for the Study of Education, pp. 23-36. Edited by Elliot Eisner. Chicago: University of Chicago Press, 1985.

Ephraim the Syrian, St. *Hymns on Paradise.* Translated by S. Brock. Crestwood, NY: SVS Press, 1990.

"Epitome of the Definition of the Iconoclastic Conciliabulum," in *Nicene and Post Nicene Fathers.* 2nd Series. Vol. XIV. Grand Rapids: Eerdmans, 1956.

Euchologion to Mega (in Greek). Athens: Astir Publishing, 1980.

Evagrius Ponticus. *The Praktikos and the Chapters on Prayer.* Translated by John Eudes Bamberger. Kalamazoo, MI: Cistercian Publications, 1981.

Evdokimov, Paul. *The Art of the Icon: A Theology of Beauty.* Translated by Fr. Steven Bigham. Redondo Beach, CA: Oakwood Publications, 1990.

Festal Menaion, The. Translated by Mother Mary and Kallistos Ware. London: Faber and Faber, 1977.

Fischer, Kathleen R. *The Inner Rainbow: The Imagination in Christian Life.* New York: Paulist Press, 1983.

FitzGerald, Kyriaki. *Religious Formation and Liturgical Life.* Ph.D. Dissertation, Boston University, 1985.

———. "The Role of the Academy in Ministerial Formation and Theological Education." *Ministerial Formation* (October 1996): pp. 17-18.

Florensky, Pavel. *Iconostasis.* Translated by Donald Sheehan and Olga Andrejev. Crestwood, NY: SVS Press, 1996.

Florovsky, Georges. *The Collected Works of Georges Florovsky, Vol. 9: The Byzantine Fathers of the Sixth to Eighth Century.* Vaduz: Büchervertriebsanstalt, 1987.

———. "The Church: Her Nature and Task." In *The Collected Works of Georges Florovsky, Vol. 1: Bible, Church, Tradition*, pp. 57-72. Vaduz: Büchervertriebsanstalt, 1987.

———. "Human Wisdom and the Great Wisdom of God. In *The Collected Works of Georges Florovsky, Vol. 12: Philosophy*, pp. 110-121. Vaduz: Büchervertriebsanstalt, 1987.

———. "The Worshipping Church." In *The Festal Menaion*, pp. 21-37. Translated by Kallistos Ware and Mother Mary. London: Faber and Faber, 1977.

Fowler, James. *Stages of Faith: The Psychology of Human Development and the Quest for God.* San Francisco: Harper San Francisco, 1981.

Frary, Joseph P. "The Logic of Icons." *Sobornost* 6:6 (1972): 394-404.

Gadamer, Hans-Georg. *The Relevance of the Beautiful and Other Essays.* Translated by Nicholas Walker. Edited by Robert Bernasconi. Cambridge: Cambridge University Press, 1986.

Gallagher, Donald and Gallagher, Idella, eds. *The Education of Man: The Educational Philosophy of Jacques Maritain.* New York: Doubleday & Co., 1962.

Geertz, Clifford. *The Interpretation of Cultures: Selected Essays.* New York: Basic Books, 1973.

———. *Local Knowledge*. New York: Basic Books, 1983.

Gero, Stephen. "The *Libri Carolini* and the Image Controversy," *The Greek Orthodox Theological Review* 18:1-2 (1973): 7-34.

Giakalis, Ambrosios. *Images of the Divine: The Theology of the Icons at the Seventh Ecumenical Council*. Leiden: E.J. Brill, 1994.

Grabar, André. *Byzantine Painting*. New York: Rizzoli International Publications, 1979.

Greene, Maxine. *The Dialectic of Freedom*. New York: Teachers College Press, 1988.

———. *Landscapes of Learning*. New York: Teacher's College Press, 1978.

Gregory of Nyssa, St. *An Address on Religious Instruction (Catechetical Oration)*. In *Christology of the Later Fathers*, pp. 268-325. Edited by Edward Hardy. Philadelphia: Westminster Press, 1954.

Gregory the Great, St. *Epistle to Serenus, Bishop of Marseilles*, Book IX Epistle CV. *Nicene and Post Nicene Fathers*, 2nd series, Vol. XIII. Grand Rapids: Eerdmans, 1956.

———. *Epistle to Serenus, Bishop of Marseilles*, Book XI Epistle XIII. *Nicene and Post Nicene Fathers*, 2nd series, Vol. XIII. Grand Rapids: Eerdmans, 1956.

Gregory the Theologian (Nazianzus), St. *Epistle 101, To Cledonius Against Appolinarius*. In *Christology of the Later Fathers*, pp. 215-224. Edited by Edward Hardy. Philadelphia: Westminster Press, 1954.

Groome, Thomas H. "Looking Back on Twenty-five Years: A Personal Reflection," *Living Light* 32:3 (Winter, 1995): pp. 73-81.

———. *Sharing Faith: A Comprehensive Approach to Religious Education and Pastoral Ministry – The Way of Shared Praxis*. San Francisco: Harper Collins, 1991.

Guzie, Tad. *The Book of Sacramental Basics*. New York: Paulist Press, 1981.

Harakas, Stanley. *Let Mercy Abound: Social Concern in the Greek Orthodox Church*. Brookline, MA: Holy Cross Orthodox Press, 1985.

———. *Living the Faith: The Praxis of Eastern Orthodox Ethics*. Minneapolis: Light and Life Publishing Co., 1992.

———. *Toward Transfigured Life*. Minneapolis: Light and Life Publishing Co., 1983.

———. "Icon and Ethics," *Orthodoxes Forum* 4:2 (1990): 195-214.

Harris, Maria, "Completion and Faith Development." In *Faith*

Development and Fowler, pp. 115-133. Edited by Craig Dykstra and Sharon Parks. Birmingham, AL: Religious Education Press, 1986.

——. *Fashion Me a People: Curriculum in the Church*. Louisville, KY: Westminster/John Knox Press, 1989.

——. *Teaching and Religious Imagination: A Theology of Teaching*. New York: Harper and Row, 1987.

Hopko, Thomas. *The Orthodox Faith, Vol. 2: Worship*. New York: Department of Religious Education – Orthodox Church in America, 1976.

Ieratikon, The (in Greek). Athens: Apostolike Diakonia, 1987.

Ignatius of Antioch, St. *Epistle to the Romans*. In *The Apostolic Fathers*, pp. 75-79. Translated by J. B. Lightfoot. Edited by J. R. Harmer. Grand Rapids, MI: Baker Book House, 1983.

Ireneaus, St. *Adversus haereses (Against the heresies)*.

Jaeger, Werner. *Early Christianity and Greek Paideia*. Cambridge, MA: Belknap Press, 1961.

John Chrysostom, St. *Baptismal Instructions*. Translated by Paul Harkins. Ancient Christian Writers. Vol. 31. New York: Newman Press, 1963.

John of Damascus, St. *De fide orthodoxa*. In *Nicene and Post-Nicene Fathers* Vol IX. Grand Rapids: Eerdmans, 1983.

——. *An Exact Exposition of the Orthodox Faith (De fide orthodoxa)*. *Fathers of the Church, Vol. 37: St. John of Damascus, Writings*. Translated by Frederic Chase, Jr. New York: Fathers of the Church, 1958.

——. *On the Divine Images: Three Apologies Against Those Who Attack the Divine Images*. Translated by David Anderson. Crestwood, NY: SVS Press, 1980.

John Paul II, *On the Twelfth Centenary of the Second Council of Nicea, Duodecimum Saeculum*, 1987.

Kadloubovsky, E. and Palmer, G.E.H., trans. *Early Fathers from the Philokalia*. London: Faber and Faber, 1954.

Kalokyris, Constantine. *The Essence of Orthodox Iconography*. Translated by Peter Chamberas. Brookline, MA: Holy Cross Orthodox Press, 1985.

Kandinsky, Wassily. *Concerning the Spiritual in Art*. Translated and introduction by M. T. H. Sadler. New York, Dover Publications, 1977.

Kearney, Richard. *The Wake of Imagination*. Minneapolis: University of Minnesota Press, 1988.

Kelly, J.N.D. *Early Christian Doctrines*, rev. ed. San Francisco: Harper Collins, 1978.

Kittel, G., ed. *Theological Dictionary of the New Testament*. Translated by G. W. Bromiley. Grand Rapids: Eerdmans, 1964.

Kontoglou, Fotios. *Ekfrasis tis Orthodoxou Eikonografias, 2 Vols.* (in Greek). Athens: Astir Publishing, 1960.

Koulomzin, Sophie. *Our Church and Our Children*. Crestwood, NY: SVS Press, 1975.

Ladner, G. "The Concept of the Image in the Greek Fathers and the Byzantine Iconoclastic Controversy." *Dumbarton Oaks Papers* No. 7 (1953): 1-34.

Lamentations of Matins of Holy and Great Saturday, The. Translated by Holy Transfiguration Monastery. Brookline, MA: Holy Transfiguration Monastery, 1981.

Lanier, Vincent. "The Unseeing Eye: Critical Consciousness and the Teaching of Art." In *The Arts, Human Development, and Education*, pp. 19-29. Edited by Elliot Eisner. Berkeley: McCutchan, 1976.

Lane, Belden. *Landscapes of the Sacred: Geography and Narrative in American Spirituality*. New York: Paulist Press, 1988.

Langer, Susanne K. *Philosophical Sketches*. Baltimore: John Hopkins Press, 1962.

———. *Philosophy in a New Key*. Cambridge: Harvard University Press, 1969.

———. *Problems of Art*. New York: Charles Scribner's Sons, 1957.

Lenten Triodion, The. Translated by Mother Mary and Kallistos Ware. London: Faber and Faber, 1978.

Limouris, Gennadios, ed. *Icons: Windows on Eternity – Theology and Spirituality in Color*. Faith and Order Paper 147. Geneva: World Council of Churches, 1990.

———. *Justice, Peace and the Integrity of Creation: Insights from Orthodoxy*. Geneva: WCC Publications, 1990

Litsas, Fotios, ed. *A Companion to the Greek Orthodox Church*, pp. 84-90. New York: Greek Orthodox Archdiocese, 1988.

Lossky, Vladimir. *In the Image and Likeness of God*. Crestwood, NY: SVS Press, 1985.

———. *The Mystical Theology of the Orthodox Church*. Crestwood, NY: SVS Press, 1976.

Louth, Andrew. *Discerning the Mystery: An Essay on the Nature of*

Theology. Oxford: Clarendon Press, 1983.

Macmurray, John. *Persons in Relation.* New Jersey: Humanities Press International, 1991.

Maguire, Henry. *Art and Eloquence in Byzantium.* Princeton, NJ: Princeton University Press, 1981.

——. "The Depiction of Sorrow in Middle Byzantine Art," *Dumbarton Oaks Papers* 31 (1977): 123-174.

Mango, Cyril. *The Art of the Byzantine Empire 312-1453.* Toronto: University of Toronto Press, 1986.

Mantzarides, George. *Orthodox Spiritual Life.* Translated by K. Schram. Brookline, MA: Holy Cross Orthodox Press, 1994.

——. *The Deification of Man.* Crestwood, NY: SVS Press, 1984.

Marcel, Gabriel. *The Philosophy of Existentialism.* New York: Citadel Press, 1991.

Maritain, Jacques. *Education at the Crossroads.* New Haven: Yale University Press, 1943.

Maximus the Confessor, St. "Two hundred Texts on Theology and the Incarnate Dispensation of the Son of God." In *The Philokalia, Vol. 2,* pp. 14-163. Compiled by St. Nikodimos of the Holy Mountain. Translated by G.E.H. Palmer, Philip Sherrard, and Kallistos Ware. London: Faber and Faber, 1981.

McBrien, Richard. *Catholicism.* 1st ed. San Francisco: Harper Collins, 1981.

——. *Catholicism.* 2d ed. San Francisco: Harper Collins, 1994.

McVey, Kathleen. "The Domed Church as Microcosm: Literary Roots of an Architectural Symbol," *Dumbarton Oaks Papers* No. 37 (1983): 91-21.

Meyendorff, John. *Byzantine Theology: Historical Trends and Doctrinal Themes.* New York: Fordham University Press, 1987.

——. *Christ in Eastern Christian Thought.* Crestwood, NY: SVS Press, 1975.

Milburn, R. *Early Christian Art and Architecture.* Berkeley: University of California Press, 1988.

Miles, Margaret. *Carnal Knowing: Female Nakedness and Religious Meaning the Christian West.* Kent, UK: Burns and Oates, 1992.

——. *Image as Insight: Visual Understanding in Western Christianity and Secular Culture.* Boston: Beacon Press, 1985.

Miller, Ron. "Freedom in a Holistic Context," *Holistic Education Review* 8:3 (Fall, 1995): 4-12.

Monk of the Eastern Church, A. *The Year of Grace of the Lord: A Scriptural and Liturgical Commentary on the Calendar of the Orthodox Church.* Crestwood, NY: SVS Press, 1980.

Murray, Mary Charles. "Art and the Early Church." *Journal of Theological Studies* 28 (1977): 303-345.

———. "The Image, the Ear, and the Eye in Early Christianity." *ARTS* 9:1 (1997): 17-24.

Nellas, Panagiotis. *Deification in Christ.* Crestwood, NY: SVS Press, 1987.

Nicozisin, George. *The Road to Orthodox Phronema: Christian Education in the Greek Orthodox Archdiocese of North and South America.* Brookline, MA: Greek Orthodox Archdiocese of North and South America Department of Religious Education, n.d.

Nissiotis, Nikos A. "The Importance of the Doctrine of the Trinity for Church Life and Theology." In *The Orthodox Ethos*, pp. 32-69. Edited by A. J. Philippou. Oxford: Holywell Press, 1964.

Nelson, James B. *Embodiment: An Approach to Sexuality and Christian Theology.* Minneapolis: Augsburg Publishing House, 1978.

Nouwen, Henri J. M. *Behold the Beauty of the Lord: Praying with Icons.* Notre Dame, IN: Ave Maria Press, 1987.

Orthodox Catechesis, Brookline, MA: Greek Orthodox Archdiocese of North and South America Department of Religious Education, mimeographed, n.d.

Orthodox Statement on Environmental Principles. Unpublished document, 1996.

Ostrogorsky, George. *History of the Byzantine State.* Translated by Joan Hussey. New York: Rutgers University Press, 1969.

Ouspensky, Leonid and Lossky, Vladimir. *The Meaning of Icons.* Translated by G.E.H. Palmer and E. Kadloubovsky. Crestwood, NY: SVS Press, 1982.

Ouspensky, Leonid. *Theology of the Icon.* 2 vols. Crestwood, NY: SVS Press, 1992.

Palmer, G.E. H., Sherrard, Philip, and Kallistos Ware, trans. *The Philokalia, Vol. 2.* Compiled by St. Nikodimos of the Holy Mountain. London: Faber and Faber, 1981.

Palmer, Parker. *To Know as We Are Known: A Spirituality of Education.* New York: Harper Collins, 1983.

Panikkar, Raimundo. "Man as a Ritual Being." *Chicago Studies* 16:1 (1977): 5-28.

Pelikan, Jaroslav. *Imago Dei: The Byzantine Apologia for Icons.* Princeton, NJ: Princeton University Press, 1990.

———. *The Christian Tradition Vol. 2: The Spirit of Eastern Christendom (600-1700).* Chicago: University of Chicago Press, 1974.

Polanyi, Michael. *Knowing and Being.* London: Routledge and Kegan Paul, 1969.

———. *The Tacit Dimension.* Garden City, NY: Doubleday, 1966.

Poulos, George. *Orthodox Saints,* 4 vols. Brookline, MA: Holy Cross Orthodox Press, 1990.

Quenot, Michel. *The Icon: Window on the Kingdom.* Crestwood, NY: SVS Press, 1991.

Report to His Eminence Archbishop Iakovos Concerning the Future Theological Agenda of the Greek Orthodox Archdiocese. Brookline, MA: Holy Cross Orthodox Press, 1990.

Rice, David Talbot. *Art of the Byzantine Era.* London: Thames and Hudson, 1963.

Rice, Tamara Talbot. *Everyday Life in Byzantium.* New York: Barnes and Nobles Books, 1994.

Rosenak, Michael. *Commandments and Concerns: Jewish Religious Education in Secular Society.* Philadelphia: The Jewish Publication Society, 1987.

Sahas, Daniel J. *Icon and Logos: Sources in Eighth-Century Iconoclasm.* Toronto: University of Toronto Press, 1986.

Schiro, Michael. *Curriculum for Better Schools.* Englewood Cliffs, NJ: Educational Technology Publications, 1978.

Schmemann, Alexander. *Church, World, Mission.* Crestwood, NY: SVS Press, 1979.

———. *The Eucharist: Sacrament of the Kingdom.* Translated by Paul Kachur. Crestwood, NY: SVS Press, 1988.

———. *For the Life of the World.* Crestwood, NY: SVS Press, 1973.

———. *Liturgy and Life: Christian Development through Liturgical Experience.* Syosset, NY: Orthodox Church in America Department of Religious Education, 1983.

Schönborn, Christoph. *God's Human Face: The Christ-Icon.* Translated by Lothar Krauth. San Francisco: Ignatius Press, 1994.

Scott, Kieran. "Three Traditions of Religious Education." *Religious Education* 79 (1984): 323-339.

Scouteris, Constantine. "'Never as gods': Icons and Their Veneration." *Sobornost* 6:1 (1984): 6-18.

Selected Byzantine Hymns According to the Tradition of the Great Church of Christ. Brookline, MA: Holy Transfiguration Monastery, 1981.

Sendler, Egon. *The Icon: Image of the Invisible, Elements of Theology, Aesthetics and Technique.* Translated by Fr. Steven Bigham. Redondo Beach, CA: Oakwood Publications, 1988.

Services for Holy Week and Easter. Translated by Leonidas Contos. Northridge, CA: Narthex Press, 1994.

Sherrard, Philip. *Christianity and Eros.* London: SPCK, 1975.

————. *Human Image: World Image, The Death and Resurrection of Sacred Cosmology.* Ipswich, U.K.: Golgonooza Press, 1992.

————. *The Sacred in Life and Art.* Ipswich, U.K.: Golgonooza Press, 1990.

Staniloae, Dumitru. *The Experience of God.* Translated by Ioan Ionita. Brookline, MA: Holy Cross Orthodox Press, 1994.

————. *Prayer and Holiness: The Icon of Man Renewed in God.* Oxford: SLG Press, 1982.

————. *Theology and the Church.* Translated by Robert Barringer. Crestwood, NY: SVS Press, 1980.

Stylianopoulos, Theodore G. *The New Testament: An Orthodox Perspective, Vol. 1: Scripture, Tradition, Hermeneutics.* Brookline, MA: Holy Cross Orthodox Press, 1997.

Taft, Robert. *Beyond East and West: Problems in Liturgical Understanding.* Washington, DC: The Pastoral Press, 1984.

Tarasar, Constance, ed. *Orthodox America–1794-1976: Development of the Orthodox Church in America.* Syosset, NY: Orthodox Church in America Department of History and Archives, 1975.

————. "Orthodox Theology and Religious Education." In *Theologies of Religious Education*, pp. 83-120. Edited by Randolph C. Miller. Birmingham, AL: Religious Education Press, 1995.

————. "Taste and See: Orthodox Children at Worship." In *The Sacred Play of Children*, pp. 43-54. Edited by Diane Apostolos-Cappadona. New York: Seabury Press, 1983.

————. "The Orthodox Experience." In *A Faithful Church: Issues in the History of Catechesis*, pp. 236-260. Edited by O.C. Edwards and John Westerhoff. Wilton, CT: Morehouse-Barlow, 1981.

————, ed. *Perspectives on Orthodox Education.* Syosset, NY: Orthodox Church in America, 1983.

———. *A Process Model for the Design of Curriculum for Orthodox Christian Religious Education.* Ed.D. Dissertation, SUNY – Albany, 1989.

Taylor, Joshua C. *Learning to Look: A Handbook for the Visual Arts* 2d ed. Chicago: University of Chicago Press, 1981.

Theodore the Studite, St. *On the Holy Icons.* Translated by Catharine P. Roth. Crestwood, NY: SVS Press, 1980.

Tolstoy, Leo. *What Is Art?* Translated by Aylmer Maude. New York: Liberal Arts Press, 1960.

Trakatellis, Demetrios. "'∞ χολούθει Μοι/Follow Me" (Mk 2.14): Discipleship and Priesthood," *The Greek Orthodox Theological Review* 30:3 (1985): 271-285.

———. *Authority and Passion: Christological Aspects of the Gospel according to Mark.* Translated by George Duvall and Harry Vulopas. Brookline, MA: Holy Cross Orthodox Press, 1987.

Vasileios, Archimandrite. *Beauty and Hesychia in Athonite Life.* Translated by C. Kokenes. Montreal: Alexander Press, 1996.

Vasiliev, A. A. *History of the Byzantine Empire.* 2 vols. Madison: University of Wisconsin Press, 1973.

Vinogradov, Alexis. "The Orthodox Christian Experience of Liturgical Space," *Ecumenism* No. 123 (September 1996): 34-37.

Vrame, Anton C. "An Exegesis of the *Epitaphios Threnos*," *The Greek Orthodox Theological Review* 39:3-4 (1994): 299-310.

———. "Forming Orthodox Identity in the Curriculum of the Greek Orthodox Church." In *Personhood:* 173-184. Edited by John T. Chirban. Westport, CT: Bergin and Garvey, 1996.

Ward, Benedicta, trans. *The Sayings of the Desert Fathers: The Alphabetical Collection.* Oxford: A.R. Mowbray, 1981.

Ware, Kallistos. "The Human Person as Icon of the Trinity." *Sobornost* 8:2 (1986): 6-24.

———. "'In the Image and Likeness:' The Uniqueness of the Human Person." In *Personhood:* 1-13. Edited by John T. Chirban. Westport, CT: Bergin and Garvey, 1996.

———. *The Orthodox Way.* Crestwood, NY: SVS Press, 1979.

———. *The Orthodox Church.* London: Penguin Books, 1963.

Warncok, Mary. *Imagination.* London: Faber and Faber, 1976.

Westerhoff, John. *Spiritual Life: The Foundation for Preaching and Teaching.* Louisville, KY: Westminster/John Knox Press, 1994.

Whitehead, Alfred North. *The Aims of Education and Other Essays*. New York: The Free Press, 1957.

Xintaras, Zachary, "Man, the Image of God," *Greek Orthodox Theological Review* 1:1 (1954): 48-62.

Yannaras, Christos. *Elements of Faith: An Introduction to Orthodox Theology*. Translated by K. Schram. Edinburgh: T & T Clark, 1991.

———. *The Freedom of Morality*. Translated by Elizabeth Briere. Crestwood, NY: SVS Press, 1984.

———. *Prosopon kai Eros*. Athens, 1976. Translated by Peter Chamberas as *Personhood and Eros: The Hellenic Approach to Ontology*. Unpublished Manuscript.

Zizioulas, John D. *Being as Communion: Studies in Personhood and the Church*. Crestwood, NY: SVS Press, 1985.

———. "Communion and Otherness." *St. Vladimir's Theological Quarterly* 38 (1994): 347-361.